A Critical Discourse Analysis
of Family Literacy Practices

Power In and Out of Print

■ ■ ■

A Critical Discourse Analysis of Family Literacy Practices

Power In and Out of Print

■ ■ ■

Rebecca Rogers
Washington University in St. Louis

Routledge
Taylor & Francis Group
New York   London

Cover photograph by Amy Blackwood

Transferred to Digital Printing 2007

First published by Lawrence Erlbaum Associates, Inc., Publishers
10 Industrial Avenue
Mahwah, New Jersey 07430

Reprinted 2008 by Routledge
Routledge
Taylor & Francis Group
270 Madison Avenue
New York, NY 10016

Routledge
Taylor & Francis Group
2 Park Square
Milton Park, Abingdon
Oxon OX14 4RN

Cover design by Kathryn Houghtaling Lacey

Library of Congress Cataloging-in-Publication Data

Rebecca Rogers.
A critical discourse analysis of family literacy practices : power in and out
   of print.
      p. cm.
      Includes bibliographical references and index.
ISBN 0-8058-4226-8 (cloth : alk. paper)
ISBN 0-8058-4784-7 (pbk. : alk. paper)
                                                                    2003
                                                                    CIP

Publisher's Note
The publisher has gone to great lengths to ensure the quality of this
reprint but points out that some imperfections in the original
may be apparent

*I dedicate this book to my parents,
Lynn and Tom Rogers, whose love and
ways of interacting sparked my interest
in family literacy at an early age.*

Contents

Foreword

James Paul Gee

University of Wisconsin-Madison

Many years ago a close colleague of mine who worked in education brought me tape recordings of stories told by certain first-grade African-American children at "sharing time" in various schools. "Sharing time" was "show and tell" without letting the children have any objects to point to. The stories were about the children's pets, their families, their birthdays, their activities, their day-to-day problems. My colleague told me that the children's teachers thought their stories were disconnected and rambling. Indeed, they thought their stories did not make much sense. The children, they felt, had some sort of "deficit."

At the time my colleague brought me these stories I worked in linguistics, not education. I knew nothing about schools and schooling. What my colleague told me and showed me shocked me. Many a sociolinguist would readily have recognized these children's stories as excellent examples of the sorts of well-formed and creative "oral stories" found in many cultures across the globe. These are cultures with long historical traditions of oral storytelling as a "cultural encyclopedia" of stored values and knowledge.

People in these cultures are usually literate now. However, they retain allegiance to storing profound cultural meanings in stories told face-to-face. Some of these stories are "repeated" in roughly the same form from occasion to occasion. But sometimes they are stories of everyday and current events that still, nonetheless, contain deeper layers of meaning germane to larger themes, meanings similar to or influenced by the more fixed stories. Indeed, this form of storytelling is often referred to as "oral literature."

Linguists knew that many African-Americans had clear ties to such a culture, both from their roots in Africa and in the development of an early, indigenous, and on-going African-American culture in the United States. Indeed, even at the time my colleague showed me the children's stories, I could pull off my bookshelves several anthologies of such stories, anthologies that treated them as "oral literature" (and compared them to the sorts of oral literature produced by the Homeric poets, the early composers of the Bible, and various other oral traditions in the past and present).

I don't know what shocked me most, though: the fact that such young children told such wonderful stories or the fact that schools could see such wonderful gifts as deficits. I certainly felt abashed at how little my own discipline had done to let others know what we knew. I never before had seen how our own failure could end up hurting even small children. But I also felt that here was not just a major practical and ethical problem, but a major theoretical one, as well: How could well-intentioned and intelligent people (like teachers) and well-intentioned institutions (like schools) come to define obvious gifts as deficits, clear sense as senselessness, manifest history and culture as non-existent, and clearly normal children as abnormal?

Furthermore, since the problem clearly had to do with the ways in which the children's language was opaque to the children's teachers, it looked potentially to be a major problem in linguistics, as well, and not just in the social sciences. Like many linguists at the time, I had not thought of education or educational research as an important area for "serious" work, especially not "theoretical" work. Yet here was an intriguing theoretical problem that clearly bore on practical and ethical concerns of the first order.

Part of the answer—although only part—turned out to be the fact that many of the teachers my colleague studied treated sharing time as early practice in school-based literacy for young children who could not yet write little essays. The teachers wanted the children to talk little essays, instead—little essays about going to the pool with one's mother or making candles with one's friends. They didn't really want stories and certainly not stories that were "literary" and not blow-by-blow linear reports of the facts and details. Nonetheless, they often asked for "stories." Furthermore, the teachers were listening for certain "ways with words" they weren't getting from some children and failing to hear and appreciate the "ways with words" they were getting.

Typical of linguists in those days, I saw literacy as an irrelevant parasite on "real language," which was oral language (because, after all, it was oral language for which humans had a biological capacity given to them by their evolutionary history; literacy was too new on the historical scene to have participated in that evolutionary history). But yet here I saw that what was important—crucial, indeed—were distinctions between different kinds of language, different styles of language: literate and oral, oral that sounded literate and oral that did not, linear and literary, stories and reports, and so and so forth through a good many distinctions that had not heretofore seemed very important in the grand scheme of things linguistic. It turned out that discourse analysis—that is, the analysis of how people actually use and respond to language in context—was crucial. In fact, it was really *critical* discourse analysis—that is the analysis of how people get helped or harmed by how people actually use and respond to language in context—that was crucial.

Educators will look at my initial reaction to my colleague's data as naïve. Nonetheless, I have now spent nearly twenty years working on the problem of how intelligent, creative, cultured children can be transformed, by social and institutional "work" in schools and society, into seemingly "slow," deficited, aculture beings, even when and where intentions are not evil (though they sometimes are). I still see the problems to which my colleague opened my eyes so many years ago as profound from both a theoretical and practical perspective. Indeed, these problems call into question the distinction between what is theoretical and what is practical, and between theory and practice.

Rebecca Rogers is, of course, not naïve or ill-educated in education, as I was. In fact, she is part of a diverse group of scholars, people adept at both linguistics and education, who have developed and are continuing to develop the movement known as the "New Literacy Studies." This movement acknowledges that it takes research in linguistics, anthropology, social, political, and critical theory, and education—not as disparate and isolated disciplines, but integrated together—to tackle the sorts of practical-theoretical problems my colleague's data brought so forcefully to my attention. But Rebecca is less naïve than me in another respect, as well: she knows that knowledge and spreading knowledge is not enough. Systems don't change unless you integrate activism and advocacy with your theory and practice.

Rebecca captures the central problem well, indeed, if I may paraphrase her own words just a bit: how does the "sticky web of institutional discourse" hold certain sorts of people, often people with the least power and opportunities in our society, "in place despite ample commitment, persistence, and cultural capital" on their part. Her book makes a signal contribution to this problem, what is now, I believe, the central problem of the "New Literacy Studies." Her book is practical theory and activist advocacy of a sort I could only have imagined when I started on this road many years ago.

Preface

This is a book about literacies, individuals, and institutions. An ethnographic case study of June Treader and her daughter Vicky, the book explores the discursive forces that impact their lives, the attendant issues of power and identity, and contemporary social debates about the connections between literacy and society.

Using participant observation, ethnographic interviewing, photography, document collection, and discourse analysis I describe and explain the complexity of the literacy work that June and Vicky, the two focal participants, engage with in their daily life. Both June and Vicky, urban African Americans labeled as "low-income" and "low-literate" negotiate language and literacy in their home and community proficiently, critically and strategically. Yet despite these proficiencies which I document, neither June nor Vicky see themselves as literate. June was defined as having "low literacy skills," reading at a "mid-fourth grade level" in her adult literacy classroom. Vicky, at the end of her sixth grade year was labeled as "speech impaired" and "multiply disabled."

To understand these and other complex contradictions, I use Fairclough's (1989, 1995) critical discourse analysis (CDA). The book shows the remarkable value of CDA, but at the same time demonstrates its limitations. The unusually rich ethnographic data within which I use CDA make it possible to extend Fairclough's theory of critical language study by demonstrating how power in language operates over time and across generations, from mother to daughter. Calling on social theories of learning (Gee, 1996; Rogoff, 1995; Wenger, 1998), I also argue that apprenticeship serves as a useful metaphor through which to examine family literacy as the space in which the ideological work of literacy is done. In the process of learning about literacy, Vicky and June learn relationships with their social world and contradictory literate subjectivities. These subjectivities are internalizations of ideologies and can be selectively invoked by discursive contexts, preventing June and Vicky from transforming their literate capital into social profit.

Methodologically, the study demonstrates the importance of embedding critical discourse analysis in ethnographic description. It also shows the reflexive value of turning the analytic tool (CDA) on the researcher as well as the other "subjects" of study. This practice allows clearer analysis of the ethical, moral, and theoretical implications in conducting ethnographic research concerned with issues of power. Through critical language awareness, educators working toward a critical social democracy may be better armed to recognize sources of inequity.

This is a timely book, for there are few ethnographic studies exploring the usefulness and limits of critical discourse analysis (for critique of this absence see Chouiliarki & Fairclough, 1999; Fairclough, 1999; Collins, 2000). Based on two years of fieldwork, this book presents the strategies, resources and histories of participation that are called on in order to gain access to social institutions and respect. It examines the deep-rooted nature of power and identity in late postmodern society. It extends both theoretically and empirically existing research on literacy, identity, and power.

This study addresses the call for researchers to be increasingly reflexive—or turning the analytic framework back on themselves—as a means of attending to credibility of research in late postmodernity (e.g., Chouiliarki & Fairclough, 1999). I address issues of researcher reflexivity in chapters 1, 6, and then again in the conclusion (chap. 8). Drawing on the disciplines of linguistic anthropology (e.g., Silverstein & Urban, Eds., 1996), New Literacy Studies (Heath, 1983; Barton, Hamilton, & Ivanic, 2000; Street, Eds, 1995) and critical discourse analysis (Fairclough & Wodak, 1999; Luke, 1995) this book develops a new synthesis. I argue that neither explanatory claims of critical discourse analysis nor descriptions of literate behaviors account for the complexity and inequity embedded in everyday interactions with language and literacy. Building on existing theories of Discourse (Gee, 1996, 1999; Knobel, 1998) the book complicates the notion of "discourse-in-conflict" and explores the boundaries of the learning and acquisition of literacies and ideologies. It intimately demonstrates and explains the ways in which people regulate and are regulated by literacy practices.

The book documents the tensions between neighborhood proficiencies with language and literacy and "schooled literacy" approaches in chapters 3 and 4. It illuminates the ways in which inner city residents who are labeled as "illiterate" are in fact using highly complex linguistic and social resources that are neither called upon nor recognized within institutional contexts. While other ethnographic/interpretive work (e.g., Cushman, 1998; Luttrell, 1997; Paratore et al., 1999; Purcell-Gates, 1995; Taylor & Dorsey-Gaines, 1988) have documented these literate proficiencies—these works have neither developed extended case studies of participants in different contexts nor combined the ethnographic detail with a discourse analysis such as CDA. This combined approach offers an explanatory framework for the stronghold of institutional discursive power and is illustrated in chapters 5,

6, and 7. The layered themes of; literate subjectivities, discursive relations, and regulation of the social world through discourse are developed on a chapter-by-chapter basis as I explicate the paradox attached to "being" literate through the Treader's lives.

ACKNOWLEDGMENTS

I am grateful to the Treaders, who welcomed me into their home and their lives. From the Treaders I learned about the complexity of language and literacy practices. I am also grateful for the committee of excellent research-ers and teachers who mentored me while I was conducting this research. It is difficult to put into words my gratitude for the guidance I received from Peter Johnston, Jim Collins, and Ginny Goatley. A heartfelt thanks to Michael Mancini who encouraged my work on this project from start.to finish. And finally, I would also like to thank Naomi Silverman and Nadine Simms for their editorial guidance and Judith Solsken and James Gee for their thoughtful review of this manuscript.

–Rebecca Rogers

Introduction: Participants in the Study and Theoretical Orientations

As no diaries or letters have been located to tell their side of the story, one can only imagine the feelings of the parents and children in the black community as they fought for fair treatment by the school system. Official documents, however, trace the victories and setbacks experienced by these foot-soldiers for equal educational rights. The story of their struggle has left scars on our hearts.   —Hughes (1998, p. 47)

The Treaders

June Treader is one of the strongest women I know. June is raising a healthy, safe, and literate family in a community faced with poverty, murders, AIDS, drugs, and gang-related violence. She handles virtually all of the literate demands of her household, from paying bills to making sure her children's homework is done. June negotiates all family communications, written and otherwise, with the school and other institutions. She even initiated and obtained signatures on a petition to change local traffic conditions. Yet, when I first met June in her adult basic education classroom, at the end of a reading lesson she asked timidly, "Did I read this good?" When she talked about her progress, tears ran down her face. There is a profound tension between June's personal and public literate lives.

There are other tensions, too. In spite of the fact that her husband, Lester, was substantially more capable at certain literate tasks—like reading the newspaper, it was June that met all of the family unit's literate demands. Standing in her kitchen one day, June handed me one of the letters that had come home from the school and commented, "I don't understand why they makin' such a big deal out of these papers." Within 3 months, June had received several form letters from her daughter's school. The school asked for parental permission to proceed with the special-education referral process on her oldest daughter, Vicky. June resisted beginning the referral process on her sixth-grade daughter, claiming, "if she put her mind to it she can do it." The urgency in her voice revealed not only her commitment to her children's education, but some of her substantial understanding of institutional practices. Like the families described by Taylor (1983), Taylor and Dorsey-Gaines (1988), and Lareau (1989), the Treaders share a commitment to their children's schooling that is unwavering (Harris, Kamhi, & Pollock, 2001). Yet, despite their best efforts, and substantial competence, they were constantly thwarted by institutional practices.

This book documents the literacies of the Treaders' lives and the sticky web of institutional discourse that holds them in place despite ample commitment, persistence, and cultural capital. As an ethnographer I wanted to document the myriad ways in which literacy is used in the texture of the Treaders' daily lives. I wanted to understand how a woman who struggled with her own literacy accommodated the literate demands of her life. Most important, I wanted to understand and make visible the norms, beliefs, assumptions, and roles embedded within what it means to be literate in different contexts. In addition, I wanted to understand how I, as a White, middle-class literacy researcher and teacher was implicated into this web of institutional discourse. To accomplish these ends, I used ethnographic field methods to capture the rich detail of their literate lives and I enlisted discourse analysis (Fairclough, 1989, 1995; Gee, 1996, 1999a) to make visible the discursive web that holds the Treaders in their place.

Selecting the Treaders

I selected June Treader and her family as focal participants in this study because I was interested in working primarily with an adult who was experiencing reading and writing difficulties and who had children enrolled in the public school system. These criteria, I believed, would allow me to explore how adults negotiated literacy in their own lives including the literacy demands of being a parent of a public school child. During the school year of 1996–1997, I came to know June, first as a member of the adult basic education (ABE) classroom that I was observing for a research project investigating the nature of literacy instruction for adults with low literacy skills. My stance in this project was that of a participant observer. I would often work one-on-one with students in the classroom. I realized this closeness offered more insight into (a) the ways adults understood reading and writing and (b) their participation in the classroom, than observations alone.

When this project was over, I accepted a position as an adult literacy teacher at the school. During this time, I became increasingly interested in the connections between literacy development and adults' participation in family and other institutional structures. All of the participants in the ABE classroom had reading levels below a fifth-grade level[1] and three-fourths of them had school-age children. I wanted to learn more about the types and extent of literacy in the lives of adults who have found learning to read and write difficult.

In the fall of 1997, I formally began the research that is the subject of this book. Already having established "insider connections," my proposal to the administration and the classroom teacher at the adult literacy center was approved. I talked with the teacher, letting him know that I was interested in working closely with one adult in the classroom who (a) attended classes regularly, (b) had children, and (c) was having substantial difficulty with reading and writing. I explained to him that the project would involve an active participant component where I would work with the adult on the individual's literacy development. He suggested June Treader first. Based on my knowledge of June as a student and the rapport I had established with her, I reasoned that her participation would lead to useful insights into the nature of family literacy with adults who have been institutionally defined as having "low literacy skills."

That morning, I sat down next to June at one of the long tables where the adults were working from their workbooks. June was working on math problems. I still remember how nervous I was about describing what my research was and why I wanted her to participate. I explained to June that I was interested in learning more about the reading and writing practices in people's homes, communities, and schools. I asked her if she would be willing to be involved in my research. In return, I would continue to work with her as a literacy teacher. She surprised me by readily agreeing and stated, "That would be real good. I don't mind. You can work with Vicky too. She havin' some problems with her readin'. She could use the extra help." From the beginning of the research, June was actively situating me as a member and participant in both her and her children's lives.

The Treaders are in many ways "at risk" in the research literature as well as in the commonsense narratives. They are an African American working-poor family living below the poverty line. June, the mother, had an eighth-grade education and was reading at a fourth-grade level as defined by the TABE. She was not, however, a popular media case of a low literate adult. June actively negotiated the literate demands of her and her family's daily lives and also used literacy in socially active ways. She accessed resources, read strategically, and thought critically. June provided a literate home environment for her four children. Furthermore, she pursued her own education at the adult literacy center, independent of government mandates.

Vicky, an 11-year-old adolescent at the start of the study, demonstrated many of the same proficiencies with literacy as her mother. Vicky attended a neighborhood school within walking distance from the Treaders' home. Vicky enjoyed reading about African American rights through the works of people such as Harriet Tubman, Rosa Parks, Maya Angelou, and Martin Luther King, Jr. She and other adolescents in the neighborhood conducted research with members of their community about what it means to live in the community and their perspectives on social justice. They planned and scheduled the interviews, wrote and asked the questions, and wrote down the responses and summarized what each person said. Vicky explained to me the procedure for applying for, and receiving, WIC (Women with Infants and Children) support. She read the local newspaper at an instructional level and made connections between texts and her own life. Nonetheless, the school district classified Vicky as having "multiple disabilities and severe speech and language deficiencies."

The Treaders speak African American language, a rule-based, systematic language that is the primary language of many of the African American people in their neighborhood. Through the stories, vignettes, and thick ethnographic description of this book you will hear the linguistic abilities of June and her children, particularly Vicky, including creative word play, improvisation of stories, extensive use of metaphor and simile, the ability to think on their feet, and adjust language to various audiences for various social purposes (Heath, 1983; Labov, 1972; Taylor and Dorsey-Gaines, 1988). This ability to use language in highly sophisticated and in a contextual manner is strongly linked to identity and is an obvious precursor to literacy development. They are, however, not recognized within the institution of the school.

Furthermore, despite proficiencies with literacy and language in their everyday lives, which I illustrate in this ethnography, neither June nor Vicky saw themselves as literate. Both saw reading as a skill done in conjunction with the institution of the school. Progress in reading, for them, was marked by test scores rather than reading for enjoyment or reading strategically and critically. Furthermore, June was highly aware of her status as one of the lowest readers in her adult basic education classroom. Vicky seemed to replicate many of June's thoughts about herself as a reader and writer.

In many ways, the Treaders resisted the cultural narratives that framed them as "deficient" or "low-literate." This fundamental tension between June's and Vicky's literate lives, what they do on a daily basis, and how institutions represent them as "at-risk" "low-literate" and "disabled" is the central theme in this book. June and Vicky have learned to see themselves through the eyes of the institution. They have learned not to recognize and value the successes they encounter on a daily basis with language, literacy, and identity resources. One promise of this book, then, is an illustration of the ways in which people learn to see themselves through the eyes of an institution.

THEORETICAL ORIENTATIONS

Theories of Literacy and Society: Social Concerns

I situate this research within the "cultural/discursive mismatch" social debate (Delpit, 1996; Erickson, 1987; Gee, 1996). Discursive mismatch is often referred to as a lack of alignment between the culture, language, and knowledge of working-class students and dominant institutions such as schools and other social institutions (Collins, 1989; Heath, 1983; Mercado & Moll, 1997). This mismatch is often explained in one of three ways. Either families do not have the "right" kind of literacy (e.g., schooled literacy), they do not have enough practice with schooled literacy, or parents do not care about literacy and education perhaps because of the lack of belief in economic opportunities associated with education (Ogbu, 1978). I demonstrate with this case study that none of the typical responses explains the "mismatch."

Discourse (Gee, 1991; 1996) is a useful construct for theorizing about the mismatch phenomenon. Primary and secondary discourses are often used to operationalize the connection or disconnection between institutional sites, the family and the school being the most readily investigated in educational research (e.g., Lareau, 1989; Moll, Amanti, Neff, & Gonzalez, 1992; Purcell-Gates, 1995). Research often demonstrates that the discourse and literacy patterns of mainstream culture differ from and are invested with more power than those of life in the community and home (Gee, 1996; Knobel, 1999; Weinstein-Shr, 1993). Social theorists and discourse analysts from disciplines including political science, psychology, anthropology, education, English, and sociology have tried to understand the "discursive mismatch" debate, a phenomenon Willis (1977) described as how "working class kids" get "working class jobs," that is, how social structures are reproduced. The explanations, both the social and linguistic theories, range on a continuum from social reproduction to individual agency. Researchers across the social sciences are increasingly turning to language and discourse as a means of describing, interpreting, explaining, and transforming social injustices (cf. Chouliaraki & Fairclough, 1999; Collins, 2001; Howarth, 2001).

Reproduction Theory

Reproduction theory is concerned with how existing social structures are reproduced through either social or cultural reproduction. Social reproduction theorists (e.g., Althusser, 1971) focus on the reproduction of class structure. Althusser directly addresses the role of schools as ISAs (ideological state apparatuses), as the place where society is reproduced. Althusser argued that ISAs, including schools, are relatively autonomous and reflect state ideology. Ideology in Althusser's theory is defined as the imaginary relationship of individuals to their social worlds, which are a reflection of their actions governed by the structure of institutions. This analysis locates schools at the center of a critique of the reproduction of capitalist society. It also opens the door to view the subject formation of individuals within schools and how this reflects larger state-driven, ideological goals.

Althusser's work has been criticized for dealing with schools and schooling at a high level of abstraction and for overgeneralizing the extent by which social structures and class stratification are reproduced. Furthermore, Althusser and other neo-Marxists do not recognize the patriarchal relationships in schools and the production of gendered subjects. In this theory of social reproduction, there is little room given to individual agency and resistance, a theme addressed in cultural reproduction theories.

Cultural reproduction theorists (e.g., Bourdieu, 1991; Foucault, 1970, 1977) concern themselves with the way class structures are reproduced through an analysis of the processes and practices, rather than through structural reproduction. Poststructuralists are theorists concerned with how certain social groups and languages are privileged over others. Poststructuralists focus on power–knowledge relationships, that is, how they are transmitted and whether people have legitimate access to them. Foucault's (1970, 1977) theory of discourse focuses on the process of transmission of genres of power–knowledge relationships and provides a broad framework for operationalizing how certain discourses become privileged, taken for granted, and seen as natural. Central in understanding the distinction between the two sets of theories is how language, as a cultural tool, mediates the relationship between the individual and the social world. In this model, individual agency and power structures are dialectically produced, transformed, and reproduced.

Locating Discourse

The same tension between structure and agency arises in discourse studies. Discourse, as a field of inquiry, is informed by multiple disciplines and includes both a theory of social life and of language. Each set of theories can be more or less focused on the autonomy of structure over individual agency.

As a reaction to structuralism in anthropology and linguistics, discourse analysts interested in the complexity of context and discourse resisted the universal categories that were inscribed on social life. Researchers who studied language as a means to understand social life originated from departments of sociology and anthropology. Sociologists included the branch of language science termed "ethnomethodology," the early predecessor of conversation analysis. Conversation analysts were interested in studying the "here and now" of interactions. They studied and described rules governing interactional patterns, including turn-taking structures and characteristics of relevant conversations (e.g., Grice, 1999). Interactional sociolinguists (Labov, 1972; Labov & Waletsky, 1966) studied the relationship between language and social context in terms of social variables such as race, class, and gender. Some conversation analysts wanted to study indepth the interactional patterns of interethnic communication (e.g., Collins, 1989; Gumperz, 1982). From this line of research, we learned of the intricacies of context as it both informs and is informed by talk in action. Conversation analysts tended to see language as structured rather than constitutive and the speaker as having intentions that the analyst could recover in their analysis.

Informed by the ethnography of speaking (Hymes, 1974), linguistic anthropology emerged in the American context in the 1970s (e.g., Silverstein, 1996). Linguistic anthropologists attended to both detailed linguistic description and theorizing and ethnographic context. At the same time, a parallel movement of attention to power relations emerged in the social sciences. Informed by structural theories (e.g., Marxism) as well as poststructural theories (e.g., Foucault, 1977), social scientists increasingly turned to a "critical" social theory as a framework to understand social interactions. The impact of this work can be traced into work in the language sciences. This work was taken up in literacy studies in the early 1980s (Barton, 1993; Street, 1984) and reflects a parallel movement away from an autonomous model of language and literacy to a model that reflects and constructs ideologically models of literacy.

Critical Discourse Analysis

Critical discourse analysis (CDA) has its roots in critical linguists (Fowler, Hodge, Kress, & Trew, 1979; Kress, 1985; Kress & Hodge, 1979) and systemic functional linguistics (Halliday, 1989, 1994; Halliday & Hasan, 1989). Fairclough (1992a) argued that CDA varies from critical linguistics in that it attends to the microlinguistic aspects of grammar including cohesion, syntactical construction, metaphors, and themes, but treats the text as a social practice rather than as a social product. CDA also has its roots in Foucault's conception of power/knowledge. Fairclough, however, critiqued this social theory as not being textually based enough. CDA is making its way into American educational context (Bergvall & Remlinger, 1996; Bloome & Power-Carter, 2001; Collins, 2001; Corson, 2000; Janks, 1997; Kumaravadivelu, 1999; Lemke, 1995; Lewis, 2001; Luke & Freebody, 1997; Moje, 1997; Price, 1999; Rogers, 2002a, 2002b, 2002c) (Rogers (Ed.) under contract).

Critical discourse analysts separate themselves from the autonomy of syntax model that dominates the field of linguistics and assumes that a study of language is always a study of language in use. In this study I use the complementary work of Jim Gee and Norman Fairclough, who both fall within the CDA tradition. Both Gee and Fairclough see language as social constitutive, that is, constructing and constructed by social life. They also privilege the multivoiced speaker and prefer to stay away from claims about individuals' intentions when they analyze discourse. Both theorists conceptualize the relationship between language bits, or the grammar of language, and social practices. And finally, both theorists see the relationship between language bits and social practices as a set of empirical questions rather than a preexisting set of social relations.

In the sense that all discourse practices are local and context specific, they construct and are constructed by ways of understanding and meaning that are more or less privileged. That is, although there is an infinite amount of meaning-making potential, some meanings are privileged over others. Gee (1996) put it this way: "It is through attempts to deny this inevitable multiplicity and indeterminacy of interpretation that social institutions (like schools) and elite groups in a society often privilege their own version of meaning as if it were natural, inevitable, and incontestable" (p. 102). Similarly, Chouliaraki and Fairclough (1999) stated, "Our view is that the links between particular discourses and social positions, and therefore the ideological effects of discourse, are established and negotiated in the process of articulation within a practice" (p. 150).

The analysis of discourse, then, is an analysis of not only what is said, but what is left out, not only what is present in the text, but what is absent. In this sense, CDA does not read political and social ideologies onto texts. Rather, the task of the analyst is to figure out all of the possibilities between texts, ways of representing, and ways of being, and to look for and discover the relationships between texts and ways of being and why certain people take up certain positions vis-à-vis situated uses of language.

Gee's (1991, 1992, 1996, 1999a) work on discourse theory was important in how I approached the situated study of language and literacy. In particular, his conceptualization of different spheres of discourse was a useful starting point. Gee's distinctions between primary and secondary discourses provide a conceptual map of the practices and boundaries that often separated the family and the home community from the domains of the school and other social institutions.

Gee makes the distinction between social language or discourse with a capital D and discourse with a lowercase d. This distinction may be compared to the distinction made between literacy events and literacy practices. Literacy events are those events associated with a text. Literacy practices include the social context and practices within which the event occurs (A. B. Anderson, Teale, & Estrada; 1980; Barton & Hamilton, 1998; Barton, Hamilton, & Ivanic, 2000; Cope & Kalantzis, 2000; Heath, 1983). Gee (1996) defined Discourse (with an uppercase D) as "a socially accepted association among ways of using language, other symbolic expressions, and artifacts, of thinking, feeling, believing, valuing and acting that can be used to identify oneself as a member of a socially meaningful group or social network" (p. 131).

Gee's conception of discourse (with a lowercase *d*) more closely resembles the micro sociolinguistic aspect of language use. Thus discourse more closely resembles a literacy event rather than a literacy practice. (d)iscourse is the "language bits" of Discourses. Gee (1990) defined discourse (little d) as "any stretch of language (spoken, written, signed) which 'hangs together' to make sense to some community of people who use that language. . . . Making sense is always a social and variable matter: what makes sense to one community of people may not make sense to another" (p. 103).

Gee (1992) reminded us of some major tenets of D/discourse systems that are shown in practice throughout this book. First, discourses are inherently ideological. That is, power is embedded in discourse. Second, discourses are resistant to internal criticism. Therefore, members of discourse form preconscious relations with Discourse and consequently are highly unlikely to critique the system in which they are a part. Third, what counts as "discourse" is defined by relationships with other discourses. In other words, it is possible to understand the properties, relationships, and values of one community of practice by holding it up to another. A clear example of such work is seen in the ethnographic research of Scribner and Cole (1981). Fourth, certain values and viewpoints are valued over others. Memberships in social groups that are aligned with the dominant class carry more social weight than others. Finally, Discourses are related to the distribution of social power. That is, membership within Discourse communities *may* result in the transformation of cultural capital into social profit or social goods.

To take this theoretical framework and put it back into the composite presented earlier, there are "language bits" in what June said and there are the spheres of Discourse of which she is a part. As I mentioned in the composite at the beginning of the chapter, those are the Discourses of primary and secondary institutions (home and school). June negotiated the demands of her own learning experiences with school and at the same time made decisions about her daughter's education. One way to investigate these "conflicts" in and between systems of Discourse is through a critical analysis of discourse in context, the approach taken in this study.

Fairclough, similar to social theorists who treat the relationship between individuals and social structures as a relatively fluid practice, envisions language as a multidimensional, hybrid construct that shifts and transforms social life and relations. Fairclough conceptualizes the "language bits" that comprise social practice through "orders of discourse." Each utterance may be analyzed through orders of discourse—or ways of interacting, ways of representing, and ways of being. Fairclough is careful to point out, using systemic functional linguistics, which aspects of the grammar correspond to each order of discourse. Though Fairclough attends to language structure (through orders of discourse) more carefully than Gee, he does not have a theory of learning attached to discourse framework, something Gee does have (Gee, 1994, 1996; Gee & Green, 1998; Price, 1998). This is an issue I return to in the conclusion.

Cultural Models, Members' Resources, and Subjectivities

Gee and Fairclough agree that the task of the discourse analyst is to uncover tacit meaning-making potential. Therefore, discourse analytic frameworks must include a way of understanding (a) how meaning is situated culturally, socially, and politically, and (b) how to study such meaning through (and in) the mediational tool of language that both constructs meaning and is an artifact of meaning. Theories of discourse and discourse analysis within critical perspectives reject the autonomy of the individual. Instead, every utterance of the individual is social—informed by voices and languages that came before it—and dialogic. Both Gee and Fairclough theorize the speaker as comprised of multiple voices—referred to in the following section as heteroglossic relations—but have sets of socio-cognitive resources drawn from the various discursive contexts of which they are a part. Gee refers to these resources as cultural models and Fairclough as members' resources.

Gee describes cultural models as the storylines or scripts that people hold in their minds as they participate in situated meaning-making activities:

> A cultural model is usually a totally or partially unconscious explanatory theory or "story line" connected to a word—bits and pieces of which are distributed across different people in a social group—that helps to explain why the word has the different situated meanings and possibilities for the specific social and cultural groups of people it does. (Gee, 1999, p. 44).

Cultural models include the social and cultural resources individuals and groups of individuals (this includes both participants and researchers) bring to bear on their understanding or their "reading" of social situations.

Fairclough (1992) referred to such scripts as "member resources." He likened members' resources to the social resources individuals bring with them to interpret, consume, produce, and distribute texts. These resources include the internalized social structures, norms, and conventions, including orders of discourse, that people bring with them into each discursive domain.

A similarity between Gee's "cultural models" and Fairclough's "member resources" is that both theorists see these as a mediation between the individual and the social, rather than as a phenomenon that resides "in the head" of the individual. Both member resources and cultural models bring the socio-cognitive dimension of interacting with a variety of discourses and texts. A second similarity is the location of the link between linguistic resources and social languages. A third similarity is that in order to understand the socio-cognitive elements of participation in discourses, the analyst must engage in both micro and macro elements of analysis that include how participants produce and interpret texts based on their members' resources and at a macro level in order to know the nature of the members' resources (including orders of discourse). This also has importance for the analyst, as I discuss in Appendix H on the role of the researcher. The analyst brings cultural models and members' resources to bear on the production, consumption, and distribution of discourse.

In this book, I use the constructs of cultural models and subjectivities in an overlapping manner. I understand the construct of cultural model in relation to literate practice to mean the story lines that people carry with them as they interact with literacy in various domains. The construct of literate subjectivities allows for a discussion of the relation between people and their social worlds and accounts for the multiple and sometimes contradictory cultural models associated with such relationships (Davies & Harre, 1990; Sawin, 1999). For example, an examination of June Treader's literate life, as we see, herein, offers insight into the multiple cultural models that are evoked as June enters into interactions with literacy in her roles as a mother and as a literacy student.

As people are immersed in discourse they are socialized into attitudes, beliefs, and values without awareness, both in the primary and secondary Discourses. These relations are highly context dependent and have physical and psychological embodiments of social positions and, thus, contradictions of the contexts that they are a part (Bourdieu, & Passeron,1977). The socialization process implies a preconscious nature of subjectivities, which is important because it means that social contradictions are not readily resisted (Krais, 1993).

Gendered lives, one piece of subjectivities that is central in this book, are what Davies (1993) referred to as story lines that have different degrees of status in the social world—a social world that is discursively constructed—and where more status and privilege are accounted to certain story lines. Davies wrote:

> We not only read and write stories but we also live stories. Who we take ourselves to be at any one point in time depends on the available story lines we have to make sense out of the ebb and flow of being-in-the-world along with the legitimacy and status accorded to those story lines by the others with whom we make up our lives at any one point in time. (p. 41)

Thus, gendered subjectivities are constructed through discursive worlds (Davies, 1993; Gilbert, 1997; Urwin, 1998; Wodak, 1997; Young, 2000). A growing body of research examines the construction of self through language and literacy (Orellana, 1999), in terms of both reading (Davies, 1993; Walkerdine, 1990) and writing (Gilbert, 1992; Orellana, 1999). As these researchers readily pointed out, gendered subjectivities are not stable sites. Rather, they are what Butler (1990) referred to as "sites of necessary trouble" (p. 14). This perspective reminds us that an individual's identity is multiple and constantly recreated as the speaker adopts subject positions in various cultural discourses (Sawin, 1999).

Research Focus

Situated within discourse studies and critical social theories, I inquire into the literate lives of the Treaders focusing on the disjunctures and paradoxes. First, from the literature and from the brief opening vignette there appears to be lines of demarcation between the home and the school. How are these boundaries constructed through participation, membership, identities, and personal and social histories? What happens when Discourses are in conflict? Second, it is widely cited in the literature that cultural capital does not always lead to social profit. The question, then, is what are the processes through which literate practices lead to (or thwart) the attainment of social resources? What roles do individuals and institutions play in the process? Finally, in what ways are literate competence and sense of self encoded in official literacies? What counts as literacy and to whom?

Concerned with access, reciprocity, and relationship building, central concerns when doing ethnographic research, I readily accepted invitations the Treaders extended into their homes and lives. I found myself continuing to find a balance between building relationships and wanting to maintain a personal distance because I continued to feel bound to maintaining objectivity and bias-free interpretations in the name of rigorous empirical social science. I worried that the Treaders would perceive my presence in their home as exploitive—but realize now that they might not have seen it this way—because they do not see their home and community's literacies and knowledge as valuable and because they saw me as a cultural resource, a set of issues I take up in Appendix H on the researcher role. I worried about how the Treaders would perceive my continued renegotiation of research boundaries and I often checked with June. June appeased my worries, at least temporarily, when she stated, "You've always done good by us and we'll do good by you." The Treaders graciously welcomed me into their home and I do the best I can in the following chapters to represent my learning and uphold the deep respect I have for them.

ORGANIZATION OF THE BOOK

Chapter 1: Introduction

This chapter introduces the participants of the study as well as engages with social theories of literacy and society. First, it grounds the study within a cultural/discursive mismatch set of issues—concerning calls for the "right" kinds of literacy. Second, it lays out the issues concerning social reproduction and how issues of identity/subjectivity are raised within the complexity of "being" literate. Third, it engages with work within critical literacy studies and power and discourse that have been part of an "ideological" model of literacy. Last, it situates the study between the boundaries of work done within the New Literacy Studies (NLS) (e.g., Barton, et. al., 2000; Barton & Hamilton, 1998) and Discourse studies (e.g., Gee, 1996, 1999; Knobel, 1998). The end of chapter 1 lays out the framework of the book.

Chapter 2: Methodology

Chapter 2 explores the intersection of linguistic anthropology and critical discourse studies in an extended case study. It lays out the specific methodological approaches—highlighting the coherence between the theoretical framework and unit of analysis. The book crosses the theoretical terrain of New Literacy Studies (e.g., Barton & Hamilton, 1998; Street, 1995), critical discourse studies (e.g., Fairclough, 1992, 1995; Luke, 1995), and discourse studies (e.g. Gee, 1996, 1999; Knobel, 1998)—each with their own unit of analysis. I highlight the points of intersection and distinguish the particular methodological approach taken in the present book. This chapter describes, in detail, the analytic procedures of conducting CDA. I raise issues of validity as they pertain to trust in language claims and introduce the concept of reflexivity, a theme running through the book.

Chapter 3: Personal and Institutional Histories

In this chapter, I put the perspective of histories of discourse and participation to work as it related to June Treader and her children in tracing the history of her participation within the institution of the school. What I offer in this chapter is a reading of June's present-day participation with various social institutions including the school that comprise her literate life. It is possible to understand June's history and trajectory of participation with school through her present day interactions with her ABE classroom and her daughter's elementary school. I argue that in June's effort to attain what Annette Lareau (1989) characterized as the "ideal" mother within the eyes of the school, she encountered roadblocks. These setbacks are not attributable to June's lack of interest or involvement in school and her children's education. They might be more justifiably connected to the intersection of June's internalization of the school experience—or her histories of experience within the institution—and the social conditions in which she currently lives (Cook-Gumperz, 1993; Gowen, 1991; Key, 1998; Luttrell, 1997). Furthermore, in participating in these communities of practice, June acquired working-class and gendered identities through her textual interactions with institutions.

Though June's participation with the school provides an entry point into how it is possible to understand her literate identity and negotiation—it is not enough to explain the complexity of her literate life. In order to attend to the multifaceted nature of what it means to be literate—I trace June's engagements with literacy into two other contexts as well—the family and the community. These contexts are not independent of each other as I have already pointed out. These are important sites of investigation I argue, because the invisibility of their practices that sustains inequities.

Chapter 4: Family Literacy as Apprenticeship

In this chapter, I shift the focus to Vicky's literacy profile in the domains of the school, the community, and the family. I interpret Vicky's literate engagements and the intergenerational transfer of ideologies around schooling and women's work in the analytic space around literacy practices.

First, I demonstrate Vicky's view of herself in relation to literacy. She has learned many of the notions of individualism with regard to reading. Second, I demonstrate how Vicky engaged with literacy in her home and community in active and strategic ways. Throughout, I build an argument for an analysis of family literacy practices to be viewed as an apprenticeship. That is, as Vicky learned literacy she also learned social roles through observation, participation, and transformation to practice (Rogoff, 1995). However, consistent with the commitment to relations of power in discourse, as presented to this point, I argue that individuals do not just learn literacy skills in this process; they learn complex and contradictory ways of being in the world (Gee, 1996; Johnston, 1999). After outlining Vicky's proficiencies and the contexts in which these are visible, I demonstrate how these proficiencies stood in stark contrast to the social identity the school carved for her. Throughout, I make parallels between June's and Vicky's cases.

Chapter 5: "I'm Her Mother, Not Them"

In chapters 3 and 4 I provide parallel cases of June and Vicky and their negotiations with literacy in their everyday lives. Two of the parallels between June's and Vicky's cases (presented in chap. 4) are relevant to the present chapter. First, both June and Vicky believe in the ideology of schooling (Bourdieu & Passeran, 1977). This belief is intact although the school does not value their local literacies. Second, there are profound tensions between their personal and their public literate lives. Each domain in which they interact with literacy evokes different aspects of their literate subjectivites—an issue that comes into focus in this chapter.

In this chapter, I explore the ideological work between June's initial resistance to Vicky being placed in special education and her final resignation to put her in it "just to get it over with." I focus on June's commitment to education as she negotiated the layers of paperwork and discursive practices that came home from the school about the special education referral process. June's insistence that special education was a wrong decision for Vicky was clear. Torn between mothering and schooling, June automatically resisted the referral process (Luttrell, 1997). This chapter represents June's torn literate subjectivities as she negotiated a decision for her daughter. After vehemently expressing resistance to the school's efforts to classify her daughter, she ultimately consented to beginning the referral process and putting Vicky into a special education classroom. The question that frames this chapter, then, (as well as chaps. 6 and 7) is how is it that individuals consent to the logic of the institution, even when they apparently believe something quite different?

Chapter 6: Into the Meeting Room

The tensions and contradictions between June's personal and public literate subjectivities come into clear focus in the last chapter. June moved from outwardly resisting the referral and the placement in special education to a quiet and submissive woman in the guidance counselor's office. Indeed, as she was confronted with the increasing stack of evidence that her daughter would be placed in a special education classroom, June was less and less able to interrupt the construction of this identity.

Through these series of interactions, it is possible to see where June's role as a mother and her relationship to the school come into conflict. Furthermore, the interactions with the school (e.g., the interaction in the guidance office and the formality of the Committee on Special Education meeting presented here) insist on one subjectivity—that with a history of public schooling—at the expense of others.

In this chapter, I present a section of the CSE meeting that occurred on June 18, 1998. I use CDA as an analytic tool to highlight contradictions embedded in the meeting that can be justified with prior ethnographic learning and textual analyses. When I look at this meeting, I am looking at it with the knowledge that June had already made her decision (chap. 5). Furthermore, I am also looking at this meeting with the knowledge of June's past and present histories with education, her active uses of literacy in her home and her community and her commitment to the educational progress of her children.

What I point out in this chapter is that the meeting is carefully orchestrated and identities constructed through official texts. However, what I point out is that failure to look at what occurred before the meeting (June's history—chaps. 3 and 5) and what occurred after the meeting, shows an incomplete picture of power and discourse. That is formalized sites, such as the CSE meeting, often become investigations of power through discourse rather than the acquisition of inequitable relations in discourse (family literacy practices).

Furthermore, having seen June's personal and public literate identities that occurred before the meeting (chaps. 3 and 5) it is possible to see how the formality of the meeting evoked June's history of schooling at the expense of what she knew to be right for her daughter. That is, I argue that this meeting evoked June's subjectivity as a person with a split and contradictory relationship with schooling. And, as I point to in chapter 8, through these interactions in the meeting it is possible to see traces of my own fragmented history of participation with the institution of the school.

Finally in this chapter, I present a CDA of one stretch of a 50-min CSE meeting. Though critical discourse analysis underlies the entire book, I have chosen to highlight the working of power through language in this meeting, rather than in some of the other events presented thus far, as a way of raising awareness of the multiple places where power operates. The complete transcript of the meeting is found in Appendix G.

Chapter 7: Through the Eyes of the Institution

In this chapter, I extend the general arguments I have made thus far concerning the acquisition of contradictory ideologies through local literacies (e.g., a family's literacy practices) that leads to continued consent to the dominant institutions. Lined up with chapters 5 and 6, this chapter examines both power "in" discourse, that is within the second-year CSE meeting room, as well as power "behind" discourse. Power "behind" discourse includes both June's and Vicky's history of participation with the institution of schools and the ways they thought about themselves as a result. I point out that the second-year CSE meeting is wrought with three contradictions, made apparent through a textual and intertextual analysis of the discourse. The first contradiction is that Vicky's discursive "deficits" were turned into "strengths." Second, the rhetoric of evidence was informal and lacking the formal presentation of the first-year meeting. The third was that despite both Vicky's and June's desire for Vicky to move out of a special-education room, they ultimately continue to consent to her placement in the self-contained classroom. I bring the second point, the presentation of evidence, to the foreground as I juxtapose the difference in meeting *style* from CSE Year 1 to CSE Year 2. This evidence extends my argument that although meetings held within institutional contexts are prime examples of power in discourse (Fairclough, 1989), there is more to individuals' consenting to the logic of the institution than what occurs in these meeting rooms. Though we witness an increase in June's participation in the meeting, ultimately June turned the decision over to Vicky to make. To understand why it is that Vicky decided to continue in the special-education classroom, it needs to be embedded within a broader framework of discourse, subjectivities, and social structures than analysis of the formal (and informal) meetings alone can provide. What is needed, I argue, is a fuller explanation of the ways in which Vicky, like June, had internalized contradictory social positions that make the ideological work of the school that much easier (Collins, 1993).

Chapter 8: The Paradox of Literacy

First, I illustrate how in this case a critical theory of discourse has undermined three common-sense assumptions about literacy in the Treaders' lives. Second, I illuminate the conceptual strengths and weaknesses of CDA. Third, I suggest the importance of thinking about ideology in relation to learning and acquisition. The book concludes by analyzing my own role in the research and the ways in which I also am implicated into institutional discourses. I argue that taken together these pieces illuminate the complexity of literacy in the Treaders' lives and suggest implications for research, policy, and practice about the literacy "needs" of children and families.

Chapter 2

Methodology

The Treaders

The Treaders are a working-poor African American family living in inner-city Albany. June and Lester Treader have been married for 13 years. They have four children. Vicky was the oldest and was 11 years old at the start of the study. Luanne, was 7 years old. Both Luanne and Vicky attended an elementary school walking distance from their apartment. Shauna, the youngest daughter, was 3 years old. June enrolled her in a federally funded preschool program during the second year of the study. Evan, the youngest of the Treaders, was born in August of 1998.

Lester has a GED (general equivalency diploma). June dropped out of school, the same school where Vicky attended middle school, at the end of her eighth-grade year. She returned to an adult literacy class so she could "pick up on her readin'." June stated that her goal was to get her GED and start a day care because she liked working with children.

Lester's family lives in New York city. June's family, her mother, father, and siblings, live in the same neighborhood as the Treaders. June grew up in an apartment a few blocks from where she now lives. The Treaders have a close network of family and friends in Albany.

The major occupations held by people in the community include retail trade, administrative support occupations, service occupations, and health services. Lester and June Treader fall into these categories. Lester was a plumber and more recently went to trade school to be an electrician. June holds a nurse's aide certificate. She has also worked as a school bus aide and as a housekeeper at a local motel. June's parents also reside in this area and fall into the general employment patterns of the neighborhood. June's mother worked as a housekeeper at the local hospital for 30 years. She rode the bus to work every day. June's father does construction work. Though June was born in this neighborhood, the Treaders have close family who live in the southern states and Vicky and her grandmother take an annual bus trip to visit these relatives.

Situating the Context

Up the cement front steps of their stoop and through an unlit entrance was the way into the Treaders' second-floor apartment. In front of the apartment a brown, ripped, leather front car seat is used for Lester's chair. He and June often sat on the front stoop, watching people walk by and keeping an eye on their children playing on the sidewalk. The red-carpeted stairs led to the apartment and the front door that was the main entrance into the Treaders' apartment. The door opened across from June and Lester's bedroom. The room had paneled walls. Newspaper clippings of family members' obituaries were taped to the walls above the main dresser. To the left of their room was the living room with a TV that sometimes had cable, sometimes not, depending on when the bill was paid. The paneled walls of the living room were filled with photographs of the three oldest children: Vicky, Luanne, and Shauna, arranged chronologically from when they were newborns to more recent school pictures with their hair carefully fixed in colorful knockers with brightly colored tops. On the side wall and on the front of a closet door were June's certificates from the adult learning center for participating in a workshop and an award she received for parent involvement from Shauna's Head Start center. A picture of Shauna with her preschool class and a finger painting she did in school were next to June's certificates. Most days June brought home a local newspaper from the adult literacy center for Lester. The paper usually was on the couch.

The living room was the place where June watched soap operas and Lester listened to music. The living room floor was also the place where they laid down old blankets for the baby to crawl on—or sometimes was a place for June or Lester to sleep. The hallway that connected the living room with the dining room and kitchen areas was carpeted with the same red carpet as the stairs leading into their apartment. This hallway was the space where Vicky, Luanne, and Shauna congregated with other neighborhood children; where they talked, giggled, and compared recently acquired jewelry charms, sneakers, or jackets (fieldnotes, 11/14/97 & 1/7/98).

June kept the house immaculate with little clutter. She said she hated having papers lying around. Once, she threw out a pad of construction paper the children had gotten for Christmas because it sat on the floor for too long. The children kept their school papers in their book bags until it was time to throw them away. June judiciously decided which school papers needed to be saved and which went in the garbage. "If I need to sign it, I know it got to be sent back," she explained to me about how she decided what to throw out (transcript, 1/98). June put away other important papers like birth certificates, award recognition letters, job certificates, and Social Security paperwork in a white grocery bag with a hole in its side.

The dining room had an old china cabinet that was missing two glass panes that was handed down from June's brother. June stored her spare set of dishes that were a part of her and Lester's wedding gifts in the china cabinet. On the other side of the room was a wooden cabinet where June kept towels. School papers that needed to be looked at, bills, and backpacks often collected on the top of this cabinet. On the paneled wall of the dining room was a "Happy Birthday" sign in different colors, which was kept on the wall for any upcoming birthday. Across the hall from the dining room was Vicky's room. Vicky and Luanne shared a room with a broken bunk bed that used to have two beds but now has only one. They slept in the same bed. Shauna slept either with her older siblings or with June and Lester. With the arrival of Evan, Shauna sometimes slept in the living room and Evan slept with June and Lester.

The kitchen was often the center of activity in the Treaders' house. In a 2-year period June redecorated her kitchen twice. The most recent time she ordered matching green-and-white tablecloths, curtains, place mats, and wall decorations from a mail-order catalog. June purchased two green-and-white crocheted religious crosses from a friend in her adult basic education class and hung them on the wall over the stove. June was attentive to the way her house looked and wanted it to be respectable and someplace that she could "show off." Often, when I would get to the Treaders' house one of the first things June would say is, "Come here, Becky, look at my new curtains" (fieldnotes, 3/4/99). Or the new burner covers. Or the matching cups she bought. She enjoyed shopping through the mail-order catalog because they had a good layaway plan where she only had to put a minimal amount of money down and then pay once a month. Often, during the first 10 to 15 minutes of my time at the Treaders' house June showed me what she wanted to get for her house, talking about the plans for redecorating or what she had already gotten in the mail. Once, as she showed me items she had bought for her kitchen she stated, "It's only $9.99 a month and they send all of this. . . I don't have to start payments till next month" (fieldnotes, 3/4/99). June kept all of her receipts for her layaway purchases, both mail order and department store, on the dresser top in her room. She spent a great deal of time looking over the receipts, doing the calculations, and figuring out how much she owed before she could pick up the items. This became particularly important around holidays and birthdays as June was often short of money she needed to pay off her children's gifts. Asking family members and playing bingo became strategic ways of making sure her children had fruitful holidays.

The kitchen is where June cooked dinner—often fried chicken, hamburgers, potatoes, beans, and collard greens. Often Vicky and I would work at the kitchen table, a spot that allowed me to observe the interactions in the house; but it also served as a central meeting spot when others came over to see if the girls could come out. During the time I worked with June or Vicky at the kitchen table, other members of the family indirectly or directly participated in the reading of books or writing letters, lists, or reflections on the readings. Realizing that a reading teacher was sitting in the kitchen seemed to spark many relatives' and neighbors' memories and feelings toward reading and school. In particular, June's younger brother would hang around the kitchen as I worked with Vicky. June's older brother told me that his daughter needed help with reading and asked if he could send her over when I was there. Another time, one of June's friends came over to the house and they held a conversation about the different schools where their children went, asking me my opinion.

June was also involved in the sessions when I worked with Vicky. Often when I worked with Vicky and she was stuck on a word, June came over to the table and looked over Vicky's shoulder at the text. On one occasion June came over to the table after hearing Vicky hesitate while reading and said, "Which word? Let's see if I can get it." She and Vicky both tried to figure it out (transcript, 2/98). Or during the time I worked with June, she brought forms or paperwork from different social service agencies or from the school to the table. During these sessions, Vicky stayed at the table and watched her mother and I as we negotiated the forms. Thus, my presence in the home facilitated the intergenerational context of literacy learning by providing a space for interactions around textual literacy.

Twice, early in the research relationship, two events raised curiosity about June's literacy. Luanne, in second grade at the time and often "showing off" her own reading, came into the kitchen when June had gone into the other room and asked me in a whispered voice, "My mother don't know how to read?" "She knows how to read," I told her. "But everyone needs a little help and practice" (fieldnotes, 10/97). Another time, Vicky came into the kitchen and was standing by the refrigerator, with the door open, watching her mother read. She asked June, "What grade you in?" June, never looking up from the book, said, "What grade I'm in? I'm not in no grade!" (fieldnotes, 11/97). With those exceptions, June's "work" on her reading seemed part of the fabric of the Treaders' life, accepted by all members of the family. Whether someone could or couldn't read did not seem to affect their status in the family and community.

The table where we worked was a black, wooden, and octagon shaped, with mismatched chairs. There were never enough chairs and we always needed to pull in at least two chairs from the dining room before sitting down. The light on the ceiling of the kitchen seemed to be always burnt-out. June complained, "Lester said he would get another lightbulb, but hasn't" (fieldnotes, 2/99). Thus, the room was dark except for early in the afternoon when the sun came through the windows.

The top of the microwave served as a spot where the Treaders placed papers, bills, documents, spelling tests, and directions. June often set things on top of the microwave that she wanted to make sure to remember to ask me about while I was there, like free- and reduced-lunch papers or forms for WIC. The refrigerator in the corner was decorated with magnetic alphabet letters, a calendar from the school and a close-up picture of Vicky with a big smile on her face. Their cat, Stanley, often used the dryer as a step stool to get to the window, where there was a hole in the screen so he could come and go onto the black tar roof.

A small room off the kitchen is what June referred to as the "library room." On my first visit to the house in September of 1997, June opened the door and showed me the room, telling me "this is where the kids do their homework" (fieldnotes, 10/10/97). In the room was a three-shelved red bookcase containing more than 75 children's books. June had collected them from the school store at the adult literacy center and the children had brought them home when their teachers were getting rid of them at school. One of the shelves held family photo albums. Vicky's, Luanne's and Shauna's certificates, spelling tests, homework papers, and awards from school covered the walls of the room. There were three spelling tests on which Vicky had gotten 100%, marked in red pen, hung on the walls. I heard June as she told the children when they were done with their homework to "get a book from the library and read" (transcript, 2/19/99). June made sure her children did their homework each night, telling them "you're not goin' outside so you might as well take your time on that homework" (transcript, 3/3/98). June and Lester decided to let their children go out after school only very infrequently because of the crime on the streets and because the neighborhood children are usually "up to no good" and act "too grown for their age" (fieldnotes, 8/98). When they did go outside, June sat on the front stoop and made sure they did not go past the end of the block where Rosemont Street intersected Herman and Shore streets. For Vicky, a rite of passage upon reaching adolescence was gaining June's permission for her to "around the corner" to her friend April's house. From the best of my understanding, based on information from the children and June and my own infrequent "hanging out" with them, when allowed out the children would stand outside, next to and on the front stoop, and watch people go by, listen to music, and generally "hang out." In the next section, I extend the context outward to the city and block group in which the Treaders lived.

The City of Albany

The city of Albany[1] where the Treaders live consists of urban neighborhoods, including North Albany, Arbor Hill, and the South End which surround the city's downtown. The local media often characterize the Treaders' neighborhood, Sherman Hollows, as one of the worst sections in the city. It is depicted as having high rates of violence, poverty, and crime, and poor relations between the police and community members. I have included an abridged history of Albany in Appendix A.

There are approximately 21,000 people in these neighborhoods, about one fifth of the city's population. About 55% of Albany's African American population and 25% of its Hispanic population live in these areas. As is the case with many urban neighborhoods, nearly one third of residents live below the poverty line, compared to about 18% in the city as a whole. The neighborhoods' per-capita income, $9,018, is approximately 34% less than the city's. About 17% of the households in these areas receive public assistance. With the exception of the South End, which includes public housing serving Albany's elderly, there is a large concentration of young people in these neighborhoods. Approximately 30% of the residents are aged 19 and younger.

Education, Employment, and Poverty

The Tract.   Tracts are defined by groups of blocks, generally three, within a geographical area. Within the tract where the Treaders live, there are a total of 2,570 people. A little over half are African American. The remainder are White. Twenty-five percent of the adults over the age of 25 in this area have less than a high school diploma. Twenty-nine percent of the people in this area fall below the poverty line. The Treaders are living below the poverty line. They receive disability payments, subsidized housing, food stamps, food and supplies from the local food pantry social services, and the children receive free lunches from the school.

The Block Group.   Rosemont Street, where the Treaders live, runs perpendicular between two parallel streets—Shore and Herman streets. It is bound on either end by central city streets. The block group in which the Treaders reside is comprised of rented apartments, old, abandoned factory buildings, and local stores. The block group of which Rosemont Street is a part stretches from Pearson to Crown Street and from Burlington to Rosemont Street. The block-group data allow us to take a closer look at what life looks like in the community where the Treaders live.

First, two thirds of the people who live in this block group are White. The rest, according to the Census, are Black. There are no other racial categories in this block group.[2] Over three fourths of the people who live in this area were born in the state of residence, whereas 40 of these people were born in the southern states before moving to this neighborhood. In terms of education, employment, and poverty, the block group differs from the overall tract figures. Thirty-six percent of adults over the age of 25 in this area have less than a high school diploma. Of these 775 people, 84 had less than a ninth-grade education, similar to June. Looking more closely at the aggregates of race and educational attainment in a block that is split in terms of Black and White reveals that of the 84 people with less than a ninth-grade education, 54 of these people are White. Similarly, whereas there are 63 White people have a 9th- to 12th-grade education but no high school diploma, there are 52 Black people with the same credentials. The numbers diverge from here. Whereas 126 White people have a high school diploma (or equivalency), only 35 Blacks have the same. There is also an interesting gap between the number of White people in this block group with a graduate or professional degree ($N = 52$) and the number of Blacks ($N =$ zero). These numbers reflect larger racial profiling in the community with regard to the number of African Americans who attend college, even with a major state university located down the road from the area.

The Census data, though over a decade old at the point of this study, indicate that the area the Treaders live in is an area with poverty, crime, "average" rates of unemployment, and low levels of education. Even with the existence of these social conditions, Sherman Hollow does not have the magnitude of destitution that is found in other, larger urban centers. The second floor of 79 Rosemont Street, the surrounding city streets, and the elementary school, middle school, and adult learning center, all walking distance from the house, comprise the setting for this research.

FRAMING THE STUDY

An Ethnographic Case Study Approach

I employed an ethnographic case study method to investigate in detail literacy events and to theorize about the relationship with social practices over time. I chose CDA as the analytic lens because it held the promise of uniting a critical social approach to the study of language and literacy with an ethnographic perspective. The case study method (Johnston, 1985; Merriam, 1997) allowed the closeness and richness of detail possible in working closely with one family. Ethnography, though, is not the same as the case study method. It is characterized by the lens through which social phenomena are investigated and is concerned with the culture and social practices of individuals or groups of individuals.

Ethnography is a set of methodological procedures as well as a means of representing the data (Richardson, 1995; Spradley, 1980; Wolcott, 1990). It is an investigative model rooted in anthropology that focuses on a deep understanding of the social and cultural phenomena under investigation. Ethnography allows researchers to capture social, personal, and institutional histories in a way that discourse analysis does not. Geertz (1973) defined ethnography as the practice of "thick description" in an effort to unearth the structures of signification in the behaviors of others, and, consequently, of ourselves as researchers, an idea I come back to throughout this book.[3] A case study approach to research is not necessarily bound to the tenets of thick description of ethnographic approaches to inquiry. A case study approach is, however, a focus on a detailed description and analysis of a single entity or phenomenon (Merriam, 1997). I combined ethnographic research methods, described later, with a focus on a case study of one family, the Treaders.

Research Design

Data Collection Procedures.   The specific data collection procedures extended over 2 years. They include participant-observations, interviews, photographs, reading group methodology, interviews with community members, document collection, and researcher journals in the Treaders' home, schools, and community. In the following section J describe each method briefly and expand on the data collection timetable in Appendix B.

I collected data over a 2-year period from the fall of 1997 through the fall of 1999. The components of the data collection involved three recursive and overlapping phases of inquiry: the home, the school, and the community. Roughly, from September of 1997 to December of 1997, I collected data on the nature and extent of literacy events in the Treaders' home. From December 1997 to June of 1998, I focused on collecting data from June's and Vicky's adult basic education classroom and sixth-grade classroom, respectively. From June 1998 to September of 1998 I collected data from the community of Sherman Hollows, a block group within the west end of Albany and the neighborhood in which the Treaders live. The first year of data collection helped me to see the nature of literacy in the Treaders' lives and to look more closely at the intersection of multiple cultural narratives about literacy. During the second year, I returned to the domains of home, school and community with the research questions presented at the end of chapter 1. Throughout both years of the research, I worked with June and Vicky as a literacy teacher. Once or twice a week I would work with each of them individually. In the middle of the first year, the one-on-one sessions turned into a small group as people in the community learned there was a literacy teacher at the Treaders' house.

Specifically, I utilized the ethnographic methods of participant-observation recorded in fieldnotes; a researcher journal; audiotapes of conversations and reading group sessions; classroom observations in both the ABE classroom and Vicky's sixth-grade remedial reading and language arts classes; semistructured and structured interviews; observations of institutional encounters; and document collection. I conducted more than 350 hours of observation in the home, the school, and the community contexts.

The nature of my participant-observation shifted from domain to domain and depended on the nature of the activity. There were some instances where I was more of a participant than an observer (e.g.,when I took on the role of a literacy teacher). There were other instances when I was more of an observer than a participant (e.g., in the ABE and elementary classrooms). I recorded my fieldnotes, depending on my place in the continuum of participant-observer, either as I observed or immediately following the observation. I analyzed my fieldnotes before going back to my research site again. I wrote down questions I wanted to follow up on. After 6 months of observing in the Treaders' home and community, I developed a data collection chart, which was categorized into the major dimensions of literacy events and practices I continually observed in those milieus. This chart served as a guide for me to record my observations in a systematic manner. I would write fieldnotes from these charts when I returned home (Appendix C). Similarly, I also developed a document summary form (Appendix D) which helped to guide my analysis of the written documents I collected from the Treaders. This document summary chart guided my construction of the vignettes of critical incidents in my analysis.

Units of Analysis: Literacy/Discourse Practices

Units of analysis are important in research because they mark the place where researchers focus their attention. The unit of analysis I employed in this study involved a merging of constructs from separate but complementary traditions. First are the constructs of *literacy events/practices* (Anderson et al., 1980; Barton & Hamilton, 1998; Heath, 1983). The second set of constructs are *discourse/Discourse* (Gee, 1996, 1999). The third set of constructs are *orders of discourse* (Chouliaraki & Fairclough, 1999; Fairclough, 1995).

The distinction between these constructs is subtle but substantive. Literacy events are defined as "any action sequence, involving one or more persons, in which the production and/or comprehension of print plays a role" (Barton & Hamilton, 2000, p. 59). Literacy events are those events in which written texts or talk-around texts have a central role. Literacy events and discourse map into each other in the sense they both involve observable instances of interactions.

The constructs of literacy practices and Discourses also have similar boundaries. Literacy practices are defined as, "the general cultural ways of utilizing written language which people draw upon in their lives. In the simplest sense literacy practices are what people do with literacy. However practices are not observable units of behavior since they involve values, attitudes, feelings and social relationships" (Barton & Hamilton, 2000, p. 6). Literacy events and practices are seen as socially situated practices that only make sense when studied in the context of social and cultural practices of which they are a part (Barton, 1994; Gee, 1996; Heath, 1983; Street, 1984, 1995).

Although the boundaries of these constructs are similar, there is also a subtle difference. Gee's d/Discourse constructs, introduced in the last chapter, assume the role of power in and through discourse. These constructs have different intellectual roots but are currently converging around the intersection of literacy practices and Discourse practices because of an increased interest in the areas of ethnography and discourse analysis (cf. Barton & Hamilton & Ivanic, 2000).

In this study, I observed literacy events in the different domains of the home, the school, and the community. It became clear there were multiple literacies corresponding with each domain. For example, there were literacy practices such as schooled literacy, workplace literacy, and family literacy, to name a few. I began with exploring the literate context of the home—or family literacy practices. Not only are the literacy events different in each domain (e.g., reading health care forms, filling out a workbook sheet) but there were different values, beliefs, and sets of interactions surrounding different literacy events. Literacy practices are patterned and structured by social institutions and power relationships. Therefore, some literacies were more dominant and visible than others. That is, dominant literacies and ways with texts carry more significance than local literacy practices. Gee's (1996) theoretical framework addresses this issue through systems of primary and secondary Discourse. However, what the constructs of d/Discourse and literacy events/practices do not do is account for the *process* through which power operates in discourse. Fairclough (1992, 1995) used "orders of discourse" as a heuristic for language and social life.

These three analytic constructs of *literacy/events, d/Discourse,* and *orders of discourse* (Barton & Hamilton, 1998; Fairclough, 1995; Gee, 1996, 1999) allow a conceptualization of power through discourse and a means of pointing to instances through a textually oriented approach to discourse analysis. When social interaction and power are given analytic priority, multivocal individuals are seen in a dynamic process of negotiation. This unit of analysis makes sense given the present set of social concerns mentioned in chapter 1 because it focuses attention on the multidimensional interaction between individuals and social structures rather than on the individual or social structures. With this in mind, literacy is not something done to individuals, nor is it something done solely by individuals. Rather, it is an intersection of individual agency and social conditions. It is at once a tool for individuals and a tool for society.

Whereas discourse and literacy practices situate local events, the starting unit of analysis is the literacy event. Literacy events and discourse are often regular, everyday repeated activities and therefore are useful starting points when researching literacy. I began this research with the Treaders' employing the literacy event as the basic unit of analysis. I documented the range of literacy events that existed and my observations were catalogued in fieldnotes and analytic charts. From this first interpretive level of analysis, I documented the sets of literacy practices with which these events were connected. The texts most frequently interacted with in the Treaders' house came from social service agencies or from the school. The majority of these texts were bureaucratic (Taylor, 1997).

These social processes of moving from a literacy event to a social practice can be inferred through literacy events that are mediated by written texts. In the following example, I illustrate the unit of analysis, the literacy event, and the sets of social practices that may be inferred from an analysis of the interaction. In this example, June and I are reading a health care form that June needed to fill out in order for Shauna, her youngest daughter, to enter preschool. Though we are both able to read the words or what Gee (1996) referred to as the "language bits," neither of us has access to the meaning of the medical terminology, or the medical discourse with which both of us struggle as we fill out the form.

6. Becky: Has she been, does she have a physical examination? ///

(I rephrase my question.)

7. Becky: Has she been to the doctor?

8. June: Uh-uh. (Shakes her head.)

13. Becky: [Okay (reading the form) this, is the child receiving topical fluoride application? Fluoridated water or fluoride supplement diet?

14. June: Oh the vitamins?

When June heard the string of words "topical fluoride application" she reduced it to "vitamins," a meaningful unit in order to make meaning from the form.

24. Becky: Is it fluoride applications? (Reading from the form.)

25. June: No, I think it is fluoride with water. I show you it.

June referred here to the pill dispenser that the vitamins were in. She went into the bathroom to get the bottle and brought it back into the kitchen where we were sitting.

26. Becky: Okay, it is not the first one (cross-checking between the orange pill dispenser and the form), fluoridated water or fluoridated supplement diet.

27. June: I think it is this one.
28. Becky: Fluoridated water. I think that would mean that she is taking the water with it. I think it is the last one that is fluoride supplemented diet. Well (. . .) I don't know.

I compared the label on the pill bottle, which described what the fluoride supplements were, with what the form asked for. They were written in different technical terms and I had trouble figuring this out. June and I talked about the vitamins that her children took and we eliminated the ones on the form that did not make sense.

29. June: (Shakes her head and disagrees with me.)
30. Becky: Is it, is it the middle one? (Referring to the form.)
31. June: Yeah, I think it is this one.
(transcript 1/16/98)

The literacy event began when June showed me the health care form and ended when the form was complete. The observable unit of analysis, the literacy event, involves interaction around the health care form where we are both consuming and producing information. There is more to this set of interactions than simply interactions with the written texts, though. In analyzing literacy events we learn more about social practices. This interaction involves social institutions, June's and my relationship, and our knowledge and proficiency with the language of the text.

Literacy is always more than reading the words. Here, neither June nor I have access to the medical discourse and we struggle with understanding what we should write for the vitamins that Shauna took. This form required June to respond to the questions and check "is" or "is not" in the boxes. It assumes that June has the necessary information and discourse.

The dominant literacy here involves the medical discourse, Standard English, and filling out a form. June's assumption in giving me the form to look at is that as a literacy teacher I will know how to fill out the form. However, June has had many more interactions with bureaucratic forms than I, a history that helps her negotiate the form. This becomes apparent in Lines 13 and 14 when June reduces the string of words "topical fluoride application" to "the vitamins." June's frustration with me *not knowing* came through in Line 29 when she shook her head and disagreed with my understanding of "fluoride applications." Therefore, as Barton and Hamilton (1998) pointed out, "literacy is best understood as sets of social practices; these can be inferred from events that are mediated by written texts" (p. 8). In the next section, I move from the smallest unit of analysis to the two complementary analytic procedures I used in this research.

Data Analysis

Ethnographic data collection can take us only so far. Thick description can help us to describe deeply contexts and actions. There were three complementary modes of analysis in this research. The first was a grounded theory approach (Glaser & Strauss, 1967; Miles & Huberman, 1984) where I inductively coded the transcripts for literacy events.[4] I coded transcripts and fieldnotes for instances of literacy events and their connecting social practices. At this level of analysis, I learned that the family literacy context was structured by institutional literacy practices, a finding cited in the research literature (Anderson & Stoakes, 1984). Without an analytic base tied to a theoretical framework, data remain piles of notes, audiotapes, and work samples. Thus, my theorizing about what I was observing in the field was also attached to the research literature. Because my understandings of what I was observing deepened and changed over time, I found myself in a continual process of moving between literature and analysis—supporting and challenging my working hypotheses.

From this point, I developed three categories to classify the type of interactions that each literacy event was a part of. These categories were "face to face," "face to text," and "text to text" interactions (Rogers, 2000). The earlier interaction with the health care form is considered both a face-to-text and a face-to-face interaction. June is interacting with the form but she has also enlisted me to help her make sense of it. Although there were not always clear boundaries between these categories, they provided a useful starting place to conceptualize the ways in which relationships were structured by institutions. It was also in these interactions that instances of power became clear. Thus, the third interpretive move involved the use of CDA as an analytic strategy.

CDA helped to illuminate *how* people make sense of their reality and understand their social positions. To these ends, Norman Fairclough (1989, 1992, 1995) presented three, intersecting domains that represent the conceptual spaces in which language functions as social practice. These domains are the genre (ways of interacting), discourse (ways of representing), and style (ways of being). Each order of discourse can be analyzed at the local, the institutional, and the societal orders of discourse (see Appendix E for the definitions and codes of CDA used in this study).

Genre is the domain where micro aspects of language are analyzed in order to understand the ways of interacting that comprise the specific genre (e.g. literacy lesson, interview, sermon). This microlinguistic analysis may include turn-taking structures, cohesion devices, tone, and information focus.

The next domain, discourse, involves the connection between texts, again either oral or written, and the social institutions connected to their production, consumption, and distribution. This domain of analysis builds on the genre and is interested in the ways of representing that are connected with any discourse practice.

Finally, style is organized in a way that allows a space for looking closely at the relationships between the texts and social structures that play a role in social positioning, identity construction, and individual agency. This domain is connected to genre and discourse and is concerned with the ways of being that are connected to a discourse practice. At this domain of analysis the analyst may look for aspects of grammar that include pronoun use, modality, transitivity, and active and passive voice. Each order of discourse—genre (textual), discourse (interpersonal), and style (ideational)—can be analyzed at the local, institutional, and societal levels.

In order to use this framework with my data set, I went through the following processes of pulling apart and piecing back together the data. First, I engaged in multiple readings of the data set. This consisted of transcripts of interviews, interactions, fieldnotes of interactions, and observations both in and out of school, as well as formal and informal written documents. In the first set of readings, I was interested in understanding or developing a sense of coherency. From here, I developed the broad analytic categories of "face to face," "face to text," and "text to text," which allowed me to talk about the shape of the interactions between the participants and social institutions. Within these broad categories, I then went back into the data set in order to select instances of each of these categories. When these categories were filled with examples, I then selected salient examples that represented "cruces" or tension spots (Fairclough, 1995). As a result of the conceptual leverage these instances played, I reasoned that they would yield rich descriptions and provide useful theoretical insights. I then chose to examine these cases, or instances, more closely.

Next, I developed critical vignettes of these instances. A critical vignette consists of a summative statement including the larger context and a CDA on the event. For example, when looking at an event in which June interacted with a community agency, I would look across the data set (e.g., fieldnotes, transcribed audiotapes, textual artifacts) and make connections across the interactions.

Taking each text separately, I broadly coded the texts for instances of discursive examples of linguistic codes, or the local level of analysis. Fairclough's (1989) framework was useful in focusing my attention on certain aspects of text. Broadly, I defined these instances as interactional patterns, vocabulary, and turntaking structure. The assumption guiding this level of analysis was that interactions are always a part of a social language or a genre that includes ways of interacting. Examples of speech genres are literacy lessons, sermons, and interviews. Genres are distinguished through their participant framework, turntaking conventions, information focus, and cohesive devices. As I was coding, I asked myself questions such as: What are the signals at the interactional level that signify a genre?

Taking the same text, I then looked to "discourses" or ways of representing. Each genre may be represented in different manners. For example, a literacy lesson (genre) may be more or less teacher-driven. This is a relationship that needs to be described using patterns of language, rather than broad descriptions of social. Because this domain is concerned with the ways of representing, the analyst looks for themes and counter themes, and the information focus of the text as well as from what perspective the discourse is taken.

The assumption with the discourse domain is that there are patterns of knowledge production, consumption, distribution, negotiation, and transformation connected to institutional spheres. These patterns signal relationships between and among discourse and social action. I read the text looking for ways in which domains of knowledge were constructed and produced. I asked myself questions such as: How is this person constructing the institution they were speaking from? What is their relation to knowledge? What is the ordering of the consumption, distribution, production of these texts?

Again, with the same text, I turned to the voice or ideational domain of discourse. The assumption that guided this level of analysis was that language works in conjunction with genre and discourse to present "ways of being" that create and sustain subject positionings. At this domain of analysis I analyzed aspects of grammar that included pronoun use, passive and active construction, modality, and transitivity. I asked myself questions such as: How are identities created and sustained in these interactions? What are the ways of being that are connected with this genre, and this set of discourse?

The crucial point of this analysis is that the three domains are overlapping. The job of the analyst is to *study the relationship* between genre, discourse, and style in order to describe, interpret, and explain the ways of interacting, ways of representing, and ways of being connected with social practices.

Next, I repeated these phases with all of the texts. I kept my notes with pencil and paper and then transferred them into the computer. Each stage of analysis proved to further refine, to add detail, and to gain increasing specificity about the level of analysis. After analyzing the texts at the genre, discourse, and style domains, I then moved to sharpen the analysis by looking across the texts to understand the ways in which the texts spoke to each other. Here, I juxtaposed the local level of analysis across events looking for instances of similarity, difference, and tension. Similarly, I repeated this process with the institutional and the societal levels of analysis.

After this stage of analysis, I started to connect things back to the whole process of events, to recontextualize.

The usefulness of this framework is that it allows the analyst to look at the data, data that is often multiple and contradictory, through multiple lenses.[5] As a result of looking at these texts through the a close linguistic lens that took into account interactional patterns as well as grammar and vocabulary, I was able to recognize patterns of language that would otherwise have been missed. This close analysis allowed me then to weave together a linguistic and social analysis that links together the individual with the broader social forces and structures.

Therefore, one of the central aims of this work is to build an argument for the necessity of theoretical models that account for the intersection and complementary work of ethnography and discourse studies. CDA promises two things. First, it promises an analytic framework for explaining the relationship between ways of interacting, ways of representing, and ways of being—a framework that provides considerable empirical leverage. Second, it provides a more fine-grained analysis of the intersection of the individual and the larger context of texts, institutions, and subjectivities. However, common uses of CDA do not fully contextualize the textual data on which it focuses (Chouliaraki & Fairclough, 1999; Fairclough, 1992). Consequently, I demonstrate in this book the value of rich ethnographic description for gaining maximal leverage from CDA.

Trust in Language Claims

Earlier in the chapter I drew on anthropologist Clifford Geertz's wisdom concerning the process of conducting ethnography. Gertz pointed out that ethnography is the process of uncovering the signification in behaviors of those with whom we engage in research. In doing so we also learn something about our own behaviors and practices. A study of culture, language, and power is always a study of self. Emerson, Fretz, and Shaw (1995) referred to the inability of researchers to separate themselves from their learning as "consequential presence" (p. 3). They believed, and I agree, that researcher involvement is not something to be avoided or denied but that it is the *source* for learning and observations. They stated, "relationships between the field researcher and the people in the setting do not so much disrupt or alter on going patterns of social interaction as reveal the terms and bases on which people form social ties in the first place" (p. 3). Because literacy is about social relationships and relationships are constructed through interactions, it cannot be argued that approaches to literacy and language analysis are valid—or trustworthy—simply because they reflect reality.

In fact, the existence of multiple perspectives and realities is one of the assumptions behind CDA and the NLS.[6] Just as language always reflects multiple realities, there are multiple lines of interpretation that might be followed as I presented in the earlier example. The analyst always interprets data in a certain way so that the data are rendered meaningful in particular ways and not in others. My intention, then, is not to convince you that this is the *only* way of seeing these data and these social circumstances, but to provide an interpretation that makes sense given the data, the theoretical frameworks, and the analyses.

Because I am combining research and analytic methods of ethnography and discourse, there are several complementary aspects of validity or credibility to which I attend. First, I strive to achieve what Gee (1999a) referred to as "coverage." That is, claims made about language may be considered more believable if they make sense of what has come before and after the situation being analyzed and allow for predictions of the sorts of things that might happen in related situations. When you see these sets of circumstances again (e.g., interactions around a health care form or a special-education meeting) you are likely to see patterns of interactions that are similar to the ones presented here. The idea of coverage is an important one in this study for two reasons. First, coverage is important because it points out the significance of looking forward and looking backward in the representation of the data. It is my intention that in moving between ethnographic and language detail I can build a rich, textured narrative of the Treaders' literate lives. However, in order to do this I need to make connections with the vignettes, examples, and composites that have come before and those that will follow. The second reason why coverage is important is because in order to build this textured narrative I need to keep one eye on June's present participation and the other eye on her socio-historical participation with the school.

Aside from coverage, there were other measures of credibility built into the research process. I built numerous "checks and balances" into my research process including member checking (Wolcott, 1990), an audit trail (Glesne & Peshkin, 1992), and triangulation (Mathison, 1988) or "convergence" (Gee, 1999). I transcribed all of the audiotaped data except for the community member interviews, which were given to a transcriber. The audit trail included conference proposals, research papers, and degree requirements, which left a trail of my analytic and methodological decisions, a process often overlooked in interpretive research. This ensured ongoing analysis as well as a consistency with transcribing local language patterns. With each paper I wrote I member checked with June and Vicky as well as with other members of the community. These safeguards helped to ensure, at the very least, that I was not misrepresenting what I had seen and been a part of for 2 years. The issue of triangulation is similar to what Gee's notion of "convergence" in that ideas from one section of the database continue to support evidence and ideas from other parts of the database (e.g., official documents, interviews, face-to-face interactions, observations). Further, I continue to support my working hypothesis about the connection between literate identities, discursive processes, and social structures with a variety of linguistic details in the text.

In order to build and maintain credibility, I have to present enough data that the reader is able (if not likely) to make different interpretations than the ones I have offered in this text (Wolcott, 1990). To address issues of credibility, or the trustworthiness of the data, I have asked the following questions of the data and representation:

1. Do the data I (re) present match the intended research questions?

2. Has the research had some sort of catalytic impact on any of the participants?

3. Have I provided enough evidence that the reader is able to make counter interpretations?

In order to address matters of consistency, traditionally referred to as reliability, I follow in the footsteps of scholars that have reframed the concept of validity contexts (Gipps, 1994; Johnston, 1998a, 1998b; Moss, 1998). Their work, from various intellectual traditions, has shifted the focus away from consistency and replicability to issues of transferability and the extent to which the data may "ring true." I posed the following questions of the data:

1. How do the multiple sources of data, over time, help to establish the consistency of the claims?

2. Where are the places where the data seemed to be inconsistent? How do these instances help me to rework the frameworks?

3. What areas of this case study are useful for making more generalized claims about the nature of literacy contexts, literacy, and language events with social institutions?

Reflexivity

The struggle with establishing the methodological safeguards mentioned previously is that they often serve to protect researchers from a self-reflexive research paradigm. Building or reformulating theories from empirically grounded data requires a reciprocal relationship between data, theory, and self (Peshkin, 1988; Peterson, 1998; Lather, 1991). Though I began the research with a set of theoretical frameworks as described in chapter 1 and in the earlier discussion in this chapter, I was conscious of the need for the data (and myself) to be open to counterinterpretations.

Therefore, in analyzing the nature of literacy and social relations, especially as they relate to issues of power, I need to illuminate my own role in the process. The writing of this research reveals as much about my own position within institutional systems, especially that of schools, as it does about the Treaders. Many of the analyses and examples provided in this study include myself as a researcher where I am closely connected to the literate interactions. My own part in this study is subject to the same analytic frames as I am applying to the discourse of others. Though the focus of the book is on the Treaders, I, in places, point to the significance of my participation in this study. In particular, aside from clarifying my shifting role and relationship in the study, I utilize the concept of reflexivity in order to look critically at my own role in this research.

There are few guidelines for reflexive practice in the research literature and even fewer examples of what reflexive practice might look like. Lather (1991) and Bourdieu and Wacquant (1992) made several suggestions with regard to reflexive research. In the rest of this book, I highlight the places where this reflexive practice comes up. In Appendix H I discuss, in depth, my role in the research and how, and in what ways, my presence has made a difference.

The first piece of reflexivity is the idea that studies situated within critical paradigms are interested in the experiences, desires, and frustrations of oppressed people. The first step in this type of inquiry is to develop an understanding of the worldview of the participants. Central to this inquiry is a dialogic research design where participants have a central voice in the structure and decision of the research.

The second aspect of reflexive practice is the notion of reciprocity and dialogue. This means that in the Freiran sense, researchers and participants learn from each other. In doing this, the present research experiences are cast against a historical background that is illuminated and at the same time challenged. The intention in doing this is so that both the researcher and the participants are able to engage in a critique of social arrangements and arrive at the potential for change in their situations.[7]

The third aspect of reflexivity relevant to the present study is that researchers and participants engage in a process of critical analysis and sustained action over time. Dialogic encounters are likely to facilitate reflexive encounters. Many of the interactions I have included in this study involve myself as a piece of the interaction. I have been reflexive on my own role in the inquiry through the ongoing process of being involved or participating, writing fieldnotes, analyzing these interactions, and writing about them.

In the next chapter, I argue that the Treaders' family and personal histories demonstrate the ways in which institutional discourse shapes people's lives. Like most families living in poverty, the Treaders have not written a personal account of their lives. Their lives, in part, can be traced through the trail of bureaucratic texts that define, shape, and grant them access to the resources they need to survive. These public documents, however, reveal a unidimensional account of their lives. Through an ethnographic case study I add the detail and the texture of life within and through systems.

NOTES

1. All of the census information presented in this chapter comes from the 1989 Census figures. Although the Census Bureau and New York's Empire State Development have updated some of the profiles as of July 1,1998, they are done at a county level. The 1989 figures are the most current at the block group level.
2. Labels presented here are representative of the language used in the national Census data.
3. I agree with Wolcott's (1995) assertions that thick description by itself is not the basis for ethnographic claims. This focus on a thick description (the level of detail) is often mistaken for the idea that if the researcher stays in the field longer, takes more and better notes, or talks with more people that they have completed an ethnography. However, Wolcott cautioned between the *degree of detail* and the kind of direction one takes with the *interpretation* of the data. Ethnographers concern themselves mainly with the interpretation and representation of culture. It is not just what participants "say" that is important but the way in which culture is symbolically represented through actions and practices. As I argue in the next chapter, literacy is inextricably bound to culture and identity. Therefore, naturalistic inquiry into literacy as a social and cultural phenomenon, extensive time spent in the field, as well as the intent of producing an ethnography (as a mode of representation) mark this work as ethnographic. However, this said, ethnography is a broad description for research. It is not to imply that there is one "ethnographic stance" that is adopted by the researcher. As I demonstrate, with examples in this book, I have adopted different positions with the research. There are a range of possibilities within the ethnographic spectrum.
4. *Transcription Notations*

   (*Italics*) for non-verbal movements
   [words] analysis comments
   / represents each second of silence
   [for overlapping utterances
   () for inaudible speech
   - for haltering or stammering
   Bold for tonal emphasis
5. CDA has been critiqued (Blommaert, 2001; Flowerdew, 1999; Kamler, 1997; Widdowson, 1998) for three primary reasons. The first is that social and political ideologies are read onto the data. Second, is that CDA is often taken out of context. Indeed, many uses of CDA involve the analysis of speeches, media text, and political documents (e.g., Bloome & Power-Carter, 2001; Wodak, 1997). The third critique is that there is often incoherence between the theory and method of CDA. That is, whereas the theoretical framework that supports

CDA assumes a dialogic speaker, language as socially constitutive, and language as enabling and constraining, often analyses view power as constraining, a univocal speaking person, and do not demonstrate language as continually reconstructed. I argue that embedding CDA within an ethnographic study situates the analysis within a larger social and cultural context. Further, the goal of a CDA is not to uncover power relationships embedded in discourse, indeed this goal would be reading social and political ideologies onto the data, but rather to systematically study the relationship between ways of interacting (genres), ways of representing (discourse), and ways of being (style).

6. The NLS was one of the many disciplinary turns toward language and mediated action as a means of understanding social phenomena. The NLS are based on the premise that reading and writing are always culturally, socially, and politically situated (see Gee, 2000, for a discussion).

7. See Gitlin (1994) and Tierney and Lincoln (1997) for a discussion around the issues of power, method, and reflexive practice in interpretive critical research.

Chapter 3

Personal and Institutional Histories[1]

June dropped out of school, in the same school district where her daughter attended, at the end of her eighth-grade year. She told me she had never been in a special-education class; although on a visit to the middle school, June remembered a red stripe on the wall that symbolized the hallway where the special-education classes used to be located. June told me her reading was "doin' good" until she dropped out of school. She complained, though, that her reading kept "goin' down." June didn't speak about her educational history often, as if she could create a new history for herself through her children. However, one afternoon in her kitchen she re-created her experience of dropping out of school:

> I just stopped going . . . I went to the high school first, then I moved to the south like in seventy-something'. Then I came back here and went to the adult learning center . . . I was about, what nineteen? I didn't have no kids then . . . I stopped goin' there after a few months because I had to start workin'. Yeah, I had to start workin' and I just went back to school in September [1996]. (transcript, 11/11/97)

Knowing June's determination to improve her own literacy, I wondered how, as a struggling reader, she had been able to negotiate the school curriculum up until the eighth grade. June explained:

> 'Cause I just was going [to school] every day. But what I am sayin' is that I was really doin' good up until the ninth grade. And then when I stopped goin' to school for that long time, that was when I was goin' down. 'Cause I hadn't been back in school. From kindergarten to ninth I was doin' just fine. But when I dropped out I was just getting lower in my readin'. I was goin' down then. 'Cause I wasn't doin' nothin'. I wasn't readin'. I wasn't doin' no type of activity for readin' or writin', nothin' like that, after I dropped out of school. (transcript, 11/11/97)

I learned from listening to June talk about her history with education that attendance at school was a significant part of what it meant to be a "good student." Attendance is an issue she reinforced with her own children.

Furthermore, June framed her decision to drop out and go back to school as her choice. When June spoke of the reason she went back to school, it was embedded in the notion that she did not want to sit around "doin' nothin'" at home. June stated:

> I was tired of sittin' home. I was tired of sittin' home and I said by sittin' home any longer I'm not goin' to get anywhere by sitting home no longer and doin' no work. And I needed to catch up on my readin' and my math, and well mostly my readin' cause math is no problem. So I'm waitin' to catch up on my readin'. (transcript, 9/97)

When I asked June to write about the reason she returned to get her GED, June wrote, "I will like to get my GED for I can get a good education on my reading and writing so I can get a good job and show my kids that I can do something for my life" (writing sample, 10/28/97). June spoke of going back to school to improve her reading, something she wanted to do versus something that was her right. This is similar to Rockhill's (1995) analysis of the relationship working-class women have to literacy and education. Rockhill stated, "Literacy is women's work, but not women's right" (p. 171). Often when women speak of returning to school, it is embedded in something they desire to do rather than as their fundamental right.

In June's discourse the metaphor "waitin' to catch up on readin'" revealed June's stance with regard to her role in her own reading and education. Often, a typical day in the classroom consisted of reading time from 9 a.m. to 10:30 a.m., a short break, and math from 10:30 a.m. to noon. After lunch was independent work time where the students could choose what they wanted to work on. Reading time consisted of working through problems in a workbook. The workbooks presented words in isolation, asked the students to match definitions with words, presented short passages with the words in context, and then presented comprehension questions for the students to answer. The workbooks progressed from lower to higher order reading levels. The teachers and the students marked their progress by their movement through the stages in the workbook series.

Ralph, June's adult literacy teacher, reported that June was one of the lowest readers in the class. However, he stated that she did her work in class and attended class every day. In the classroom, June participated by the rules. She worked out of her reading workbook during reading time and her math workbook during math time. When she was done with a section in her workbook, she would ask the teacher to correct it. I often observed her following the words in the workbook with her pencil as she read to herself. June never rejected one-on-one help from any of the volunteer tutors in the room. She seemed to enjoy the reinforcement that reading aloud to a more knowledgeable other gave her.

When the classroom instruction shifted to include discussion groups around multiple copies of trade books, June resisted this type of learning, stating that she was not going to become a better reader by talking about books (fieldnotes, 10/98). When the rest of the class discussed books, June and a few other students sat at the back table and worked out of their workbooks. Similarly, when the rest of the class participated in a language experience approach to literacy instruction, telling and writing family stories, June refused to be involved stating that she "didn't have no stories to tell" (fieldnotes, 4/8/98).

From observations of these various literacy events, reading the workbook in the classroom, resisting discussion groups, and a language experience approach to literacy education, it seemed that June saw reading as something that was measured incrementally and was an individual endeavor. Indeed, an analysis of the ways in which June represented the discourse of reading (discourse) and her ways of being (style) demonstrates that she saw reading as an individual endeavor, something that was practiced.

June stated, "I wasn't readin'. I wasn't doin' no type of activity for readin' or writin'. . . . I was just getting lower in my readin'. I was goin' down then." It was not just her reading that was going down, but symbolically her sense of self was also diminishing. She added to this stating, "I was tired of sittin' home and I said by sittin' home any longer I'm not going to get anywhere by sitting home no longer and doin' no work." Reading symbolized her movement into doing something. The irony in this was that whereas June saw reading as something done by the individual, it was measured by an authority outside of one's self, that is, a teacher or guidance counselor. June positioned herself as passive in terms of her deepening of literate understandings. She stated, "I'm waitin' to catch up on my readin'."

June believed that reading and writing was mastery of a set of skills rather than a sociocultural tool. Indeed, June believed the route to better reading was through reading. As a result, she practiced in many different contexts including the grocery store, when she took walks, and at the health clinic. One afternoon I accompanied June and her three children to a doctor's appointment at the local health care clinic. June was in her second trimester and was scheduled for a routine check-up on the progress of her pregnancy. We sat in the waiting room of the clinic. Lori and Shauna played with the brightly colored toys that were stacked in the corner. Vicky sat in the chair and observed people coming and going. I was taking note (in my mind) of the types of literacy events and practices available to the patients of the health clinic. There was print on the walls, informational brochures and handouts, magazines, and a rack of children's books. I picked up a magazine and started to look through it. Shauna, watching me, picked up a book and brought it over to me to read. Holding her on my lap, I read the children's book to her. I sat next to June and June watched as I pointed to the words in the book, talked to Shauna about the story, and asked Shauna to help me read. June picked up a children's book off of the coffee table and began to read it to herself (fieldnotes, 6/98). When I asked June if she read to her children, she said, "they know when I mess up on a word" and that "Vicky is a better reader." Although she never stated this, it seemed that part of why she picked up the children's books, the pamphlets, and read the street signs was so she could become a better reader and read to her children. Many of June's thoughts, beliefs, and desires about literacy framed how she interacted with the school on behalf of her children.

"Pushin in a Time Clock" : Discipline, Authority, and Timeliness. June often included vignettes about Curt, the guidance counselor, as she talked about her experiences at school. Curt was responsible for attendance and for scheduling of tests. When June spoke about Curt, she often referred to him as someone who monitored her actions. June stated, "He comes in and sit in the class to see whose doin' work and whose not doin' work." By June's again evoking the metaphor of work to describe her interaction with literacy and education, I recognized that Curt's behavior bothered June, because she felt as though she *was* doing her "work". "June stated," Ralph [ABE teacher] he know I do readin' in the mornin' or do math in the mornin' and then 'round 'bout, I just get tired. I just get tired readin' or writin' or doin' math. Ralph know I be doin' work up in the classroom" (transcript, 3/26/98).

The notion of June's whole body getting tired aptly characterized the lack of stimuli of the ABE classroom and the embodiment of this experience. The 25 to 30 students in the classroom sat at long tables with workbooks in front of them. They passively filled in the pages until it was time for their break.

June was resentful of the connections Curt, the guidance counselor, made between discipline, timeliness, and order in school. June told me she was not mandated to return to school and she did not see the connection between school and having a job like Curt reinforced at the school. June wanted control and autonomy over her learning. She told me about one of the tense interactions between herself and Curt at the school:

> I came to school yesterday and soon as I came to school he talkin' about you bein' late. "You late." It was ten minutes after [the hour school starts]. I said, "that's nothin' new 'cause I'm late." I come to school yesterday, after one o'clock (after lunch break) and fifteen minutes after I got there he say, "You're late." I say, "So what, Curt, I'm late. I'm late. I'm not mandatory to come here

so why you keep bein' on my back talkin' 'bout "I'm late?" Then he talkin' 'bout "well I'm not sayin', I'm not on your back." I say, "Yes, you is on my back this mornin'; now you on my back this afternoon. What's your problem?" Then he got to talkin' 'bout, "well, um, if you was the teacher" and I said, "I am not no teacher." He went on 'bout callin' my caseworker. I said, "go ahead and call her, call her . . . I'm not mandatory to be here." (transcript, 12/11/97)

June reiterated that she did not have to be at the school. The department of social services (DSS) had not mandated that she go to school. June stated:

I'm, not mandatory to be there . . . I went on my own. When I stopped working, they [DSS] either tol' me to get a job or to do something'. So what I did when I left from up there [DSS], I called her [caseworker] and tol' her I was goin' to school and then she said that's good you goin' to school on your own because 'round 'bout January they was gonna cut people off or get 'em in school [referring to welfare reforms]. (transcript, 12/11/97)

The fact that June was not obligated to be at school, but that she chose to go, was important for her. She resented Curt's behaviors that suggested she was owned, like an employee, and that he therefore had a right to tell June what to do. June wanted autonomy over her educational decisions and resisted being told what to do:

So I just tol' Curt, I tol' him to leave me alone. I ain't got time to be bothered with him. He sits in class all day yesterday waitin' for somebody to say something'. You know how he just comes in the classroom, I mean he just sits there, he sits in that class, all day yesterday [June laughed at the absurdity of this]. And then when we got back yesterday afternoon he was siting in the hallway on a chair by the time clock. Just waitin' for us to be late. (transcript, 12/11/97)

Curt's presence, especially by the time clock that sat on the dark hallway wall leading to the office, suggested discipline and authority that June did not think it was necessary to contend with. June went on:

He gonna talk about you suppose to be here on time or if you had a job, you'd be here on time. I said, "But let me tell you something'. This is not a job. Now if I had a job, yeah I'd be there on time like I suppose to be. But this is not no job. You not payin' me to come here so what you need me to be pushin' in a time clock for when you're not payin' me." (transcript, 12/11/97)

June's desire to have control over the procedural aspects of her education is important because she had very little control over curricular aspects of her learning, a pattern similar pattern to other working-class parents (Lareau, 1989). This control and assertiveness stood in contrast to June's fragility as a literacy student, an issue that becomes apparent in the next section. Furthermore, this theme of being involved in the procedural aspects of education rather than the content or the curricular aspects is a theme that frames June's involvement with her children's school.

"Goin' Up" and "Goin' Down": Progress With Literacy. June stated on an inventory for her school that her educational goals were to get upstairs to the GED room. Her occupational goals were to start her own day care because she liked watching children (inventory, 10/98). June often used the metaphors of "goin' up" and "goin' down" when she discussed her progress toward these goals at school. June had learned this from the value placed on standardized tests that measured her gains in literacy through sets of scores and grade-level equivalents. These cultural beliefs about literacy and about measuring worth were deeply ingrained in June. This cultural stronghold, a piece of intergenerational literacy, is a theme I demonstrate in future chapters. Often, when June referred to her own literacy it was in terms of the last test she just took. When I asked June how she was doing at school, she would say "I just got a 3.7." Schooled literacy seemed to be a measured phenomenon, controlled by external authorities and not connected to her life. Many of June's present-day experiences with the adult literacy center signified her past educational history.

Tests were a significant part of June's experience in her adult basic education class because it was evidence to her that she was making progress. Her understanding of the purpose of these tests, to measure her reading and math to see if they had "gone up," influenced how she interpreted the testing Vicky would undergo during the special-education referral process. In the following narrative, told to me in her kitchen with tears streaming down her face, June linked her past educational experiences with her present:

> I mean it was a problem [reading]. When I first went back to school my readin' was down to like a one. I was down to a one in readin'. Yulp. I went down to my readin' was down to like a one point three. And that was like a first grade or something like that? 'Cause I couldn't read but I could read but I couldn't read that good. I was down to a one point three. Then I took another test and it went up to like two point something' like that. And then I just kept on goin' to school every day and doin' my work and you know then that Tim and Joanne was in that project and we had to do a lot of reading with that project. Then you was workin' with me and Ellen was too. So now it's a four point seven when I took my last readin' test (transcript, 3/98).

The themes of reading as an individual endeavor and evaluated by an external authority are apparent in this quotation as well. Similar to the analysis I presented of June discussing her experiences in her ABE classroom, a CDA of this narrative demonstrates the relationship between ways of interacting (genre), ways of representing (discourse), and ways of being (style).

The genre or the "ways of interacting" is an interview. The genre is marked by June's repetition throughout the interview. She stated, "down to like a one . . . I was down to a one in readin'. Yulp. I went down to my readin' was down to like a one point three." Repetition works as a cohesive device that serves to remind the reader or the listener that important things are not said in unimportant ways. At the domain of discourse or "ways of representing," the themes of "reading", marked by going up and down, and measured by tests are clear. June represented these themes through an individual perspective, that is, reading and progress is done through practice and "goin' to school every day and doin' my work." In the domain of style or "ways of being," June couched her discussion of self in relation to literacy in terms of deficit language. For example, she stated, "I mean it was a problem. When I first went back to school my readin' was down to like a one." She also stated, "I couldn't read that good." Many of June's "I"statements are followed by deficit statements. Further, she positioned herself as a passive recipient of the tests, the teachers, and the guidance counselor in terms of knowing when she made progress with her reading. She stated, "Then I took another test and it went up to like two point something'."

Looking at this quotation through the lenses of ways of interacting (genre), ways of representing (discourse), and ways of being (style) makes visible the relationship between orders of discourse. June's positioning of herself as passive in relation to schooled literacy comes into clearer focus as we see her negotiate literacy in other domains—especially with her children and the community—in more active ways.

June's fragility when she talked about her progress with literacy stood in stark contrast to her assertions of control and autonomy over the procedural aspects of her learning. Though June wanted to be in control of her choice to be at the literacy center and wanted to make the decisions about when she would get there and when she would do her work, she was not very confident about assessing her own growth. June's thinking about her progress in school was dominated by references to going "up"and "down"on tests. June counted on these periodic tests—"We take 'em once every three to four months," June told me—to tell her if she had made progress (transcript, 3/18/99). They did report progress, as June reported she had moved from a first-grade level to a mid-fourth-grade level within 2 years of being in the classroom. Aside from learning about the role of learning as measured by tests, June learned that reading was an individual endeavor, practiced for mastery of skills.

As June talked about her progress, there were echoes of her belief in reading as an individual endeavor, a reliance on external authority figures, and a significant emphasis placed on standardized tests. In following example, June talked about what she needed to do in order to get upstairs to the GED room. I have underlined the places where June emphasized her current status with literacy and education through markers of moving up or going up to the GED room. I have also bolded the places to mark where June made reference to Curt as the person who is responsible for her movement upstairs:

> I just, I have to pick up on my reading. 'Cause **he [Curt]** said I got to go up like to the seventh level, like the seventh. 'Cause I'm at a 4.7 right now and **he** want me to go up, to the seven. I think it's like readin', up to a seven. Seven point. Yeah, **he** said that once I get up to a seven then I'll go upstairs (transcript, 11/11/97).

June values education and literacy. This significance is problematic, I argue, because June's memories of schooling were laced with what Cook-Gumperz (1986) and Hicks (2001) referred to as "schooled literacy." Schooled literacy aptly characterizes the context-free learning that is evaluated by tests and whose progress is determined by outside authorities. June believed in the evaluation of her progress from outside authorities such as the guidance counselor and her classroom teacher. She seemed to believe in the power of the test scores to reveal whether she had made progress. Indeed, as June described what she needed to do to get upstairs, she revoiced Curt's, the guidance counselor's, expectations. She stated, "He [Curt] said I got to go up like to the seventh level, like the seventh . . . Yeah, he said that once I get up to a seven then I'll go upstairs." She also exhibited a strong control over the procedural aspects of school including the discipline, timeliness, and work ethic connected with school. She demonstrated a solid voice when talking about these things. This stood in contrast to June's talk about her progress with literacy. It is clear that June was not willing to sacrifice her personal integrity in the process of becoming literate.

As Luttrell (1997) pointed out, being "somebody" with regard to schooling operates at both psychological and social levels. And Collins (1996) wrote about the embodiment of contradictions that are inherent in literacy and education in a capitalist society. That is, identities are often organized and performed at a textual level within schools and other educational settings. This is relevant because June has formed an extremely strong connection, in both values and aspirations and everyday literacy practices and events, with school. As a result, the school as a set of Discourse practices had a strong influence on June's identity. This history helps us to understand June's participation with her children's education and the subsequent decisions she made.

Negotiating Literacy in the Community

As is the case historically with African American families, complex language and literacy practices were part of the fabric of the Treaders' daily lives (Foster, 1998; Gadsden, 1998; Moss, 2001; Harris, Kamhi, and Pollock, eds., 2001). The interactions June had with literacy practices in her home and community did not match her literacy participation in the classroom. In her home and community context June actively negotiated the literate demands of her life. Unlike reports of other adult education students who avoided literacy in their daily lives (Fingeret & Drennon, 1997; Gowen, 1992), June both negotiated and initiated literacy in her home and community. The paradox, though, was that these interactions did not count toward June's status within the school nor did June view them as literacy.

The Community Petition.   From June's front stoop, the place where many of our conversations took place, you can look across the street and see a corner store. People are in and out of the store day and night carrying lottery tickets, soda, beer in paper bags, and various colored pop sold in plastic barrel-shaped containers that turns children's faces colors. The store was on the corner of Rosemont and Herman streets and, because Rosemont is a popular shortcut from the interstate to a main avenue, the traffic on the street is heavy, especially during rush hour. Often, Vicky, Luanne, and I walked across to buy ice-cream bars, bags of chips, and soda. During these times, I observed the girls in their community, how they negotiated people and, sometimes, written texts such as advertisements, newspapers (there were no magazines or books sold in the store), or print on packaged baked goods. This store was owned by people who lived outside of the community, not uncharacteristic of many of the corner stores in the neighborhood (alderman, interview 8/98). Vicky and her friend told me that even though the stores served the Black community, there was often discrimination against Black adolescents who came into the store (transcript, 3/99).

During one of my first visits to the house, I asked June what "community" meant to her. She responded by saying, "like when people help each other out?" She said, "like when I did that sign." "What sign?" I asked. She got up from the kitchen table, went into her room, and brought back a white plastic

July 2, 1997

Hon.
Mayor,
City Hall
_____   New York . _

Dear Sir:

Attached please find a petition calling for the placement of a traffic light at the intersection of   Street and   Street which is being submitted by concerned area residents.

The safety of our young people, and the failure of your admin- istration to effectively respond to traffic issues which were previously raised, has led residents to submit this petition and I ask you to respond effectively to it.

In Fact, the speed of the cars going through this portion of our city has already led to dangerous conditions and the growing number of young people who live in the area is being threatened by the excessive speed which automobile drivers use on our local streets.

Therefore, I am asking your administration to take prompt action to address this important matter by placing a needed traffic signal at this much used intersection. I am also renewing my request for your administration to enforce speed limits along   Street particu- larly at;   Street,   Street,   Avenue, and   Street.

I look forward to your action on this matter.

Sincerely,

cc. Traffic Safety Division
        Street Area Residents

Figure 3.1a   Letter to City Hall.

48

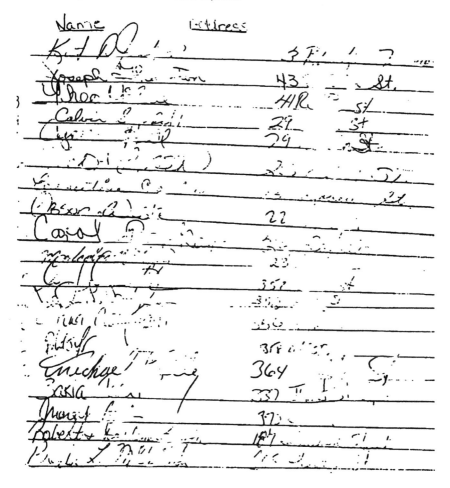

As concerned residents of the _____ Ward, we the under-signed feel that there is a dangerous situation being ignored due to lack of a traffic light at the corner of _____ and _____ Streets. The Stop Sign there does nothing. It is ignored. There have been several accidents at this intersection in recent weeks. We feel the safety of our children is at risk. We urge the City of Albany to correct this situation as soon as possible.

Figure 3.1b   Petition letter.

shopping bag with a supermarket logo on its side. This bag held all of June's important records and documents including bills, her children's birth certificates, the lease to her apartment, and pay stubs. After digging in the bag, she pulled out two pieces of paper. One was a petition, the other a letter (see Figs. 3.1a and 3.1b; fieldnotes, 10/8/97).

June, aware of the unsafe city streets, was afraid her children might be hit by a car. She decided in the spring of 1997 to write a petition to get a traffic light put at the corner of Rosemont and Herman streets. As she took the petition out of the white plastic bag in her kitchen, she explained to me how she took this idea to her ABE classroom. She explained to her teacher that the traffic conditions on her street were bad and that there had been many near-accidents on the street. June's classroom teacher helped her to write the purpose of the petition. June told Curt what she wanted the petition to say and then they codrafted it. She then asked the school secretary to help her type it. June spent several afternoons, after she got out of school and before her children got home, walking around her neighborhood, explaining the reason for the petition, and asking people to sign. June stated, "I just walked and asked everyone to sign." June collected more than 100 signatures. June then elicited the support of the alderman of her ward, explaining what she had done and that she needed to make sure the petition got to city hall. The alderman drafted a letter of support on official city letterhead and he and June took the bus downtown to deliver it to city hall.

June's petition expressed concern with the safety of her street, and that there had been many near-accidents on the street at the intersection. The unpredictable parking and large, city-owned and -operated vehicles often restricted the view of traffic from the side street. The streets were frequently busy with bicycle riders, adolescents carrying younger children and older men, presumably riding to and from work. Lester also rode his bike to and from work and to the store.

A traffic light never was put up at the corner of Rosemont and Herman streets. However, in the process of actively seeking better safety on her street, June negotiated textual resources, employed strategies, and utilized social resources. She demonstrated an active orientation toward written texts in her life as she negotiated the fair-hearing paperwork and planned and implemented a petition in her community. Her engagement with these events illustrated a number of strategies.

For instance, June described her case to a social service agent. She elicited signatures from more than 100 people in the community. She had access to the social network of leaders in the community. Furthermore, she showed knowledge of various social resources. For example, she had knowledge of the institutional organization of her adult learning center. She knew who to ask her to help with the petition. She got access to a computer. She also demonstrated the rhetorical skills or persuasion as she informed people of the unsafe city streets. June's skepticism, though, is apparent in her statement, "Everyone know these streets are unsafe and yet they won't do anythin'. They got more important things to do" (interview, 2/98).

June had knowledge of the organization of three different organizational structures: the adult learning center, the local government, and her neighborhood. She also accessed literate resources through a strategic network. Furthermore, and most impressive, I believe, is the deep-rooted sense of social activism that drove her to initiate the petition in the first place. However, as becomes clearer with other examples, June's activation of cultural resources often was not turned into social profits—either material or educational.

Falsely Labeled as HIV.   It was a Sunday afternoon in the middle of July and Shauna, June's youngest daughter, went out to ride her bike on the sidewalks of her street. Shauna, 4 at the time, got on her bike and rode to the corner. June was on the front stoop trying to get a glimpse of a breeze. Shauna hit a pothole and fell off of her bike. When she landed she was not seriously hurt, although the fall had shaken her up. However, when she looked down at her hand she realized that she had a hypodermic needle stuck in her ring finger. The vision of having this needle in her finger must have hurt worse than the actual needle. She screamed. Her older sister, Luanne, on seeing her fall, ran over and took the needle out of her finger. She threw it in the gutter. June called a taxi and immediately brought Shauna to the emergency room. Shauna was given blood tests and the physicians showed Shauna and her older sister a series of needles asking which one it might have been. Luanne pointed out the one she thought it might be. They told June that the chances of contracting a disease were slim—it would have to be an infected needle and thrown out within the last 48 hours. The doctor prescribed two different types of medicines that she needed to take every day to ward off an infectious disease. She would need to take this medicine twice a day for 2 weeks (fieldnotes, 9/98).

When I asked June what the medicine was she said that she did not know the name of the medicine but that Shauna needed to take it so she did not get AIDS. After a series of intermittent blood tests, the doctors confirmed that she did not have the disease. A few months later when Shauna entered preschool, June was called for an appointment with the teachers and the director. They told her that Shauna's medical records indicated that she was HIV positive. At this point June told them that it was a mistake—that her blood tests came up negative and that the forms were wrong. The directors of the preschool assured her that it was confidential and that no one else would see the records. In this case, the officials of the preschool took the official label from the health care form and assumed that it was correct. The encoding of Shauna's identity as HIV positive was taken as a "reality" when, in fact, it was an error in processing the forms.

Meanwhile, June was not given access to the records. She was given another medical form and was told to give it to the health center in order to fill out another form indicating her correct health status. June then brought

it back to the doctors who apologized and made the appropriate corrections. The doctor's office faxed the form back to the preschool center. This
maze of inaccuracies and misrepresentations that appeared in the health
form papers is similar to that which appears in the fair-hearing paperwork.

There are two significant points to make with this example with regard to
June's engagements with literacy. First, literacy in the Treaders' lives was
consequential. As Shauna's mother, June was deeply concerned about her
daughter's health status being misrepresented as HIV positive. Second,
through a trail of official documents, such as the health care and the
preschool records, it is possible to see how individual identities become
encoded into texts, texts to which June did not have access (Taylor, 1997).

These two examples, the community petition and making sure Shauna
was not falsely represented as HIV positive, show June's active and proficient engagements with literacy. June used literacy to access better social
and material resources for her and her children. Both negotiations were
done in conjunction with her role as a mother. Independently, June
demonstrated many of the engagements with power and privilege that
characterize parent involvement programs with an underlying commitment
to critical action and social change in the community (Delgado-Gaitan,
1992; Rodriguez-Brown, & Mulhern, 1993; Shanahan, Mulhern, & Rodriguez-Brown, 1995). June demonstrated proficiency with multiple ways of
interacting with texts (genre), she represented her family and herself from a
strengths perspective (discourse), and she took on the role of an advocate
for her family (style). Still, June did not see herself as literate, nor did she
count these interactions as examples of literacy. June defied many of the
cultural narratives of people who have been defined as having low functional literacy skills—through her negotiation of literacy in the context of
the community. Furthermore, June defied the school's and the more
general societal vision of the "uninvolved" parent.

Literacy at Home

June took care of most of the literacy demands of the household even
though Lester was the more competent of the two in terms of literacy. In
American society, women are expected to be involved in the "work" of
raising "literate" children who will be productive and sustain themselves
within the workforce (Edwards, 1995; McNemar, 1998; Morrow, Tracey, &
Maxwell, 1995; Neuman, Celano, & Fischer 1996).[2] Literacy in the Treaders'
home did not always consist of book reading—the common conception of
family literacy practices (e.g., Morrow, 1995). June's home defied two
common cultural "mismatch" narratives that frame the lives of families,

often nonmainstream, whose children do not do well in school. The first is that there is no literacy or there is lack of literate competence in the home. This, as I have demonstrated, was not the case in the Treaders' home. The second cultural narrative is that the home has the wrong kind of literacy. That is, that there is no schooled literacy present. This, as I have demonstrated, was also not the case in the Treaders' home. In fact, schooled literacy was a large portion of the literacy available in the Treader's home (recall the "library room" and its contents). However, in this section, I illustrate two examples of literacy that characterize the Treaders' "family literacy practices" that do not involve books but are examples of the connection between institutional and family literacy practices.

Magnet School Letter. At home, June continued to negotiate documents and texts that did not count as progress with schooled "gains." Each time I visited the Treaders' home, there was a new form to be read, signed, and sent back to various social agencies. In the spring of 1998, June received a number of form letters from the school with regard to the special-education referral process and Vicky's transition to the middle school the following year. One of the letters sent home from the school informed June that Vicky

Dear Parent/Guardian:

Welcome to the We are pleased to inform you that your child's name was drawn in the Magnet School Lottery by on March 24, 1998. We would like to invite your child to enroll in Academy.

Please Note: Once a child attends a Magnet School requests to transfer back to his/her former school should first be in writing to the school principal. Requests must be put in writing before November 1st and will be honored provided there is space available. After November 1, transfers will only be considered on a case by case basis, depending upon space availability. Final determination will be made by the Superintendent of Schools.

Due to the length of the waiting list we are requiring parents to return the attached form by April 3, 1998. If we do not receive the attached form by April 3, 1998, we will continue to the next student on the waiting list and offer him/her an opportunity to attend Academy. Your co-operation is greatly appreciated.

Please remember that the Lottery Procedures do no apply to self-contained Special Education Classes. Students identified by the Committee on Special Education are assigned to a school by the Committee on Special Education.

We are delighted that your child may join us at

Sincerely,

Figure 3.2   Magnet School Letter.

had won the "lottery" to attend the magnet school next year (see Fig. 3.2). June's perception of the magnet school was that it was "like a Catholic school" (3/26/98). She didn't know why the school was making such a big deal out of the magnet school because, she told me, it had been a magnet school for a few years. June was, however, excited that her daughter won the lottery: "that's good she got accepted up there" (3/26/98). It was clear as I listened to her talk about Vicky's acceptance into the magnet school that she did not know the specifics of the magnet school. She had heard of it and knew only that it had existed for some time. June let Vicky decide if she wanted to go to this middle school. June said, "I just asked her did she want to go to this [middle school] and she say yeah. I say you passin'? [sixth grade] She said yeah she said her teacher read off all the names that was passin' and who ain't passin' . . . That's what she say, I'll just wait till her report card come" (transcript, 3/26/98).

June was led to believe from the form letter that her daughter had "won" a place for herself at the middle school. Based on the letter that informed June this was a decision, June let Vicky decide. June believed in giving Vicky autonomy in some of the decisions she made about school, a belief she valued in her own education. June seemed more willing to grant Vicky this control as Vicky neared the middle school. However, when I talked with Vicky's classroom teacher, she told me that all of the children in that neighborhood would go to that school, regardless of the "lottery system" (interview, 3/98). The façade of institutional decision making evoked June's strong sense of the need to have control and make decisions.

June showed me the form letter, told me that she already read the letter, and that Vicky had been accepted into the magnet school. June suggested that we read it together during the tutorial part of my time at their home. "This the note that came for her for up to the middle school." I looked at the letter and said, "Oh, this is for the magnet school." June responded, "Uh huh, that what they made the school, a magnet school." We discussed where the school was located. "I got to fill out the application and send it in, send it back over there. This is for if I want, like transportation if she want to catch the bus." I asked June if Vicky would take the bus and June said she asked her and Vicky stated, "I don't want to be catchin' no yellow bus."

As June read the letter, I took a running record of her reading (Clay, 1993). This reading and the subsequent record of her oral reading raised a number of interesting issues concerning the presence of literacy in the Treaders' home and her involvement with the school. First, the letter was too difficult for June to read and understand. June made sense of the overarching purpose of the letter—to inform her that the magnet had school accepted Vicky. However, based on an analysis of the errors she made as she read, June did not read the letter with understanding. She substituted many words based on initial visual cues. For example, she read *envision* for the word *inform*. When June made these substitutions she kept reading even though they did not make sense.

Analysis of June's reading of this form (see Fig. 3.3) suggests her goal was to read the words to get it done, rather than to read it for understanding. This was consistent with how June viewed the purpose of reading in her ABE classroom. June saw reading as a subskill process to be measured rather than a process of interacting with texts. Furthermore, June's pattern of reading this form suggested a history of interacting with similar texts. In particular, analyzing June's errors provides insight into this history of participation. Whereas June did not read sight word vocabulary such as *would, once,* or *should* correctly, she did read words such as *Superintendent, enroll, form, identified* and *special-education* without hesitation. Indeed, some of June's substitutions of words suggested a history of experience with bureaucratic texts that use similar types of language. For instance, as June read she substituted the words *accept* for *attends, contact* for *continue, opportunity* for *co-operation, communication* for *committee* and *self-assistance* for *self-contained*. These errors suggest a difference between her speaking and reading vocabulary and a knowledge of institutional language.

As June read this form, Vicky sat at the kitchen table and watched. Vicky had a look of curiosity on her face as she watched her mother problem solve unknown words. Vicky was interested in what the letter said because it was about her transition to the middle school. She also wanted to make sure that June knew she would walk to school rather than take the "big yellow bus" (transcript, 3/26/98). When June filled out the accompanying form, she asked Vicky how to spell the name of the middle school. Vicky told her mother to just write the abbreviation of it.

Aside from demonstrating June's interactions with literacy in the home, the letter also speaks to the type and quality of parent involvement initiated by the school. The letter was written at a level that potentially excludes parents from the meaning of the letter. The narrative structure of the letter did not promote meaning making. There are three major topic shifts in the letter that are not coherently connected. The letter begins with inviting the student to attend the magnet school. It then shifts to explain the parameters of returning to an old school. Then, it gives the deadline for returning the form. Last, it shifts to the provisions that are made for students who are in self-contained special-education classes. Students placed in a self-contained classroom, the letter states, "are assigned to a school by the Committee on Special Education." There was no phone number on the letter in case June had questions about the magnet school her daughter would attend the following year.

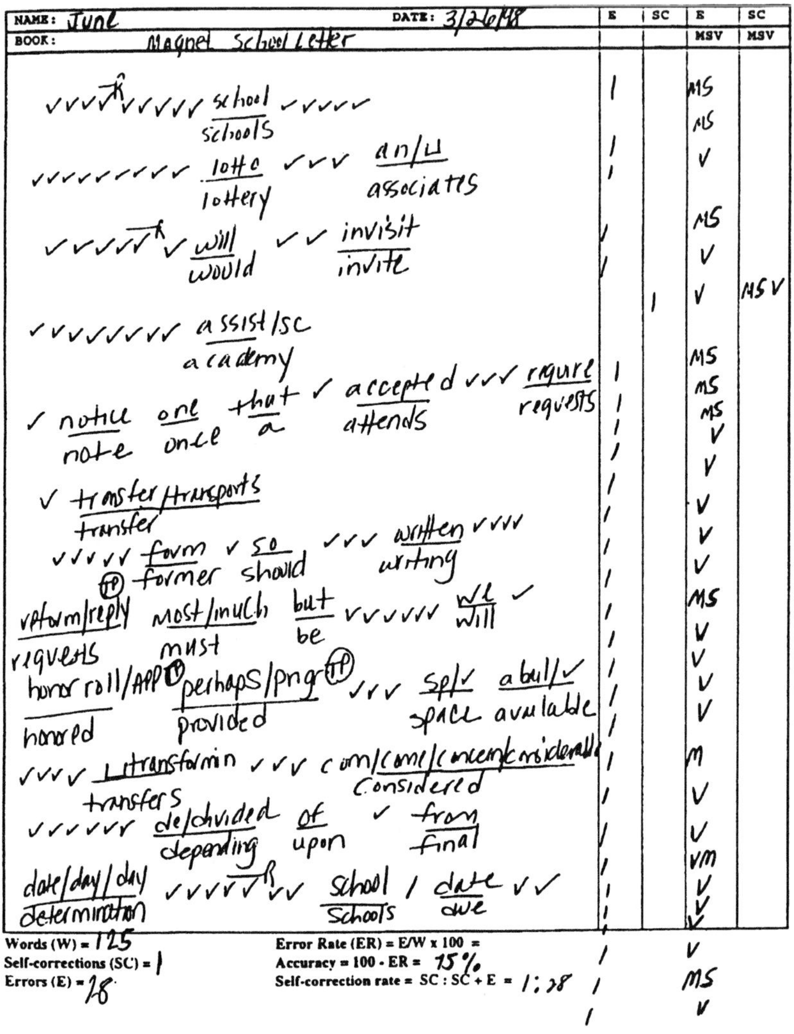

| NAME: June | DATE: 3/26/98 | E | SC | E | SC |
| BOOK: Magnet School Letter | | | | MSV | MSV |

(Running record form with handwritten marks and scoring; see figure below.)

Words (W) = 125	Error Rate (ER) = E/W x 100 =			
Self-corrections (SC) = 1	Accuracy = 100 - ER = 75%			
Errors (E) = 28	Self-correction rate = SC : SC + E = 1 : 28			

Running Record Form from *Knowing Literacy: Constructive Literacy Assessment* by Peter H. Johnston. Copyright © 1997. Reprinted with permission of Stenhouse Publishers.

Figure 3.3   Running Record of Magnet School Letter.

The presence of literacy from the school—though not the book type of reading—provided an opportunity for June and Vicky to interact around written texts. Rockhill (1995) aptly characterized the role of literacy as women's work, which is appropriate for this example and the following. She stated, "Women do most of the literacy work of the household. In addition to the uses of literacy involved in housework, they attend to the purchase of goods, as well as the transactions around social services, public utilities, health care and the schooling of children . . . through detailed repetition, [they] acquire sets of literacy skills" (p. 167). I extend this assertion and suggest that June and Vicky are learning their role in relationship to texts and discourse. Furthermore, Vicky learned that it was her mother, not her father that took care of the literacy demands.

Fair Hearing.   One day when visiting their home, I watched June read a five-page, typewritten form. I asked her what she was reading and she retold her experience with social services, including that she took social services to a fair hearing (fieldnotes, 2/98). June noticed that the family's social service check was half of the amount that it should have been after Lester had been laid off from his job because of lack of work. Similar to the health care form presented in the last chapter and the magnet school letter, this bureaucratic text was similar in the density of its readability.

June read the check and accompanying letter critically to realize the gap in payments they should have received. She assumed social services had included the time period when Lester was working in the calculations. However, the dates on the check did not match up with the time period during which he was employed. June called social services and asked for a fair hearing, an institutional safeguard in place so recipients are able to voice their disagreement with allocated payments. She scheduled a fair-hearing trial at the downtown court. The day of the appointment she gathered the necessary paperwork: her social security card, past records of employment including pay stubs, and her social security stub that showed the amount of money allocated to her. She took the bus downtown and represented herself in front of the judge, explaining her case. Two weeks later June received a form letter in the mail explaining that she has lost the case. It read: "At the hearing, the Agency explained its calculations of the Appellant's budget, the Appellant did not refute the Agency's figures. The record established that the Agency applied with appropriate allowances and disregards in calculating Appellant's household with a monthly grant of $184.00 was correct."

However, June had not received $184. The check she received was for the amount of $51 dollars, less than a third of the correct amount. The document further stated under "Decision" that "The agency's determination to provide the Appellant's household with $184.00 in monthly Public Assistance benefits is correct." However, when June went to collect this money, there was no additional money available. She again called a social service representative and the woman at social services told her that she had lost the fair hearing. Nowhere in the text of the document sent to her does it say she lost the fair hearing. Furthermore, both the letter and the decision made at the fair hearing state that June is eligible for $184. June again tried to make the point that she had not receive the correct amount of money.

June did not have access to the legal discourse yet she had knowledge of the institutional organization and felt comfortable negotiating the system. She demonstrated local power as she attempted to persuade the court that she should have received more money. As June and I discussed this event and the form, Shauna and Vicky sat in the kitchen. June's children, through this event and others like it, learned long before going to school, that in their family reading was connected to learning. Forms such as the fair-hearing paperwork, the community petition, and health forms and documents from the school, provide many opportunities for talk in the Treader family. In front of her family, June explained, described, asked questions, or contradicted written texts in an authentic manner. Nonetheless, similar to the petition, June did not get the resources she expected—or deserved—yet she conceded to both the local government and social services.

Although these interactions provide practice with literacy, there is always something more being acquired than literacy skills (Gee, 1996; Hicks, 2001; Johnston, 1999). In the process of acquiring literacy skills through official texts, people acquire stances toward texts including whether or not their literacies matter and the gender, class, and race relations embedded in texts (Brandau & Collins, 1994; Collins, 1996; C. Luke, 1997).

June's Involvement With the Elementary School

June's involvement with the elementary school was a central theme in her literate life. June simulated "schooled literacy" at home. She was also an active presence at the elementary school, contradicting other research literature that suggests that parents with low literacy skills may have fears about going to the school (Lareau, 1989). In trying to meet the requirements of what June believed it meant to be a "good mother," June also retained skepticism toward the school, a skepticism that reflected her own past experiences with school.

The Presence of Schooled Literacy at Home.   One of the first things I observed about the Treaders' home was the presence of schooled literacy. There was a plethora of literacy materials. For example, there were books in the library room and pencils and paper readily available to the children. June allocated a space and a time after school for her children to do their homework. Furthermore, she reinforced the school's rules at home and told the children to read a book when they were done with their homework. June also supplemented the children's education at home by finding tutors for her children and going to the library to get books out for her children. The younger children would often "play school" with the extra papers their older siblings did not want or need.

Many of these resources are what Bourdieu (1977) called "cultural capital." Cultural capital refers to the cultural resources closely aligned with the school. It is not just the existence of these resources that matter, according to Bourdieu and Passeron (1977) it is the embodiment of the values and beliefs attached to these resources. Solsken (1992) extended the analysis done by Bernstein (1975) of middle-class parents and codes of power. She stated that:

[Being a good parent] "requires the extension of invisible pedagogies into childrearing practices, transforming the nature of mothering by demanding total surveillance of children and the adoption of particular modes of inter-personal communication. Thus as primary care givers women are expected not only to take responsibility for the physical and emotional nurturance of children, but also to play a direct pedagogical role in the development of their cognitive and social capacities (p. 61).

Schooled literacy is very much a part of the lived experience of the Treaders. Every afternoon when Luanne and Vicky came home from school, June asked her children if they had homework. June told me, "I ask her, ask her every day when she come home. Do you have homework? She tell me if she have homework or if she don't have homework. And then if she don't have homework I ask her to read a book" (transcript, 3/3/98).

I also observed the children as they sat at the kitchen table or on their bed and did their homework. June told them they could not go outside until their homework was finished. When Vicky's birthday came in February or Luanne's in March, June brought a cake or cookies to the classroom for their birthday. When I asked June what she thought her role with the school was, she stated, "I help them do their homework, do it neat, get it right and don't be sloppy or anythin'. Don't be sloppy so the teacher can understand what you wrote. Then I just need to stay on top of 'em about doin' their homework. Takin' their time doin' it, don't be rushin" (transcript, 3/25/98).

Once, when June had looked over Vicky's math homework and noticed she had done it incorrectly, she made Vicky leave the paper at home. June described the incident: "One of Vicky's math sheets, I didn't let her take it back to school because she rushed and did it and it was all wrong. The whole math sheet was wrong and so I made her leave it [the work sheet] at home. Then when she came home from school I made her go upstairs and do it all right" (transcript, 10/9/97).

I later asked June what had happened with the homework paper and she told me that she had fixed a lot of the mistakes on the paper before Vicky got home. June also asked April, one of Vicky's friends from around the corner, if she would work with Vicky on her reading after school. June identified April as a smart girl who gets A's in school and finished all of her homework in school (fieldnotes, 2/5/98): "I had asked April if she can ask her mother if she can come over here and read with Vicky. I know she [April] don't have no homework to do because she do it all in school. So like I said, I tol' her, she don't have to read to Vicky, just let Vicky read to her. Or they can read a page for each other" (transcript, 2/5/98).

Significant to note is the difference in June's language as she discussed her own education and when she discussed her daughter's education. When she talked about her daughter's education she took an active role using cognitive statements such as "I know." She also positioned herself in active ways. She stated, "I ask her, I ask her every day when she comes home"; "I ask her to read a book"; "I help them do their homework"; "I need to stay on top of 'em"; "I didn't let her take it back to school because she rushed and did it and it was all wrong." June saw herself as an active participant in her children's education.

June was concerned about Vicky's progress in school and was involved with her education in a number of ways. She also helped Vicky study for spelling tests every Thursday night and helped her with her math homework. However, in the middle of sixth grade, the spelling words Vicky brought home were too difficult for June and June told her she was not able to study with her anymore (fieldnotes, 1/98). Contrary to June's involvement in and commitment to Vicky's education, Vicky's teachers told me in an interview that June was not involved in her children's education (interview, 1/98). They further stated there was virtually no literacy in the Treaders' home, similar to the other children in their classes, who were dealing with issues of violence, poverty, and drug trafficking (interview, 1/98).

Based on my observations, June was not only involved in her children's education but was involved in school-defined ways (Leichter, 1984). June set a time and a space for her children to do homework, made sure there were no interruptions during this time, checked homework, helped them to study for tests, and made unexpected visits to the elementary school. June knew the surface "rules" of the school game. She knew she had a right to check on her children's progress at school, that they were supposed to read every day, that their homework needed to be done, and that they needed to be on time for school each day. Much of June's struggle was done within the existing discourse of the school, an argument that extends beyond African American theorists and researchers—Delpit (1988) and Edwards (1995), in particular—who argue for the directions and rules of school to be directly explained to parents. That is, June understood the rules of the school, similar to how we heard her describe the discipline, timeliness, and authority connected with her ABE classroom.

June's Presence at the Elementary School

June often walked from her ABE class on her break or during lunch to her children's school, two blocks away. She would poke her head in one or the other of the girls' classrooms, without an appointment, to see how Luanne or Vicky were doing. Once, when I accompanied June to the elementary school, she went to Vicky's sixth-grade classroom, which was on the second floor. She opened the door and walked in. The teacher, Mrs. Smith, was sitting at her desk and the children were in their seats working. Vicky, at the time, was talking with a girl sitting behind her. June asked Mrs. Smith how Vicky was doing in class. Mrs. Smith told her Vicky often talked too much in class and that she needs to be reminded to pick a book up during free-reading time. June, from the back of the room, said to Vicky in front of her classmates, "Turn around and stop talking. Where your glasses at?" She asked Mrs. Smith if she had been wearing her glasses in class. Mrs. Smith said "no" and June told Vicky to get them out of her book bag and put them on (fieldnotes, 11/97).

Another time, with somewhat different results, June and I made an appointment and sat down and talked with the reading teacher at the elementary school to find out what Vicky was doing during reading time. As we sat at the table in the remedial reading room, June kept looking out the door and saying "hi" to the different children she recognized. June seemed to be at ease in the school. June looked at the books Mrs. Matthews had put on the table. Mrs. Matthews told June that Vicky was reading at "level b of a fourth-grade level" in the workbooks she used (fieldnotes, 10/14/97). Mrs. Matthews then discussed a systematic phonics program that included flash cards and stated that, if she had more time with Vicky, and if she were sure that Vicky did not have an auditory discrimination problem, she would work systematically through this program from the beginning. As she explained these things, June listened attentively.

Mrs. Matthews took flash cards out of the boxes to demonstrate how the systematic word analysis program worked. She held up a card in front of June and asked June to read the word. The word was *expedition*. June was unable to read the word. Mrs. Matthews continued with the activity. Anticipating where this was heading, I was torn between intervening and running the risk of June thinking I did not think she was competent or not intervening and letting her appear unable to do the word-decoding task.

Still holding the card up, Mrs. Matthews directed June to, "look at the word. Spell 'ition' in expedition." June paused, unfamiliar with the activity, both the language of it and the directions, and unsure of what to do. Mrs. Matthews gave her the answer and spelled "i-t-i-o-n" and then pronounced the ending of the word.

"Now" she directed, "spell 'ex' in the word." June, falling easily into the role of the student, looked at the word and spelled "ex."

Okay," Mrs. Matthews continued, "say the middle part without saying the beginning." June stumbled over this, as did I, again unsure of what she was asking her to do. Mrs. Matthews modeled what the middle part of the word would sound like and asked June to repeat her after she said it. June followed her lead.

Frustrated, and embarrassed for June, Mrs. Matthews, and myself for sitting through that, I interrupted and took over playing the role of the student. Mrs. Matthews demonstrated how the children worked on Reading for Understanding cards (RFU) and how they had to read a cloze passage and choose the correct answer. Again, she asked June to be the student in order to demonstrate what she expected the students in her remedial reading classes to be able to do. Mrs. Matthews handed the passage to June, expecting her to read it out loud. June started but got stuck on the first word in the passage, the name "John." I could tell June was nervous from the way she looked at the card, knowing she should respond quickly and not understanding the intention of the activity (fieldnotes, 10/14/98).

I took the passage from her and read, "John got a new flashlight for his birthday. He liked the flashlight so much that he decided to use it even during the _____." The choices were "day," "night," "baseball game," or "winter." I needed to reread it in order to answer it correctly. Mrs. Matthews then told us that Vicky had answered that he would use the flashlight at "night." Mrs. Matthews explained that Vicky doesn't visualize what she is reading. She exemplified this deficit further by showing us another RFU example that had to do with a deer. "If she would just get a picture of a deer in her mind, then she would do all right." Looking back, I should have said many things during this meeting, one of which is that it is hard to visualize something you have never seen (fieldnotes, 10/14/97). We left this meeting without much further damage, and June seemed to be impressed with the reading teacher's knowledge of Vicky and about reading. June did not seem to be intimidated by the teachers at the school, nor did she "look up to them" as did the "lower-class" parents in Lareau's (1989) study.

From these examples of June's involvement with the school it is clear that, in many ways, June strove to be the "ideal" parent Lareau (1989) described in her study of social class and parental intervention in elementary education. Despite June's status as a lower-class parent based on the family's income level and educational background, June's actions and involvement with literacy at home characterized many of the examples of the middle-class parents in Lareau's work. It is also clear that whereas June's participation with her own literacy and education are laced with feelings of doubt and passivity, she positioned herself as an agent with regard to the literacy work done on her children's behalf.

That is, there was interconnectedness between the home and the school in terms of both June's physical presence as well as setting up "schooled literacy" at home. This stands in contrast to the lower-class parents in Lareau's (1989) study, who were supportive of the school but felt that the school was where education takes place, not the home. Whereas working-class parents assumed that the school and teachers would provide an equitable education for their children, the middle-class parents believed they had to supplement the school's curriculum. Similar to the middle-class parents, June supervised, supplemented, and intervened in her children's academic work at home. When she was not able to help with certain aspects of their learning, she found outside tutors. June set up a time for the children to do their homework, she told them to read a book when they were done, and when they were struggling in school she found tutors to help them. Whereas the lower-class parents in Lareau's study trusted the teachers' decisions about their children's education, the middle-class parents often monitored the school's performance. Similar to the middle-class parents, June monitored the actions of her children's school. As I demonstrate in chapter 5, June disagreed with the school's decision about Vicky and complained about the instruction she received as well as the placement decisions that were available to Vicky. This skepticism about the intentions of the school blended into how June understood her daughter's placement in special education.

Up until this point, Lester has been absent from my analysis. This is not because he was not physically present. As I said earlier, Lester was, in fact, the more capable of the two parents with regard to formalized literacy. He held a GED and read various texts including the newspaper. Given this evidence it might make sense if he were to handle the literate demands of the household. Despite his proficiency with written texts, however, it was June, the woman and mother of the household, who remained highly involved in her children's education. June did not resist this cultural narrative of family literacy as women's work.[3] As an African American woman and mother of four children, June thought a great deal about the education of her children.[4] Indeed, it is intricately connected to her own identity as a mother, a woman, and a literacy student. Many of the decisions June made for her children were connected to her "ways of knowing" (Belenky, McVicker-Clinchy, Goldberger, & Mattuck-Tarule, 1986), both as a mother and as a woman struggling with her own literate history and emerging identity.

Each of these spaces, the home, the school, and the community, helps to situate June's past and present literate life. Each of these contexts reveals the tensions between June's relationship to literacy through schooled literacy (e.g., her past and present experiences as a student) and her relationship to literacy through her interactions for and with her children (e.g., magnet letter, petition, fair hearing). It is possible to see the shifts across contexts through ethnographic description and an analysis of the ways of interacting, ways of representing, and ways of being that are connected with literacy in the domains of the school, the home, and the community. These tensions between personal and public literate lives and engagement with literacy in a range of contexts also situate the literate life of Vicky, June's daughter. The web of literacy extends into her daughter's literate life—an issue I take up in the next chapter.

NOTES

1. Some of the data presented in chapters 3 and 6 appeared in an earlier version in Rogers (2002a).
2. The Adult Education and Family Literacy Act, Title II of the Workforce Investment Act (Public Law 105-220) restructured ABE so that it funnels directly into employment training, progress toward employment and self-sufficiency, and assisting parents in gaining educational skills to become full partners in the educational development of their children (Sparks, 2001). The majority of participants enrolled in family literacy programs are women. The rhetoric of family literacy promotes a traditional view of what counts as literacy. Regulating practices such as parenting classes use curricula that focus on "family values," "schooled literacy," and being a "good parent."
3. Extending this analysis along class lines, German (1989) examined the history of women's work—their productive and reproductive "work"—and argued for the connection of gender and socioeconomic class. Literacy may be seen as part of the private labor division of the family that is unseen and unvalued and yet serves an important predictor in the success of children in schools (Teale, 1986; Teale & Sulzby, 1986).
4. Women's domestic labor contributes to the reproduction of labor power and indirectly to the surplus produced for the capitalist class by lowering the value of labor power (German, 1989). Women's wages are also affected by the existence of the family. On average, women earn two-thirds to three-fourths of the average male wage (Kessler-Harris, 1990). This inequality is brought about in different ways: part-time work, grading, and the division of labor along gender lines. However, the overwhelming reason for women's unequal pay lies in tacit assumptions of the existence of the family, and that women have other means of support (primarily men) other than their own wages.

Chapter 4

Family Literacy as Apprenticeship

> Children [are] apprentices in thinking, active in their efforts to learn from observing and participating with peers and more skilled members of their society, developing skills to handle culturally defined problems with available tools, and building from these givens to construct new solutions within the context of sociocultural activity.   —Rogoff (1995, p. 7)[1]

June and Vicky taught me that intergenerational literacy learning is a delicate balance of textual encounters, institutional arrangements, and subjectivities. I learned from them how literate identities are embedded within legacies, transmitted across generations.

June's literate life, demonstrated in the last chapter, may be defined in relation to "schooled literacy," her own and her children's, and to her identity as a "mother." June's belief in the power of literacy over her and her children is seen in her assertion to Vicky, "How you gonna get somewhere without readin'?" Further evidence of this commitment to her children and to school is seen in her evoking my role as a literacy teacher for her daughter.

KNOWING VICKY

I came to know Vicky, in part, through reading the expressions on her face. Vicky's smile shows her dimples etched into her face. Her eyes, a deep brown, reveal how she is feeling and thinking. Her eyes light up when she is proud of herself or when she realizes others are proud of her. Knowing how important school is to her mother, she came home from school and reported that she had made the "effort" honor roll or that she got a 100 on her spelling test her mother had helped her to prepare for. June's pride in her daughter reflected onto Vicky's face as a sheepish grin crawled across her face. When Vicky felt good about herself she was playful, witty, and creative.

When Vicky talked to me about things that did not go well at school, or when she had been unsuccessful at something, she cast her eyes downward. When she told me about going into a special-education classroom, she did not make eye contact with me, slouched in her seat, and mumbled. Once I experienced this look, I tried to avoid it at all costs, making sure she had plenty of choices in what she read, and that the books were never too difficult for her.

When she held her baby brother, a look of seriousness washed over her face, in her eyes, and around her mouth line as she attended to his needs. Vicky was not easily fooled. She carried a look of disbelief and skepticism handy for when she thought she was being conned or when she was unsure about a person or a social scene. Her "looks" made me believe she had seen more and understood more than a White woman who grew up in a small town would think a preadolescent knew.

Vicky attended an elementary school in walking distance from the Treaders' house. She attended this school for 3 years, from third to sixth grade. Prior to that Vicky attended another school, further into the south end of the city, within the same school district. At the adult literacy center, June told me many stories about Vicky.

Vicky had an affectionate relationship with her siblings. She enjoyed harassing her younger sisters, as older sisters do, but she also helped them with many things. Part of her relationship with her siblings was connected to literacy and education. Vicky helped Luanne, a second and third grader during the period of this research, with her homework. Vicky was particularly proud to help Luanne with words she did not know when she was reading. Vicky's participation as a family member and as the oldest sibling also included watching the younger children when June went on errands or to the store. Vicky would watch the children from the front stoop, just as June did, making sure that they did not go around the corner. In the house, Vicky would respond if Shauna cried—by giving her a drink of water or helping her to locate a lost toy.

When Evan, the youngest of the Treader children, arrived in the late summer of 1998, Vicky acted as the primary caregiver for him. She often gave him baths, changed his diapers, put him to sleep, fed him, and played with him. She seemed to enjoy the closeness she experienced with him. June told me that this caregiving was a relief for her because it gave her time to sit outside, to play bingo, or watch TV by herself.

June showed a strong belief in the ability of her children. When June asked me to work with Vicky as a reading tutor and told me she needed extra help in reading she did not frame it as a deficiency. Instead, as June stated, "Vicky is smart if she put her head to it. Vicky is really smart, really smart, she is. She just need to keep readin'" (transcript, 9/3/97).

When I first met Vicky she was shy but attentive. Vicky seemed to be more of a listener than an initiator of conversations. She demonstrated fragility as a literacy learner. When I asked her to tell me about herself as a reader, she told me that she was the "lowest reader in the class" and that she "can't read." Vicky had learned from school that literacy meant completing exercises and passively participating in other, teacher-driven activities. Though she completed her homework assignments, they did not seem to hold any meaning for her.

Literacy as an Individual Endeavor

Part of how I grew to know Vicky aside from my observations of her at home, in the community, and at school was through a reading and discussion group that occurred over the course of 2 years (Rogers, 2002b).

The reading time started as I worked one-on-one with Vicky and June in the Treaders' kitchen, on the living room floor, or in a quiet space in the house for an hour to an hour and a half twice a week. During this time, other neighborhood kids would come in and out looking to see if Vicky, Lori, and Shauna could come outside and play jump rope, hopscotch, or "hang out." They would look with interest at the books we were reading and look quizzically at me. The looks on their faces stated "Why is she here?" "Who is she?" I would introduce myself and June would tell them that Vicky could come out when she was done with reading.

All of the participants in the reading group were African American children and adolescents, ranging from elementary age to 16 years old. June would often sit down with us to read but told me she would rather I spend my time with them because they "need it more" (than she did). Vicky, Taz, April, and Lori were regular participants in the literature discussion groups and chose the literature we read. Vicky was a sixth grader when I first met her. She had been in a remedial reading class since the third grade and had been referred for special-education testing because of her "second grade" decoding skills. Taz was also a sixth grader when he joined the discussion group. He was Vicky's cousin. Taz's mother requested that Taz join the reading group because he needed extra help with his reading. Lori was Vicky's younger sister and in the fourth grade when I first met her. Like her sister, she also started remedial reading classes when she was in third grade. April was a friend and classmate of Vicky. She lived around the corner with her parents and two sisters, one older and one younger. June explained to me that April is a very smart girl, who always gets A's in school and does her homework at school. There were a total of eight adolescents who joined the reading and discussion group at various points.

I would bring a range of books I considered to be at their instructional reading level. Though Taz's comprehension, both literal and interpretive, was good, he needed to work on his fluency. Vicky needed support with comprehension. When we finished a book, either I or the three of us would go to a local bookstore to pick out the next book. The adolescents often chose literature where there were consequences attached to the characters and the situations in which they were involved. Many of their choices were historical biographies. Along with the multiple copies of books, I would always bring a selection of picture books that connected to the theme of the guided reading book we would read. I started every session with a read-aloud. During this time, Shauna and Lori along with the other children June was looking after would come around the table to listen to the story. June, too, was often present in the kitchen. She was usually washing dishes or sweeping the floor. Sometimes during this time, Vicky would take over the reading. Vicky, Taz, and I would often go to the library together. Here, their enthusiasm for picture books was again evident as they combed through the shelves of children's books looking at the illustrations (for a complete discussion and analysis of the reading group through a CDA framework, see Rogers, 2002b).

The literature reading and discussion group was a rich source of learning, for both the Treaders and myself. Through these discussion groups I learned about the contexts in which June and Vicky were proficient—an issue I return to at the end of this chapter. I also learned about their anxieties and fears with regard to literacy and how they negotiated the everyday literacy demands of their lives. Furthermore, this group allowed me to observe how June and Vicky interacted around literacy in a way that would not have been possible if I only took the role of a more distanced participant-observer.

Vicky and several other adolescents from the neighborhood selected books they wanted to read from a range of selections I brought over to the house. Vicky was adamant about making choices with her reading. She enjoyed reading nonfiction and historical fiction, and often chose books that had strong African American people such as Jackie Robinson, Maya Angelou, Harriet Tubman, Rosa Parks, Martin Luther King Jr, Malcolm X, and Fredrick Douglass.

One of the books she selected was *The Last Safe House: A Story of the Underground Railroad* (Greenwood, 1998). This book is a narrative of a family escaping from slavery. Because of the mixing of genres (nonfiction, historical fiction, and map reading), the content, and the sophistication of vocabulary used, the text is around a fourth-grade level in difficulty. Vicky read this text at an instructional level.[2] Her background knowledge and interest in the subject of the Underground Railroad facilitated her reading of the text. Her interest led us to have many conversations about the topic. In the following discussion, Vicky was concerned with two girls her own age who were not allowed to learn how to read. Vicky explained to me how the slaves might have taught themselves to read. I have bolded the sections of the text where I focus my analysis. These are the sections where Vicky described reading as an individual activity, as practice, rather than as a sociocultural tool.

V: Easy just get a piece of paper, if they didn't have no piece of paper, just write in the dirt, get a stick write in the dirt and just write your name.

B: You think so?

V: And then they just, like, do they have books back then?

B: Uh huh.

V: They had libraries. **If they didn't know how to read just go to the library and just get a book and teach themselves how to read.**

B: How would you teach yourself how to read?

V: **Uhm, say the words that's in the book.**

        And then just keep readin' and readin'.

        Or when they run away from slavery, they might meet somebody and that person can teach them if they don't know how to read, that person can teach them how to read. Yeah like when I'm in the field, picking cotton and the master, the guy who own slaves, they're not there, I just go back in there and run away.

B: What if they caught you?

V: I be like Harriet Tubman. She never got caught (transcript, 3/9/99).

In this conversation, Vicky's interest in the subject of the Underground Railroad is apparent. Also apparent was her belief in reading as an individual endeavor. Vicky stated, "If they don't know how to read they just go to the library and teach themselves how to read . . . say the words that's in the books. And then just keep readin' and readin'." Vicky's comments illustrated her view of reading that coincides with her belief in reading as a subskill process that is done by individuals—rather than a social endeavor.

These comments corresponded with how Vicky talked about reading in an interview I conducted. When I asked Vicky how she would describe reading to someone in a younger grade, she told me, "just read the words." Also, several times I sat in Vicky's language arts and remedial reading classes during her sixth-grade year. As I observed, I was better able to understand why Vicky might "hate reading," not see herself as a reader, and think that reading is something tied to practice and repetition, and is an individual endeavor. In Vicky's remedial reading class, there was an emphasis on defining words out of context, filling out sheets from a program called Reading for Understanding (RFU). When there was time the class read a book, as a group, out loud (Appendix F). I did not observe any instances where Vicky read a book she had selected herself, read a book at an instructional level, or sustained reading for any length of time. In the language arts classroom, Vicky was exposed to books that were mainly too difficult for her. The books were read aloud as a class. There was very little introductory work done around these books. How Vicky learned to see herself as a reader was practiced at school and reinforced through her mother. That is, reading is something that is done by individuals, is evaluated through tests, and is not something in which there is a lot of choice. The paradox for both June and Vicky is that they learn that literacy is attached to the individual and yet it is something over which they have little control.

Vicky's comments about the power of literacy over individuals were similar to her comments as she read the account of *Night John* (Paulsen, 1993), a narrative written about Night John, a freed slave, who returns to slavery so that he might teach other slaves how to read. As we discussed the social and historical context of the book, Vicky explained to me that slave owners had an interest in not teaching slaves how to read in order to, "keep them dumb slaves." She told me that if slaves knew how to read they would, "escape, go up north or find someone to teach them to read" (transcript, 5/99). When I asked her why this might matter, Vicky told me that when you can read, "you can do anythin'" (transcript, 5/99). Embedded in Vicky's discussion about learning to read and the function of illiteracy as a tool of oppression is not only Vicky's interest in the Underground Railroad but also how she viewed literacy as an individual endeavor. She stated that if the slaves did not know how to read they could just go to the library and teach themselves how to read; just "say the words that's in the book. And then just keep readin' and readin'." This is similar to June's assertions that when she is reading a book that is difficult for her she will, "read them and even if I look over, even if I have to read the words twice, I read them until I get them right" (interview, 10/98). Vicky learned, like her mother, that reading is a subskill process, an individual endeavor that is assessed through standardized tests, is measured by grade-level equivalents, and is determined by an external authority. Furthermore, she seemed to see her deficits in reading as an individual shortcoming rather than a social issue, tied to instructional circumstances.

READING THE SOCIAL WORLD: LITERACY IN CONJUNCTION WITH LOCAL LIFE

Action Research Project. After reading and discussing the book *Oh Freedom!: Kids Talk About the Civil Rights Movement With the People Who Made It Happen* (King & Barrett-Osborne, 1997), Vicky and the other adolescents in the reading group initiated an action research project. *Oh Freedom!* is a book arranged as a set of interviews conducted by adolescents with people who participated in the civil rights movement. As a result of our discussions, Vicky and the other adolescents in the reading group became interested in social issues in their own community. They were impressed that other children their age had developed interview questions and interviewed people that were a part of the civil rights movement. This interest led them to develop an action research project wherein they interviewed people in their community to learn more about what "everyday heroes" in their community looked like.

They went through a number of stages in order to develop the research plan. First, they brainstormed the people they wanted to interview. With these people they had to think about which people would be home at what part of the day and who would want to be interviewed. Vicky's initial selection of people to interview consisted of their downstairs neighbor, a cousin at the high school, a friend of the family who grew up in the South and "probably knows a lot about racism" (Vicky, fieldnotes, 2/13/99), the alderman, the barber, and Taquisha, their friend's mother. Then, using the interview questions in the book as a model, they brainstormed the questions they would ask the people they had identified. From here, they set up times to talk with the people. Sometimes these appointments were set up via the phone and other times they walked to the person's apartment to ask.

During this time, I brought examples of interviews from the book Oh Freedom! (King & Barrett-Osborne, 1997) so Vicky, Taz, and the other adolescents had a model for writing interview questions and to see what an interview sounded like. I also troubleshot the interview schedule, attending to when people might be available, if we needed to call ahead of time, and how long we might need for the interview.

Before the "real" interviews, they practiced interviewing their cousin, who came over to the Treaders' apartment. The interviews lasted from half an hour to 2 hours and all took place in various apartments in the community. The adolescents took turns asking the questions and they were all responsible for keeping a written record of what had been said. Sometimes when Vicky interviewed, she listened so intently she forgot to write notes. After the interview, I made sure we had time to write down our fieldnotes, which were not only a summary of what we had learned but observations and questions that would guide the next interview.

I transcribed the interviews and used them as the reading material for the next reading session. Reading the interviews they conducted allowed the adolescents to do what Freire and Macedo (1987) referred to as "reading the word and the world" (p. 32). Vicky loved to read the transcripts and was surprised how her words "sounded" on paper. She often asked, "Did I say that?" (transcript, 3/9/99). Through this project, Vicky demonstrated making connections between their everyday life and the life of books. She illustrated the ability to listen, speak, read, and write for meaningful and social purposes.

One interview in particular is worth recalling because of Vicky's engagement with the literacy event and her subsequent reflection on her own life. When we spoke with Taquisha, their mother's friend, she told them about her experiences when she lived in the South. Vicky was interested in this subject because Vicky's mother lived for a while in the South and Vicky and her grandmother had taken several trips by bus to the Carolinas to visit relatives. Taquisha explained the racism in the South and what it was like when she went to school there. She described how she had been spit at and how she saw crosses burnt into people's front lawns. This interview led Vicky to think more deeply about the conditions of racism in her community and in her life. On our way back to the Treaders' apartment from this interview, Vicky talked about how she did not trust any White people. After she realized she was riding in a White woman's car, she stated, "I'm not talkin' 'bout you, Becky, I'm talkin' 'bout in the back, in the way back [meaning a long time ago]." Her second comment, intended to show me that she did not mean me, did not hide the raw distrust she felt for White people, and I continued to wonder how as a White researcher and teacher I was implicated into these sets of social relations.

As a young adolescent Vicky was aware of conditions of inequity in her community and demonstrated a street-wise knowledge of local life. She had mentioned racist conditions in stores and with the police on several occasions. Vicky told me about the worst streets in terms of violence and where the drug dealers were located. In the next vignette I demonstrate another example of Vicky's knowledge of institutions within her community through her engagements with literacy.

"She Was Just Goofin' Around" : The Pepper Spray Incident.   A theme that has become apparent by now is that all of the literacy examples involving June and Vicky in each domain of their interactions connected with the family. The same is true for the following example, in which Luanne, June's middle daughter, was sprayed in the eye with pepper spray.

When Luanne was sprayed with pepper spray, June decided to withdraw Luanne immediately from the summer program. The following example involved June's retelling of the incident, Vicky's reference to the written text (the newspaper), and Vicky's counterinterpretation of the event. June had worried about sending Luanne to summer camp at all because of her knowledge of the unsafe streets and the groups of children Luanne might encounter on her way to the program, just two blocks away from their apartment. June was torn between sending Luanne to an enrichment program that would stimulate her socially and academically and her knowledge that "no good parent lets their child cross the boulevard alone" (transcript, 9/13/99).

The enrichment program opened during the summer of 1998 for the first year. It was part of an urban restoration project. June spoke with the alderman of the ward to ask him if she might be able to get Luanne into the program. He assured her that it would not be a problem. June called the program and reserved Luanne a spot on the list. One summer afternoon, a counselor at the program sprayed Luanne and several other children in the eyes with pepper spray. The paper reported the spraying as an accident but it made the front page of the paper, in part because it was the first summer the program had been running.

When I got to the Treaders' apartment the following afternoon, Luanne complained that her nose and eyes still hurt. At the time, June and I were in June's bedroom where June was showing me the gifts she had received at her baby shower. She had a crib filled with diapers, bottles, baby oil and lotions, and toys for the child she expected to deliver in July. I asked June what had happened to Luanne. June responded, "Didn't you see the news or read the paper?" I told her that I had been out of town. June shook her head, surprised that I had not heard about it, and explained what had happened at the program. She told me that one of the counselors, a teenager, sprayed pepper spray and it got into Luanne's eyes. The director of the summer school program called June to notify her about the incident. June rode with Luanne to the emergency room in the ambulance. Luanne was taken to the emergency room, treated, and released. The director of the summer school program fired the counselor.

As June explained it to me, she told Luanne to get the paper out of the garbage to show me the article (see Fig. 4.1), which included a picture of her daughter, with an oxygen mask over her face. As Luanne brought the newspaper into June's room, Vicky intercepted her, took the newspaper, and went into the living room to look at it. Because of the unbearable heat in the apartment, Vicky and I went to the local library, which was air-conditioned, for reading instruction that day. Vicky brought along the paper and asked if she could read it first. I did not introduce the text because Vicky was anxious to start reading. Vicky was motivated to read it because her sister was on the front page of the paper and because she had an alternative interpretation of the situation. Vicky was convinced that Luanne was just "goofin' around" and that "she wanted to go to the hospital for attention" rather than really being hurt by the pepper spray (transcript, 7/99).

I took a running record on Vicky's reading of the newspaper article as she read (see Fig. 4.2). The newspaper is written at between a fifth- and sixth-grade level and Vicky read it at an instructional level. Vicky's background knowledge of what happened with the pepper spray and her interest in the story aided her understanding of the story. In addition to being able to read the text, Vicky asked a number of questions, made personal connections with the text, and added several insights to the article that were not included in the text. For instance, Vicky told me the counselor who sprayed the pepper spray thought the pepper spray was perfume and that is why she sprayed it. She also commented that Nora Porch, the president and owner

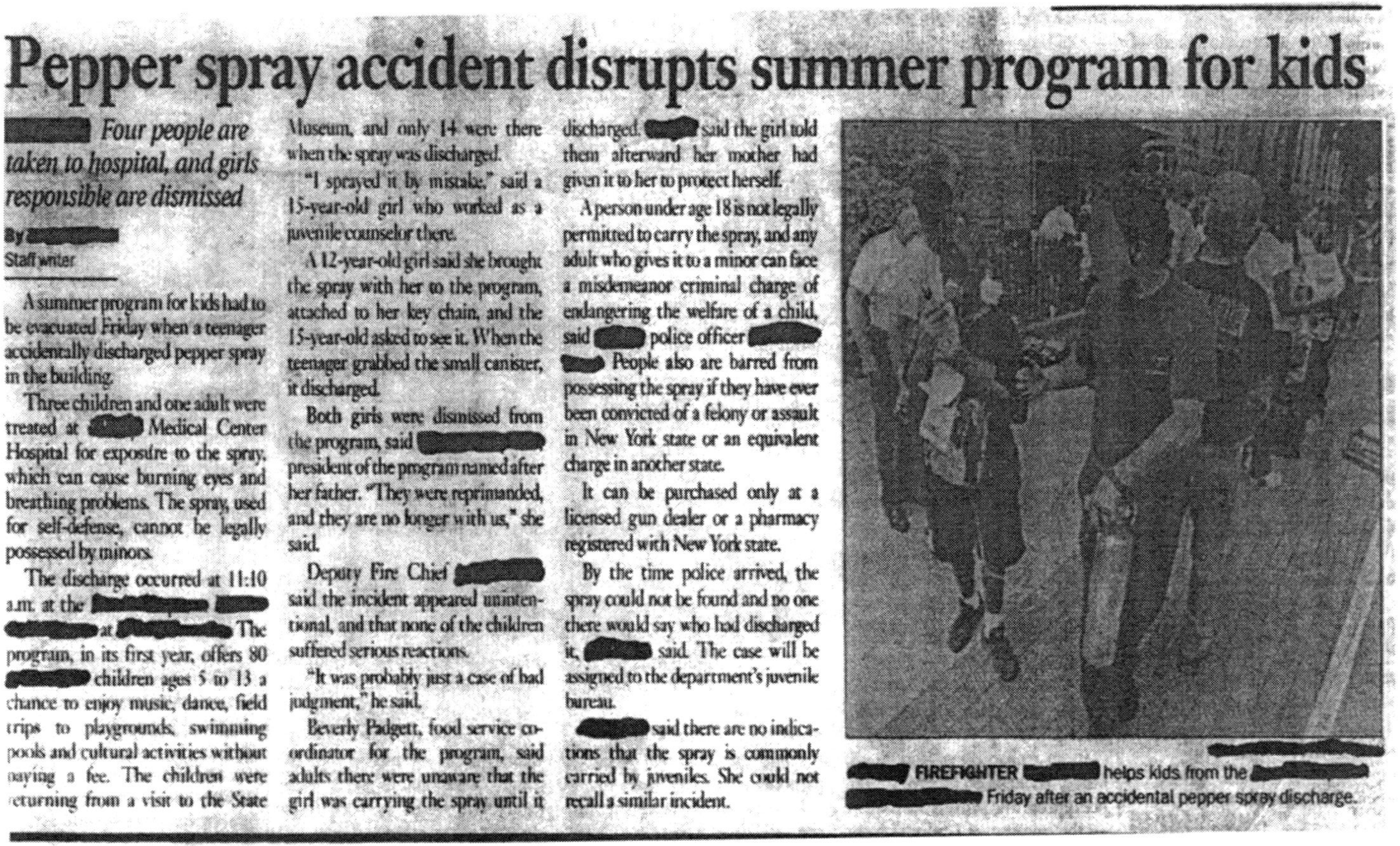

Pepper spray accident disrupts summer program for kids

Four people are taken to hospital, and girls responsible are dismissed

By ▇▇▇▇
Staff writer

A summer program for kids had to be evacuated Friday when a teenager accidentally discharged pepper spray in the building.

Three children and one adult were treated at ▇▇▇ Medical Center Hospital for exposure to the spray, which can cause burning eyes and breathing problems. The spray, used for self-defense, cannot be legally possessed by minors.

The discharge occurred at 11:10 a.m. at the ▇▇▇▇▇▇. The ▇▇▇▇▇▇ program, in its first year, offers 80 ▇▇▇ children ages 5 to 13 a chance to enjoy music, dance, field trips to playgrounds, swimming pools and cultural activities without saying a fee. The children were returning from a visit to the State

Museum, and only 14 were there when the spray was discharged.

"I sprayed it by mistake," said a 13-year-old girl who worked as a juvenile counselor there.

A 12-year-old girl said she brought the spray with her to the program, attached to her key chain, and the 13-year-old asked to see it. When the teenager grabbed the small canister, it discharged.

Both girls were dismissed from the program, said ▇▇▇▇▇, president of the program named after her father. "They were reprimanded, and they are no longer with us," she said.

Deputy Fire Chief ▇▇▇ said the incident appeared unintentional, and that none of the children suffered serious reaction.

"It was probably just a case of bad judgment," he said.

Beverly Padgett, food service coordinator for the program, said adults there were unaware that the girl was carrying the spray until it

discharged. ▇▇▇ said the girl told them afterward her mother had given it to her to protect herself.

A person under age 18 is not legally permitted to carry the spray, and any adult who gives it to a minor can face a misdemeanor criminal charge of endangering the welfare of a child, said ▇▇▇ police officer ▇▇▇▇▇▇.

People also are barred from possessing the spray if they have ever been convicted of a felony or assault in New York state or an equivalent charge in another state.

It can be purchased only at a licensed gun dealer or a pharmacy registered with New York state.

By the time police arrived, the spray could not be found and no one there would say who had discharged it, ▇▇▇ said. The case will be assigned to the department's juvenile bureau.

▇▇▇▇ said there are no indications that the spray is commonly carried by juveniles. She could not recall a similar incident.

▇▇▇▇ FIREFIGHTER ▇▇▇ helps kids from the ▇▇▇▇▇▇ Friday after an accidental pepper spray discharge.

Figure 4.1 Pepper Spray Article.

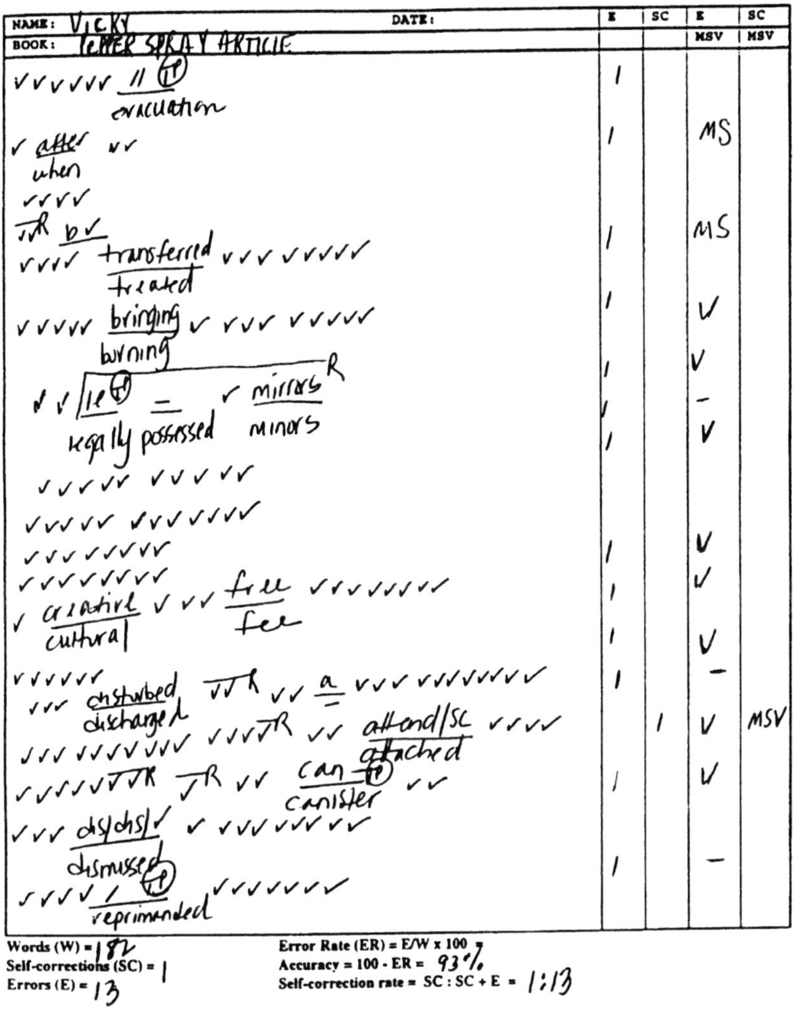

NAME: Vicky   DATE:
BOOK: (Pepper Spray Article)

		E	SC	E	SC
				MSV	MSV

(Running record of hand-scored reading, with handwritten checks and corrections.)

Words (W) = 182
Self-corrections (SC) = 1
Errors (E) = 13

Error Rate (ER) = E/W x 100
Accuracy = 100 - ER = 93%
Self-correction rate = SC : SC + E = 1:13

Figure 4.2   Sheet for Running Record Analysis.

of the summer school program, had worked with her uncle, Steve, on a community institute and was a nice lady.

Vicky demonstrated knowledge of networks in the community, including who the owner of the summer school program was and how that connected to her family. Like June, Vicky read a range of texts from her life—often ones that represented her and her family in "official ways"—as in the present example. As Vicky interacted with these everyday texts with meaningful and socially purposeful intentions, she understood what she was reading and the range of social implications. In addition, she learned that her mother took care of issues related to the children in the house, and that her mother made the decisions in the household. In this example, June made the decision to enroll Luanne in the summer school program and she made the decision to take her out of the program. This assertion connects to an issue I explore more fully in the following section. That is, through interactions connected to the family's literacy Vicky learned a number of things, including the role of literacy in their lives and the relationship between gender and literacy.

"You Fill Out These Papers" : Acquiring Social Relations

Explaining WIC.   "Becky, you like this kind of juice?" June asked me one afternoon as she opened her cupboard and pointed at the surplus of cans of Juicy Juice she received from WIC and from the local food pantry. I told her I did. Taz, seeing the juice, said that he wanted to take a can of the juice home for himself. Vicky, at that point, took ownership over the discussion. First, she told Taz he couldn't bring any of the juice home because he received WIC himself. Then, she explained to me the process of applying for and receiving WIC resources.

1. V: [to Taz] No, ya'll get them off your own WICS.
2. B.   Where do you get them from?
3. V.   From the store.
4.   From Price Chopper off WIC.
5. J: Yeah you get them off your WIC.
6. B: What does that mean?
7. J: Off your WIC check, your WIC check
8. V: = your WIC check
9. B: What does it look like?
10. J: It's just like a piece of paper.
11. V: [Like a check.
12. B: And its written on it what you can get?
13. V: Yeah. Like milk, eggs, juice, peanut butter, dairy.
14. B: So can I get WIC?
15. V: No WIC is for babies.

16. T: When you have a baby then you can get WIC.

17. B: Really?

18. V: You get WIC for yourself and the baby too.

19. B: Who do you call to get it?

20. V: She's gonna have a baby

21.   to get WIC. [to Taz, laughing]

22.   You got to go down to Whitney Young [health center]

23.   and fill out the papers.

24.   Then once a month

25.   you get these checks

26.   to use at Price Chopper.

Unfamiliar with the specifics of the process, I asked open-ended questions to which I did not know the answer. For example, I asked them where they got WIC from (Line 2) and where they called in order to get WIC (Line 19). Vicky explained the process clearly, using language proficiently to describe an event with which she was familiar and comfortable. In addition, she also managed to make a joke at my expense, saying, "She's gonna have a baby to get WIC."

This interaction indicates a number of issues about Vicky's history of practice with these institutions and these texts. First, the relationship between the need to have children and the ability to receive support is clear to Vicky. Second, she knew that Taz and his family also received WIC and therefore he would not be able to take any of their supplies home with him. Third, she demonstrated, through repetition of what she had seen her mother do, that the literacy work of the household, including filling out forms, is women's work. Recall Rockhill's (1995) reminder that, "in addition to the uses of literacy involved in housework, [women] attend to the purchase of goods, as well as the transactions around social services, public utilities, health care and the schooling of children" (p. 171). Vicky learned that June attended to these things and that eventually, so would she.

Similarly, Kessler-Harris (1990) wrote about the connection between women's work and social consequences. A statement she made is relevant to this situation:

[G]ender defines the source of one's identity . . . in the end it serves as both a justification of female behavior and as an explanation of its consequences . . . It explains the consequences in terms of home attachments and attitudes. And it carries the ring of inevitable repetition since it offers up a picture of female work culture that relies heavily on women's own values to identify acceptable parameters of female behavior" (p. 63).

From observing June and participating in the activities of the home, Vicky learns the "inevitable repetition" and contradictions embedded in literacy as women's work. Just as June was involved in the aforementioned WIC discussion, throughout the 2 years June was, in many ways, involved with the tutoring sessions. Each of these informal learning situations added to my learning about the Treaders' use of texts in their everyday lives. Sometimes June's involvement with the reading group took the shape of participation in the reading and discussing of books, something she was reluctant to do in her classroom but willing to do in her kitchen. Other times her engagement with a literacy event, seen in the next example, led to an intergenerational conversation around literacy.

Free- and Reduced-Lunch Forms. June also negotiated forms in the kitchen as the children read at the table. At the beginning of each school year, a free- and reduced-lunch form was sent home with the children to be sent back if they qualify for assistance. June brought the paperwork over to the table where we were working and showed it to me. Our conversation went as follows:

J: Only thing I really need to fill out is this [takes the form and flips through the pages] household, size, what's that? What they mean income ca, chart?

B: [looking at the form] Okay. Household size. Number of people in your house. Is how many?

J: Five.

B: Well let's read this. Okay. Income chart. [hand the form back to June]

J: The following chart lists income lev-lev-level

B: Uh-huh

J: as, according, according to household size and income level receivin' each year, monthly or weekly if you, if you total in house income is the size, same of less than one amoun' on the income chart below your child can get reduced?

B: Uh-huh

J: Reduced-price meal and maybe eligible to receive free meal.

B: Okay so now you have to, what's your house-hold size? How many of you are there?

J: Five.

B: No, there's six of you. Right? Four kids and two adults?

J: You ain't countin' the baby, is you?

B: Well why not?

J: Well six. (transcript, 9/98)

Similar to June's negotiation of the magnet school letter—seen in chapter 3—June read "income level," "house income," and "eligible to receive a free meal" with fluency. June demonstrated a history of experience with these forms exemplified in her automatic recognition of these terms. There is more to this interaction than just the textual level, though.

June received the document from the school. She knew she needed to fill out the form in order for her children to get lunch at school. Through this interaction, it is reinforced to June and Vicky that literacy is filling out forms. In fact, June stated, "Only thing I really need to fill out is this." Unsure how to negotiate the form by herself, June accessed her social network, which in this example was me as the researcher and literacy teacher, as a way to ensure she filled out the form correctly. As we read the document, Vicky looked over June's shoulder and read it alongside June.

B: Okay so if you're six people in your house and you're under that, that means that you are eligible for reduced meals. Okay.

J: So what I put? Just mark six?

B: Yup.

I could tell from the way June gripped the pen tightly, with her correction fluid placed next to the paper and the pen wavering between putting the "6" on two different lines, that she was anxious about filling out the form incorrectly (fieldnotes, 9/98). In this literacy event, June's role as a mother and a literacy student are evoked. In the first set of interactions she was ready to put "five" down for the number in her household. June did not count her newborn, Evan, as a member of the household. Because free and reduced lunches are figured on an equation of the number of people in the house and the amount of income, choosing "5" instead of "6" would have lowered the amount of money they received. As a result of these forms being connected to the family's nutritional status, there is a sense of consequences or evaluation connected with filling out the forms correctly.

In the preceding example, an "error" in her reading of five versus six children may have had serious consequences. It may be that June and Vicky have learned that reading means reading the words "correctly" because of the detail connected with bureaucratic texts. In this example, June understood the meaning of the document. She needed to fill in the number of people in the household in order to get her children free lunches. This is similar to June's negotiation of the health care form for Shauna's preschool in chapter 2.

These intergenerational interactions around literacy in Sherman Hollows concur with Heath's (1983) research in the Piedmonts of the Carolinas with children and families in Trackton, a Black working-class community. Heath wrote, "[j]ointly or in group affairs, the children of Trackton read to learn before they go to school to learn to read" (p. 191). There are many opportunities for talk around these documents and forms. Furthermore, they provide the context for intergenerational literacy learning as we saw in the WIC example, where June and Vicky jointly explained the process of applying for and receiving social services. Aside from reading to learn in early interactions with literacy, the Treader children are also learning expectations about texts, the consequences of these interactions, and about their own social roles.

Vicky, in Rogoff's (1995) theory of learning, is being apprenticed into a number of discourses including how literacy is used in their daily lives. She learned through observing her mother interact with these forms over time. Vicky was then guided through participation as she reminded her mother she could use the abbreviation when filling out the magnet school form (chap. 2). Finally, as I illustrate in the following interaction, Vicky transformed this knowledge of free- and reduced-lunch forms into a way that made sense to her. That is, the knowledge and social roles connected with each of these literacy events are a part of Vicky's subjectivity as a daughter, a student, and an emerging adolescent. In making this knowledge her own, as shown in the next example, it is possible to recognize traces of the intergenerational transfer of ideology of women's work entextualized into the bureaucratic forms (Collins, 1996).

Extending the discussion around the free- and reduced-lunch form, Vicky and Taz, her cousin, began a discussion about what they had for lunch at school that day. Being at different schools, Vicky and Taz reported different lunch items such as peanut butter and jelly sandwiches, milk, salad, and a brownie. I asked them how they got their lunch. Taz informed me, "I stood in line and they gave me my lunch. I told them my number and I got my lunch." Vicky expanded on this and stated, "He got it for free if his mother signed a paper." They both tell me they have "numbers."

L: There's a lunch number.
V: What's your number?
L: 485.
V: 485? Mine is 319.
B: So what do you mean? How do you get your lunches?
L: You got to tell the person, you got to get your lunch and then you go up to the lady and
V: [they ask you for your number and then
       then they say what's your number and then you tell em your number and say if you got peanut butter on your tray, /// then they look at your number and if peanut butter not by your number that means you don't got peanut butter so you got to tell your teacher you want peanut butter then you got to get your number ... Everybody in my classes got numbers. (transcript, 2/99)

Vicky described to me how each year their mother signed a paper so that they can get a number and then get their "free food," just like the one she just filled out. She told me that if "your mother don't sign the paper you got to pay." Vicky showed an awareness of her mother filling out the forms. However, as is clear from the earlier interaction with June filling out the free- and reduced-lunch form, there is more "work" being done than just "signing the paper." In order to successfully fill out this form, June had to have knowledge of the financial status of the family (something she takes care of) and of the organization of the school. Furthermore, she learned that the literacy in their daily lives has the power to regulate.

Family Literacy as Apprenticeship

In each of the aforementioned examples (*The Last Safe House* reading and discussion, the action research project, reading the local newspaper, explaining the process of applying for and receiving WIC and free lunches), Vicky is actively and strategically using language and literacy as a sociocultural tool. She demonstrated proficiency with language and knowledge of social arrangements as she explained how to apply for and receive WIC. Indeed, her proficiency with language in explaining things with which she is familiar and comfortable can readily be seen in the free- and reduced-lunch form example and as she discussed the book *The Last Safe House*. In one case, Vicky went beyond a literal understanding of the process and demonstrated empathy toward the slaves who were not allowed to learn to read. In the other, she made a joke at my expense suggesting I might have a baby in order to get social services.

In the conversations about *The Last Safe House* and *Night John*, Vicky demonstrated an understanding of the text as well as an interest in issues of social justice and a questioning beyond the literal text. Her reading in a meaningful, connected text that is at a fourth- and a fifth-grade reading level demonstrated her proficiency with written texts. This contradicted the school's report of Vicky's severe speech and language deficits —which I illustrate in chapters 5 and 6—as well as demonstrated what she can do in meaningful, authentic social situations. Vicky also wrote a diary entry where she stepped into the persona of Harriet Tubman (see Fig. 4.3).

This writing illustrated her ability to step inside of the literature, to make connections between her writing and her reading and to write in different genres. In addition, she knew a number of conventions and took risks in her spelling. Though she needed instructional support in her writing, it is not a "below average piece of writing," the claim of the special-education committee report, nor was she just attending to mechanics such as being "proud of her penmanship" (CSE meeting, 6/18/98).

Vicky's discussion of *Night John* and *The Last Safe House*, two of the many books she read, demonstrated her negotiation of literature at a fourth- and

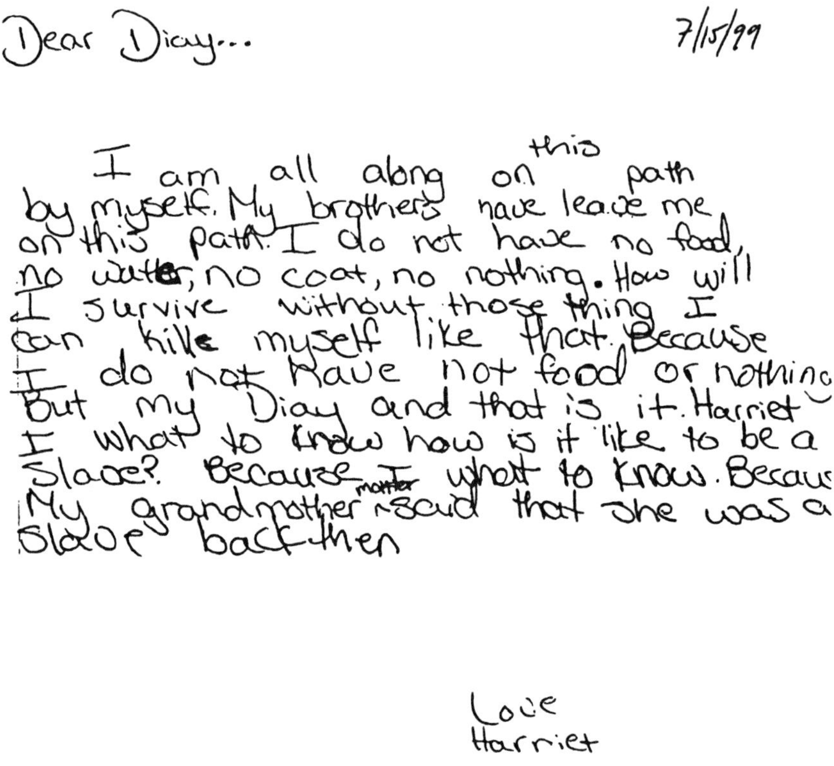

Dear Diary...   7/15/99

I am all along on this path
by myself. My brothers have leave me
on this path. I do not have no food,
no water, no coat, no nothing. How will
I survive without those thing I
can kille myself like that. Because
I do not have not food or nothing
But my Diay and that is it. Harriet
I what to know how is it like to be a
Slave? Because I what to know. Becaus
My grandmother mother said that she was a
Slave back then

Love
Harriet

Figure 4.3   Vicky's Letter.

fifth-grade reading level. Vicky not only comprehended these texts; she made connections between the world of books and her world by suggesting we embark on our own interview project.

The interviews, initiated by Vicky and her peers, indicate how Vicky used language to learn more about her social world. These interviews also show Vicky's reflection on the conditions of racism and her own life. Vicky's knowledge of institutional organizations and social arrangements is apparent in her reading of the local newspaper with the news story on Luanne and through her explaining the process of WIC to me. Vicky was set up to be successful in these examples because she, not I as the researcher and the teacher, had the answers.

This instructional context leads to different results about the proficiency of Vicky's language and literacy abilities than we see in the next chapter. Vicky demonstrated proficiency with reading a range of genres and writing. I argue, however, that Vicky's engagements with literacy extend well beyond a schooled literacy approach—certainly as it is practiced in her school—and enter into the arena of "critical literacy" in terms of her knowledge and questioning of social arrangements.

There are several common threads through each of these sets of literacy practices. First, Vicky was apprenticed into these engagements. That is, in each of the interaction she has (a) observed the literacy practice carried out by a more knowledgeable other (i.e., her mother or her peers), (b) participated in the social practice in a guided relationship (i.e., interviews, WIC), and (c) carried out the practice independently. Second, each of these sets of literacy practices involved the use of language and literacy as mediators of sociocultural experiences. That is, Vicky used literacy and language proficiently in authentic and purposeful situations. Third, Vicky has ownership over the interaction. Thus, she had much to contribute.

This exemplifies an important point about Vicky as a learner. Vicky was highly successful as she moved from apprenticeship (watching and observing her mother fill out the form), to guided participation (helping her mother with the abbreviation of the middle school), to transformation of how this knowledge plays out in her social world.

Intersecting Points: June and Vicky

Embedded in theories of discourse and power is the assumption that different domains of practice carry more value and weight than others (Fairclough, 1995; Gee, 1996). Though Vicky interacted with many different genres, she continued to see reading as a subskill process and did not see herself as proficient with literacy.

I have developed the argument that the reason why June and Vicky did not see themselves as literate was because they identified so closely with the notion of "schooled literacy." That is, instead of being a "mismatch" between the home and school, there was an alignment of beliefs and values. Within this institutional framework they had learned to see themselves not as literate but as people who had literate failure. Despite this, June and Vicky believed in the value of education and demonstrated a substantive commitment to literacy education. This contradiction is an important tension in June's and Vicky's lives because it influenced the decisions they made within the school.

There are many parallels between June's and Vicky's cases. Both June and Vicky view reading as an individual endeavor and a value in schooled literacy. However, as I point out in chapter 5, this view is paradoxical because whereas reading is done by individuals (thus not incorporating social relations), it is evaluated, measured, and reported by authorities other than themselves. June and Vicky both have fragile literate identities. They do not see themselves as readers and demonstrate profound tensions between their personal and their public literate lives.

June and Vicky demonstrate a local activism with literacy. In their engagements with literacy in their home and community, they portray a use of literacy as a sociocultural tool in order to mediate their daily lives. Whereas June engaged in activism through her organization of a petition for a traffic light, Vicky set out to interview "local heroes" in her community. However, the role of literacy at home as part of the texture of their lives seemed to be "invisible." June demonstrated and Vicky learned that literacy is women's work, connected with household tasks and raising children. Connected to their literacy work are the contradictory subject positions that are asked of them as women and as students, that is, their relationship to literacy through schooling and their relationship to literacy through their family (in June's case to her children). Another intersecting point in June's and Vicky's learning trajectories is that despite the proficiencies noted earlier, their local literacies go unnoticed and unvalued by the school. June was defined as the "lowest reader in the class" and Vicky, at the end of her sixth-grade year, was defined as "multiply disabled" including severe speech and language deficits.

In the next two chapters—5 and 6—I shift to focus on power embedded in language, both spoken and written, as a trace the discourse trail of the special-education referral process. That is, the school represented Vicky's academic learning identity in deficit terms that constructed her social identity. This analysis makes it possible to explain why Vicky believed she is not literate and that her literacy does not count. This de-valuing occurs day after day at the school. Despite Vicky's proficiencies, Vicky was referred for a special-education evaluation during the middle of her sixth-grade year. When I spoke with the reading teacher about the decision to begin the referral process, she told me that they really did not know what was "wrong" with Vicky. She was a borderline student who was not "dumb" but that they see so many cases "like her" that they are never sure what to do. She stated, "Vicky has a kind heart. If she does not get pregnant too soon, she'll make out okay. Vicky will be happy. She's the type of person who does not have to be a doctor or a lawyer. She will be happy with the simple things in life" (Reading teacher, informal conversation, 5/19/98). This teacher, who certainly cares for Vicky, almost certainly structures her interactions with her around these constructs. It is within these interactions that Vicky builds her literate subjectivities. When I spoke to the classroom teacher about the referral, she told me that the intention was to get Vicky into a "grade-level special-education class"—an institutional intention I take up in the next chapters.

NOTES

1. An earlier version of this chapter received the National Reading Conference Student Research of the Year Award and appeared in Rogers (2001). *National Reading Conference Yearbook, 50,* 96–114.
2. Clay (1993) defined an instructional level as a level of reading at between a 90% and 94% accuracy rate. At this level, children make productive errors in using what they know to facilitate their literacy learning.

Chapter 5

"I'm Her Mother, Not Them"

> If they argue with me they argue with me. She [Vicky] will not be in no special education class. I'm the one who has to sign the papers. I'm her mother, not them. So they can argue with me all they want to.   —June (transcript, 3/26/98)
>
> I guess I let them put her into it [special education] just to get it over with. —June (transcript, 6/13/98)

INTERSECTING HISTORIES

In January of 1998, the school sent home a form letter asking for parental permission to begin the special-education referral process on Vicky. June stood in her kitchen and told me the reading teacher had called her to explain what the paperwork was. After the phone call with Mrs. Matthews, the reading teacher, June told me what she viewed as the school's intention for testing Vicky. June stated, "She just say that she wanted to, test Vicky and see how she, how she goin' before she gettin' into the middle school. And then she just gonna show me what she gonna be test on if I want her tested."

"What is the purpose for the testing?" I asked.

June responded, "She just said to just see how, you know, see how she goin', what her level and stuff is, before she get into the middle school. I tol' her I'd think about it. She said don't worry about it now because it ain't until just like, before they get ready to get up outta school."

"So," I asked June, "what is your view on the testing?" June responded:

> *I don't know, I want to see* the papers and stuff first before *I decide* what she gonna be tested on. *I want to see* what the paper is and what, you know, and what they is about and stuff. And if *I feel* she need to be tested on that, then *I let her* go ahead and test her. But she said that she can't do it unless *I'm concerned about it. You know, I sign it* and stuff.[1]

Embedded in this quotation, similar to all utterances, are orders of discourse including genre, discourse, and style. The genre of this quotation is part of an interview. The discourse—or the ways of representing— includes how June understood the institution of the school. These phrases are underlined and include phrases such as "papers and stuff" and "tested." June understands the Discourse of the school from the perspective of a testing paradigm. In her own experiences with school she expressed a belief in tests and what they tell her about her progress, and therefore she acquiesced to the tests. However here, in the context of making a decision for her daughter, June positioned herself as having more control over the process of educational testing and decision making.

Style, or the order of discourse that includes ways of being, indicates the relationship between June and her relationship to literacy when she interacted with literacy on her daughter's behalf. An analysis of her "I" statements illustrates that June believed the testing process was in her control, evidenced by the series of "I" statements in the preceding excerpt (Fairclough, 1989, 1995; Gee, 1997, 1999; Wortham, 2001)[2]. Action, affective, or cognitive statements follow June's "I" statements. Her "I" statements reflect her wanting to be in control of the situation that impacts her daughter. The form of June's answer is cast in terms of her practices and beliefs as a mother (e.g., "unless I'm concerned about it"; "I sign it and stuff.") June, as the mother, could sign the form in order to start the process. This is relevant to June's subjectivities because June was constructing one piece of her identity to literacy through her position as a mother. This analysis demonstrates that the relationship between linguistic resources and social identities varies depending on the context from which June spoke.

June believed that the referral and the testing would not begin until the end of the school year. The school failed to articulate to her that the battery of testing would begin almost automatically. June did not seem concerned about the testing at this point. She stated she wanted to know about the specifics of the tests and then she would think about it. June viewed the testing, *if* she were to allow it to happen, as exploratory—to learn more about Vicky. The reading teacher and the classroom teachers, who began the referral process, saw it as a way to get Vicky into a grade-level special-education class. This is an important point because it concurs with Mehan's (1996) research that illustrated the process through which ambiguities about student achievement move to clarity through the testing process. Yet both the reading teacher and the classroom teacher told me in interviews that they wanted to get the paperwork done so that they could get Vicky into a special-education class before she got to the middle school.

June and I sat in her kitchen, at the small oval table, before the children got home. I asked June what she thought about the testing and told her what I knew about the process. I told her that a "group of teachers would get together and decide if there are any instructional changes they can make for Vicky." June interrupted me, and for the first time initiated a discussion about special education. She said, with fervor in her voice:

She, she didn't say anything else, she didn't say nothin' about a special. She didn't say nothin' to me about a special. No special ed class when she get into the other school. She didn't mention nothin' like that . . . If *I don't want* her in a special then she don't have to go into a special. If *I feel* she don't need to be in no special then she won't be goin' into no special . . . Like *I said, I don't know* till *I see* the test, the test papers and see what kind of test papers it is before *I jump* up and say, "Yeah" *I'm goin' to let* them come in and test her. 'Cause if *I feel* that she is doin' better with you working with her, why do I figure she needs to be tested? (transcript, 3/3/98).

Embedded within the larger discursive context of mothering, June's "I" statements are either affective (e.g., I don't want; I feel), action (e.g., I said, I jump up), or cognitive (e.g., I figure, I don't know), with the majority being affective and action statements. This indicates her emotional connection to the decision and her relationship to the school and testing. June's relationship to the testing process was characterized by a pattern of affective and action statements within the context of the home.

One of her action statements, "before I jump up and say," is an enactment of her strong physical resistance to this process. June seemed to mock that the school thinks she would readily sign the papers and send them back, consenting for her daughter to be placed in a special-education classroom. Instead, she wanted to examine the text and then make a decision. June further revealed her knowledge of the school system through her abbreviation of the phrase "special education," referring to it as a "special."

Furthermore, June's statements about the tests, in conjunction with her "I" statements, illustrate her own history with testing (chap. 3), one that was evoked through this referral process. For example, June stated, "I don't know till I see the test, the test papers and see what kind of test papers it is" ; "before I let them come in and test her"; "why do I figure she needs to be tested?".

In this passage, June moved from my statement about a group of teachers to fervently denying her daughter's placement in special education. It is clear that this issue weighed heavily on her mind. June's speech evoked the metaphor, from her own ABE classroom, of "coming in" to test her, again a connection to her history of education. In her own classroom, Curt, the guidance counselor, would come into the classroom and ask the teacher to see certain students, and then he would take them to the guidance office and give them the test to take. June did not want this for her daughter. Her resistance to even begin the referral process stemmed from her strong desire to be a good mother and protect her daughter.

As June talked about Vicky being tested, she was the most passionate I had ever seen her be. She continued:

If she's comin' along, and her teacher tol' me that she is coming along real good, then all she need to do is pick up on her spellin', be needed to be more improvin'. If she, figuring that, then *I figure* she doin' real good in school. Then *I don't figure* that she probably need to be tested or see because she got four or five months before she get out for spring vacation so *I just see* how she does between now and June. And what *I'm sayin'* is that *I don't want* her in a special ed class, *I don't* want her in it. That's my opinion (transcript, 3/26/98).

June retraced a conversation she had with the reading teacher and the classroom teacher. She recognized the contradictions between narratives about Vicky in terms of what the teachers had told her informally—"the teacher tol' me that she is coming along real good"—and that they now want to test her. In the preceding quotation, June recounted that the teachers told her Vicky had made progress and that she needed to continue to study her spelling words. June was very confident in her ability to help Vicky study spelling words. She and Vicky would sit down with the list of words and June would read the words and Vicky would spell them. June would stop her if she got a letter wrong and make her start over until she spelled the word correctly. They would often practice in the kitchen, after dinner. When Vicky studied and brought home "A" spelling tests, June hung them on the wall in the library room. Further contradictory evidence to Vicky's not needing special-education testing, not mentioned in this conversation, was that the teacher granted Vicky an effort award at the midyear honor ceremony held at the elementary school.

June called on her role as a mother to monitor Vicky's progress and to decide if she needed testing. She stated, "I figure she doin' real good in school . . . I don't figure that she probably need to be tested . . . . . So I just see how she does." In contrast to the working-class parents in Lareau's (1989) study, in this context (June's home), June believed it was her right to make educational decisions and to monitor her daughter's progress with school.

Trying to understand her strong stance on this, I asked her, "how come?" June responded:

'Cause Vicky don't need to be in a special ed then she don't need to be in a special ed. Special ed is like, for a slow person and she is not slow. She is not slow at all. The only things that it is that when she gets around a lot of people, she just don't concentrate in her work. Now if it's just her in a classroom working and she don't know anybody in the classroom she will do the work. But like I said, special ed is for slow people and she is nowhere near slow. She is not slow (transcript, 3/3/98).

It is evident listening to June that she has a working knowledge of special education. June stated, "special ed is like, for a slow person and she is not slow." June called on her knowledge of special-education and the knowledge of her daughter ("she just don't concentrate on her work") to make the assertion that she did not want her in a special-education class. Whereas when June talked about herself as a reader, she attributed her problems to internal deficits (i.e., that she couldn't read), when she talked about her daughter she referred to external distractions as the source of the problem. June's commitment and dedication to her daughter is apparent. Surprised and excited by June's passion as well as thinking about Vicky's strengths with literacy over the year, I responded, "I agree with you." Before I had a chance to say much more, June intervened again: "And my opinion right now is that she is not goin' into a special-ed class. She's not. Even if she takes the test or if she don't take the test. She's not goin' into special ed. She's not" (transcript, 3/3/98).

June seemed to shake the cultural belief that the test will tell her whether or not her daughter should be in a special-education classroom. Her knowledge of her daughter as a "smart girl" counted more than what a test could tell her. June stated, regardless of what the test "says" she is saying something different. June repeated herself, "She is not going into a special ed class."

Curious about where she has learned about special education, if she had not been in special education herself, I asked, "Do you know other people that have been in special education?" June responded:

> Yes. My niece, my niece have been in special ed ever since last year and she in special ed this year. So everything that she in special ed last year and special ed this year she must not be doin' too good in the special ed class . . . They must not be teachin' anything in the special-ed classroom. You know? So why would they want to put her in last year and then she in the same school, in the same special-ed class. So, no, she not goin' in no special-ed class. No and I mean it (transcript, 3/3/98).

The narrative June drew on to inform her thinking about the special-education process came from her niece's experiences. June told me that her niece had been placed in special education and had not come out of the class. June told me directly that once you go into a special-education class, you will never come out, a statement she explicitly made later on. She directly questioned the assumptions behind that going into a special-education class will move a child up to grade level, when, in fact, that rarely happens (Harris, 1992; Gartner & Kernzer-Lipsky, 1987; Patton, 1998). June demonstrated an understanding of the organization of the school system and questioned the legitimacy of the institution of special education. June wanted more and better instruction for her daughter. Again, this questioning of the legitimacy of an instructional decision and the instructional circumstances tied to this decision is a pattern rarely found in studies of working-class parents and schooling (Lareau, 1989). However, a point I draw upon later is the discursive context, that is, the home in which June made these assertions.

June's insight into more and better instruction is insightful as she again defended her position about Vicky not being put into a special-education classroom: "She [Vicky] can learn just as good in a regular class than goin' into a special-ed class if she has to be tutored or with just another teacher and her but not goin' into no special-ed class though . . . I didn't ever go in one so why should she go in one?" Here June made the distinction between a "regular" and a "special-ed class," a theme that runs through chapter 7. Further illustrating her involvement as a parent she reinforced that she would have Vicky tutored or request that she be with another teacher. June was willing to change the instructional conditions so that her daughter would not have to go into a special-education classroom. Another important element of this stretch of talk is June's linguistic signal to her educational history. She stated, "I didn't ever go in one so why should she go in one?" Here, the discursive contexts of mothering and schooling come into alignment.

June then reiterated that the reading teacher told her not to worry about it because they weren't going to do anything right now. They probably would do something in 4 or 5 months and then "she'll [the reading teacher] get back in touch with me if I want her to be tested before she come out of that school" (transcript, 3/26/98). June made it clear she believed that placement in a special-education class would not only be a wrong instructional decision for Vicky but would symbolize that Vicky had actually done *worse* than her own experiences within the same school district.

Throughout the process, June clung to the vision that her daughter was not being placed in a special-education classroom. She stated on another occasion, "She have to scrub just to get through. She will. She's not going into no special ed class" (interview, 3/8/98). As June negotiated the forms and letters sent home from the school, forms that pushed her to the edge of her own literate competence, she was faced with the intersection of her own literate identity and the responsibility, as a mother, of opening different possibilities for her daughter.

SPEECH PAPERS

As June and I walked back to her apartment from church on a Sunday in March 1998, we discussed the letter the school sent home. We walked up the street parallel to June's apartment. At one o'clock in the afternoon the street was still quiet, with a few people sitting on their front stoops. Boards covered many of the windows we passed on the way to June's house. As the children passed the parked cars, ranging from new to decades old, they used the car windows as mirrors. Vicky, Luanne, and Shauna were a block ahead of us, walking carefully, mindful of their Sunday clothes. June seemed relieved to talk about the referral process in private, outside of the range of her children's earshot. At this point, she had sent back the initial referral form and had agreed to begin the referral process. She and Lester decided to let the school test Vicky so they could "learn more about her."

Another form letter arrived at the Treaders' house a week after June sent back the first. This time it was a letter asking permission for the speech therapist to test Vicky's speech and language. June told me the reading teacher called to follow up on the note. The reading teacher told June she wanted to make sure June knew what the note meant. June told me that there was "nothin' wrong with Vicky's speech" (3/25/98). This was similar to June's outward rejection that Vicky needed to be tested. In both cases, June called on the discursive context of mothering, in order to assert that there was "nothin' wrong with Vicky's speech."

June reiterated that she did not want Vicky in a special-education class. June also told me that the reading teacher *still* had not mentioned anything in the phone conversation about special education. The reading teacher only stated that she wanted to get Vicky's speech tested, just to see how Vicky was doing (fieldnotes, 3/24/98). June stated:

> *I don't want* her in a special ed because once she gets in to the special ed and the simple fact she get in there she never come out of there. Until she get to the 12th grade and then she come out of special ed. But special ed don't teach you more than the classroom teacher. *I think* she is improvin'. *I see* her workin' with Luanne and workin' with you. She even help me out. If *I don't know* the word, she helps me with it. That's why *I think* she's really improvin' with what she doin'. . . . *I'm going* to tell them if *I have to* take her out of that school, and put her in another school she will not go to a special ed. *I know* that [middle school] has a special ed up there.

June's last statement foreshadows our trip to the middle school where she also attended school before she dropped out. Similar to prior statements about the construction of "I" statements in June's speech, here, they are action, affective, and cognitive statements. Here, however, the action gets stronger as she continues to narrate her decision. June moved from stating an affective reason ("I don't want her") to a cognitive statement of her improvement (e.g., "I think she is improvin'") to an action statement (e.g., "I see her workin'"). She then stated that she would "take her out of that school and put her in another school," a physical action. As June talked through her thoughts about the special-education process, she not only represented how she thought and felt but enacted her position through her words as well (Wortham, 2001).

The overlap between orders of discourse (discourse and style) is visible in the italicized and underlined phrases in the previous quotation. The discourse dimension refers to the ways of representing larger narratives such as the Discourse of schooling or the Discourse of reading. When June referred to her daughter she noticed the progress she made as a reader both at home and at school. She drew on this information from her observations of her daughter as a reader. Style calls on subjectivities and how people are positioned and position themselves within discourse (e.g., through pronoun use and active and passive construction). In conjunction with June's "I" statements were her assertions of what she would do so Vicky would not be placed in special education. I have italicized these places in the text. For example, when June stated, "*I think* she is improvin'. *I see* her workin' with Luanne and workin' with you. She even help me out. If *I don't know* the word, she helps me with it," she called on her role as a mother and the observations she had made of Vicky's improvement in the home. Each of these examples called on the discursive context of mothering, or June's understanding of literacy through her relationship with her children.

The second area that indicates the overlap between June's role as a mother and the institution of the school is exemplified in the following statement: "I'm going to tell them if I have to take her out of that school and put her in another school she will not go in a special ed." June called on her *right* as a mother to make educational decisions for her daughter. June told me she would even go so far as to withdraw Vicky from the school in order to make sure Vicky was not placed in special education. While June continued to resist, her concerns moved from resisting the testing to resisting placement, a step further into the process.

It is this gradual chipping away and June's realization that although the discursive context of mothering is strong, the discursive context of the school is stronger. It is possible to trace this turning of the tide through linguistic evidence. Noting June's stance about the placing Vicky in a special-education referral process and also knowing how the school might respond to this, I tried to help June anticipate what the school might say to her. I told her that the school personnel might suggest that one option for Vicky would be for her to go into a resource room. June responded, "resource room is still like special ed." June was right that in order to receive support from the resource room a child needed to have a special-education label. June agreed that if Vicky needed "special help" that was okay, but she would not be placed in a special-education classroom. She stated, "Well if she needs special help then yes I can go for that. But if it's just putting them with other special-ed kids, Vicky is smart if she put her head to it. You know, but if she just sit there and let them [the other kids] do it what they want to do, she gonna go for it, but if Vicky put her head to it, Vicky is really smart she is." (transcript, 3/26/98).

Again, June calls on the discursive context of mothering, how she knows her daughter and what she believed was possible for her daughter. She and Lester discussed the speech papers one afternoon on their stoop. Shauna sat with the three of us as we talked. Lester asked me what my opinion was about the speech papers. I told him I did not know what they were and June asked Luanne to run upstairs and get her mail. I explained that often, as part of the special-education process, the teachers would test various components of the child's intellectual resources—including speech and language. Lester, hard of hearing in one ear, also had slurred speech because of his hearing. He seemed concerned and transferred this concern to his youngest daughter. He told me that he was concerned she was not saying her words the way she was supposed to and that sometimes he had difficulty understanding her. June, looking down the street at the people walking to and from the store shook her head and said, "There's nothin' wrong with any of them speech." Although they agreed to send back the papers to start the initial testing, June disagreed with the speech papers and never sent them back to the school. Whereas June's discourse is a clear and audible resistance to the process, not sending back the speech papers is also a clear form of resistance—one that should not be overlooked. This "silent resistance" symbolized that June was involved and did not agree with the process. Even though June did not send the papers back to the school, the school personnel went ahead with the testing, claiming that parental consent was embedded within the first set of forms sent home.

AN "INVITATION" TO ATTEND THE COMMITTEE ON SPECIAL EDUCATION MEETING

A few months after the psychologist and speech therapist conducted the testing on Vicky, another form letter was sent to the Treaders' home. This letter "invited" June Treader (the letter was addressed to June) to a committee on special education (CSE) meeting held on Vicky's behalf. This document called on June's conflicting relationship to literacy through her relationship to her children and to school. I presented a similar theme in chapter 3. That is, through these literate demands, June is reminded that literacy is filling out the forms. Furthermore, the jobs of corresponding to the school and attending educational meetings are women's work. I had also spoken with the reading teacher at this point, and she had informed me that Vicky's test scores were very low, confirming their decision about her placement in special education. The following interaction occurred between June and I, again in her kitchen:

B: So have you called to tell them that you are coming?

J: No. Why are they making such a big thing out of it [the CSE meeting] then?

B: What do you mean?

J: This [she picks up the letter that was sent home and shows it to me].

B: Because they want to go over the test scores with you. They showed that she was low and they will probably recommend that she go into special ed.

J: She's not goin' in no special ed. She's not goin' in no special ed class and I mean it. I don't care what they talk about, she's not goin' in no special ed.

(transcript, 5/9/98)

The meeting was to be held on June 18. The stated intention of the meeting was to discuss instructional options available for Vicky for the following year. However, the underlying purpose of the meeting—as I point out in the next chapter—was an invitation to accept their legitimate place in the social structure.

At this point, June still believed that even though they did the testing, Vicky would be in what June referred to as a "regular class" for her first year in the middle school. As a result of this belief, she didn't understand why the school was making "such a big deal out of it" and why they wanted to hold a CSE meeting. June held on to her initial assertions that placement in special education was a bad option for Vicky. June stated four concrete reasons why Vicky should not be placed in special education: First, Vicky was not slow, she was a bright girl. Second, Vicky just needed to put her mind to it. Third, June believed that if she never had to go into a special education class then why should her daughter? Fourth, she had seen Vicky make improvement in her reading as she worked with me, with Lori, and with her at home.

What is remarkable in these examples is June's sense of involvement with the school. She believed she had a voice and could make a difference in the educational lives of her children; indeed, the school convinced her she could. However, this voice never left the context of her family and her community. It is only heard in the context of the home. If she believed this, educators and other "gatekeepers" must also, and attend to the institutional structures that permit this to be the case. That is, attention must be given to what Key (1998) referred to as "literacy shutdown," a term that symbolizes the processes, emotional and cognitive, through which women find themselves at odds with their womanhood and their aspirations for literate achievement. I expand on this point in later chapters. June saw herself as key to her children's success in education and yet, at the same time, as inadequate because of her own limited literacy proficiency.

THE MIDDLE SCHOOL VISIT

In May of 1998, June and I walked into the middle school for an appointment with the guidance counselor. We went there to talk with her about the instructional options available for Vicky at the middle school for the following year. Prior to the meeting June and I generated a list of questions we wanted to ask about the resources that were available to Vicky at the middle school. I had June ask me a few of the questions and pretended I was the guidance counselor. At the time, Vicky was in the middle of a series of tests, part of the special-education referral process, because of her "low achievement in reading and math" (teacher interview, 1/98; CSE meeting, 6/18/98), an issue I take up in chapters 6 and 7.

As we walked down the corridor of the middle school, June pointed to the red stripe painted midway up the wall and said, "These are the same color stripes as when I was here" (fieldnotes 5/98). She told me that when she attended this school, the students in the red wing were those who went to "special" classes. Later, she asked the guidance counselor if the special-education classes were still held in the hallway with the red stripes. The guidance counselor assured June that the classes were physically integrated and were not separated by colors as they used to be. Similar to June describing the special-education process, seen earlier, when her memories and knowledge of the school were evoked, here being in the physical context of the school evoked her past participation in the same school building.

When we walked into the guidance counselor's office on that spring day in May, June was reminded of her own experience at the school not only by the red stripes on the wall but by the location of the guidance counselor's office, set off from the main office. She commented as we walked into the office, "This is the same place it used to be" (fieldnotes, 5/3/98).

June told the guidance counselor that her daughter was being tested at the elementary school. After hearing this information, the guidance counselor immediately explained the special-education program to June even though Vicky had not yet been classified as a special-education student. The guidance counselor, similar to Vicky's teachers, made the leap from being tested to being placed in a special-education class—a leap June was still not willing to make. The guidance counselor described the categories of available instructional support rather than the support Vicky might need.

Periodically, June stated, "I don't want Vicky in no special class." The guidance counselor explained the block schedule and the electives available to Vicky through the magnet school. At one point, the guidance counselor asked June why she felt so strongly about not placing Vicky in a special-education classroom (fieldnotes, 5/3/98). June responded, "I just don't want her to be in there." At that point, filled with emotion, June started to cry. Sitting in the guidance office, the same office she had to go to when she was in middle school, facing her dwindling hopes of Vicky not being placed in special education, June just put her head down and cried. The guidance counselor and I exchanged glances and there was a silence in the room. I put my arm around June's shoulders, also wanting to cry. The guidance counselor handed her a tissue and began again in a softer, gentler tone, as if she could modify the content of her words with her tone. From listening to her strong assertions about Vicky not going into special education to this moment, it is possible to see the tensions between June's personal (mothering) and public (schooling) literate subjectivities.

Though June's resistance to the process entered the school in her statement, "I don't want Vicky in no special class," and in the not spoken, her tears, it is substantively more silenced than how we heard June resist the placement in earlier quotations. Earlier she discredited the placement based on it being a wrong decision. June stated at least five different pieces of evidence. First, she said Vicky was not slow. She was, as June stated, "smart if she put her head to it." Second, once a person goes into special education they never come out and therefore they must not teach anything in there. Third, Vicky would not learn anything from a special-education teacher that she could not learn from a regular-education teacher. Fourth, June specified areas of improvement she had observed at home. She read at home, helped Luanne with her reading, and even helped June out when she had difficulty with a word. Fifth was June's statement, "I didn't ever go in one so why should she go in one?" This question exemplified her belief that Vicky is smarter than her and therefore should not be in a special-education classroom. Despite these five reasons why Vicky should *not* be placed in a special-education classroom, many of which are linked with her own personal experiences with education, all June was able to say during that meeting was, "I don't want Vicky in no special class." The institutional setting silenced her.

CONSENT

A month later, I visited June in her ABE class to observe her in class and also to work with her on her reading. I would spend half an hour observing in the classroom during language arts time and then work with June for an hour.

June told me that she found it easier to have reading instruction in the school setting than at home because her attention was often split between the books and tending to her children, cleaning the house, and making dinner. Furthermore, she preferred that when I was at their home I work with the kids because, "they need it more."

As June started to look through the books I brought with me, she told me about the informal meeting she had with the reading teacher and the psychologist at the elementary school the previous afternoon. This surprised me because I had asked the reading teacher to inform me of the meeting. The reading teacher had assured me it would be the following week and she would call me to let me know the date and time. June told me that Mrs. Matthews, the reading teacher, had called her in the morning and the meeting was held that afternoon. June had to leave her own classroom in order to attend. The last-minute meeting was with the reading teacher and the school psychologist, and the focus of the meeting, they told June, was to go over the results of the test scores. With resignation in her voice, June described to me what happened at the meeting:

J: I went up there yesterday and talked to them.

B: The both of them? What did they say?

J: Nothin'. They just went over the test scores and stuff. That's all. They called me yesterday morning and I went up there about two o'clock.

B: And what did her test scores say?

J: They was low. The only one, the highest one that she got was in math. She got like an eighth grade level . . . the rest of them were like below average.

B: So was there anything surprising in what they said?

J: No, they talked about that she really need to be in a special ed for her to pick up on her reading and her vocabulary and stuff like that. That's about it.

B: Oh.

J: What I figure is that I just go ahead and put her into a special ed just to get it over with. So she can pick up on her reading and vocabulary and science and stuff like that (transcript, 6/98).

After months of resisting this decision, June agreed "to get it over with." My heart sank as I heard June say this. I felt, again, another missed opportunity to make a difference. I worried that when June was presented with the test scores she would acquiesce to Vicky's placement in special education because she so adamantly believed in tests from her own educational history. Biased against culturally and linguistically diverse children, the standardized tests administered to Vicky did not show what she could do and in what instructional contexts (Harry & M. Anderson, 1994; Johnston, 2000). June's decision, I realized, had been more in opposition to the process continuing than in her belief that Vicky was "disabled." It seemed as though she had reached her personal limit. Determined to make Vicky's educational career different from her own and yet faced with her own literate limitations, June conceded to the school. In the face of test scores, the school evoked June's past experiences as a student with failure rather than one who had a right to make a decision about her daughter's placement. A similar pattern was seen as June talked about her experiences with returning to school. That is, as a woman she had desires and opinions about education and literacy but not rights to decent and equitable instruction for her and her daughter.

June's convictions raised earlier are effectively replaced with her statement, "They [the test scores] was low. The only one, the highest one that she got was in math. She got like an eighth grade level . . . the rest of them were like below average." Similarly problematic is that although June continued to not want Vicky in special education, she never regained the enthusiasm and conviction she showed in the beginning of this chapter. This phenomenon is one contextualized example of what Moss (1998a) and Johnston (1998a) referred to as the often invisible "consequences" of testing.

Both June's and Vicky's educational futures hinged on the results of test scores. As June relayed Vicky's deficiencies to me, as they were reported to her through the language of the tests that were administered to her, I was struck by the similarities between Vicky's and June's reported "deficiencies." The issue of "vocabulary" was interesting because it was the weakness that June has told me about herself. She stated, "[w]hat I need to work on is my vocabulary words." Even more striking than the fact that both June and Vicky struggle with vocabulary, according to standardized tests, was the way June revoiced the language of the school, repeating what they had told her about her daughter's weaknesses. This stood in stark contrast to what she had previously told me about Vicky's areas of improvement and the specific examples of why she should not be placed in a special-education classroom. This exemplified June's internalization of the linguistic codes of the school, even when it was not in her or her daughter's best interest (Collins, 1993).

I argue that the logic of Vicky's deficiencies, reported by the reading teacher and the psychologist, convinced June because she believed those same things about herself as a learner and a literacy student. When the psychologist told June that Vicky's test scores were low, June could relate; hers were also low. They told June that Vicky's reading and vocabulary were "below average" and she needed to "pick up" in these areas. This resonated for June, because she too needed to "pick up" in her own reading and vocabulary. She believed these diagnoses because how could she do otherwise? They were what she already believed about herself. In other words, her subjectivity as a literacy student was evoked in the context of this meeting.

As June lost voice with her daughter's placement, she also lost voice and belief in her own education. A week after this meeting with the school officials, June stated, "I don't care what Curt say. I'm about ready to quit school anyway. I'm just tired of it. Been there too long and I ain't movin' nowhere." I disagreed with her and recounted the progress she had made, using many of the examples from her "local" literate life. I recounted how she had studied for and taken her driver's permit test. I reminded her that she had written a note to Vicky's teacher to get a dictionary sent home and how she took social services to a fair hearing. June's response to my reminder of these strategic and authentic uses of literacy was, "But it seem like to him, I'm not movin'; if I was movin' I would be upstairs in the GED class." Again, June did not see the literacy she engaged with on a daily basis as counting toward her progress with literacy. She did not see her local literacies as valuable or important. June's use of the "movin' up" and "goin' down" metaphors signified her final resignation. If the test scores had gone up, she would have been in the GED room, literally upstairs. Therefore, in June's mind, she had not made progress.

June had been effectively "shut out" of both her children's education and her own (Fine, 1995; Key, 1998). June's decision to drop out of school was a decision made so that her literate identity would no longer be compromised. She was also 7 months pregnant at the time and did not seem to be able to attend to everything. She chose mothering over schooling. Ironically, June's decision to drop out of school, this second time around, was an act of resisting one regime of "discipline" and "authority" while acquiescing to a different regime—husband, children, and mothering (Luttrell, 1997). As part of these assertions, June separated her desire and right for intellectual freedom from her obligations as a mother and wife.

Luttrell (1997) highlighted this internalization of the success or failure of children by mothers as one of the effective mechanisms regulating and reproducing social inequalities. That is, because June believed it was her role to be a good mother in relation to schooling, when she was unsuccessful at advocating for Vicky, she doubted her own competence—both as a mother and as a person interacting with literacy and education. When all was said and done, June believed that she, not the school or the teachers, was responsible for the decisions made in the special-education process.

Two of the parallels between June's and Vicky's cases (presented in chap. 4) are relevant to the present chapter. First, both June and Vicky believe in the ideology of schooling (Bourdieu & Passeron, 1977). This belief is intact even though the school does not value their local literacies. Second, there are profound tensions between their personal and public literate lives. Each domain in which they interact with literacy evokes different aspects of their literate subjectivites—an issue that comes into focus in this chapter.

NOTES

1. The analysis of each order of discourse is represented in the quotation through the use of boldface, underlines, and italics. The genre, or ways of interacting, marked by turn taking, participant structures, cohesive devices such as repetition, and information focus, is coded in boldface. The discourse, or ways of representing, is coded with underlines. This domain includes larger narratives as well as the perspective from which the narratives are told. The domain of style, or ways of being, is represented with italics. The aspects of style include transitivity, modality, pronoun use, and active and passive construction of the sentence.
2. Analysis of the syntactical construction of language can offer insight into the connection between the linguistic resources used and the social positions they occupy or hope to occupy (Bucholtz, Liang, & Sutton,1999; Fairclough, 1995; Gee, 1999). Pronouns, and the clauses that follow, demonstrate the link between June and social languages. I analyzed the pronoun and construction of the verb and came up with the following categories of pronoun use: affective, cognitive, state, action. The action statements could be either passive or active; the cognitive statements include believe, think, know, and remember. The affective statements reflect want, desire, hope, or need. The state statements reflect a physical or mental state of being or relationship.

Into The Meeting Room

THE MEETING

The meeting took place on June 18, 1998, at the Daybreak School, which is a
school used in the district specifically for special-education purposes (see
Appendix G for a full transcript of this meeting). I reviewed the case report I
wrote on Vicky's progress as a reader and writer over the time I worked with
her and gave a copy of it to June. I planned on presenting this report at the
CSE meeting. I gave the report to June a week earlier and went over Vicky's
strengths and growth as a reader and writer. June told me she would share
the report with Lester. I asked Lester what he thought of the report and he
told me, "you doin' real good with her. She just need to concentrate and put
her mind to it and stop tryin' to act so grown. When I tell her she can't go out
after she school, she gotta do her homework, she gotta listen to me." Like
June, Lester did not think Vicky should be placed in a special-education class.

The morning of the meeting I picked up June and Shauna at their
apartment. In the car I handed June a list of the questions she and I had
brainstormed, compiled, and gone over the last time she and I worked
together. Unfamiliar with the programs and policies of the school district,
this was an authentic list of questions for both June and me. She told me,
"You can hang on to those" (fieldnotes, 6/18/98). When we got to the
school there was a 10-minute wait before we were invited into the meeting
room. During this time, Shauna played with the toys in a cardboard box that
were tucked under a table and June picked up a few children's books and
flipped through the pages, reading the words out loud.

When the chair of the committee called June into the meeting room,
Shauna and I followed her lead. I had called to speak with the chair of the
committee ahead of time to ask permission to record the CSE meeting as a
part of my research. She told me she would discuss it with the committee
and let me know prior to the meeting. Before we went into the room, the
chair told me that everyone had agreed to the tape recording. I placed the
tape recorder in the middle of the table and asked each member of the
committee to sign a consent form before I left the building.

The meeting lasted approximately 50 minutes. The participants in the
meeting included the psychologist (AB), the chair of the committee (DT),

the special-education liaison (SL), a parent representative (PR), the speech therapist (SS), June, myself (BR), and Shauna, June's youngest daughter. All of the participants, except for the parent liaison, June, and Shauna, were White women. Figure 6.1 illustrates where each of us sat during the meeting time.

Of the school officials in attendance at the meeting, no one knew Vicky outside of the tests they administered to her. The reading teacher and the classroom teachers who started the referral did not show up for the meeting. However, given prior ethnographic evidence, even if they had been present at the meeting, their evidence would have confirmed the results of the testing[1].

In the following sections, I present a portion of the CSE meeting that occurred on June 18, 1998. I utilize CDA as an analytic tool to illustrate the relationships between orders of discourse and the contradictions embedded in the meeting that can be justified with prior ethnographic learning and textual analyses. I knew from conversations with June before the meeting that when she entered this meeting on June 18, 1998, she had no intention of resisting a label being placed on her daughter. That was apparent in the conversation she and I had at the adult literacy center when she told me she would, "put her in it, just to get it over with." June knew

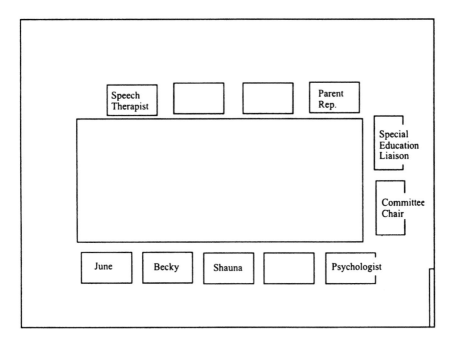

Figure 6.1   Seating Chart of CSE Year 1 Meeting.

going into this meeting that her daughter would be labeled. I believed that my report that documented Vicky's growth and her strengths could interrupt the labeling process. Even though June did not plan on resisting the label, neither she nor I knew the specific label that would be used to construct and represent Vicky's literate identity.

ORDERS OF DISCOURSE

Here, I return to the critical discourse framework I introduced earlier. Conceptually this diagram illustrates the intersection between orders of discourse and context. This illustration, and the framework, assumes that discourse always contains multiple levels. Some of the points I have made along the way in this book are illuminated in this meeting.[2] Through an analysis of multiple layers of discourse, it is evident that discourse is a process rather than a product. It is always context dependent and subject to the ways in which texts are produced and consumed. Each utterance can be understood and analyzed on at least three levels or "orders of discourse." This assumes the utterance is a social construction, not a property of any one individual.

Figure 6.2(a), Context, represents what Fairclough (1995) referred to as "local," "institutional," and "societal" domains. The local domain represents the CSE meeting. The institutional context represents the norms, policies, and regulations of the school system within which the CSE operates. The societal domain represents the national policies governing the

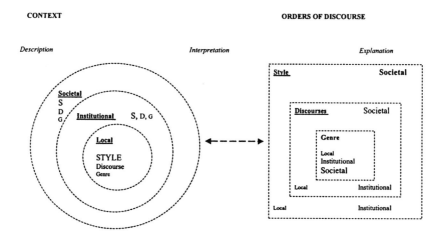

Figure 6.2   Critical Discourse Analysis Heuristic.

institution of special education as well as the values, beliefs, and meta-narratives that construct and maintain the legitimacy of special education. Each of the domains overlaps and is informed by the others. Embedded in each of the contexts are orders of discourse—or genre, discourses, and styles.

Figure 6.2(b), Orders of Discourse, is in a dialectic relationship with Fig. 6.2(a), Context. As the diagram demonstrates, each context (local, institutional, and societal) is embedded within each order of discourse.

Each order of discourse works together in a network to form social practices. The task of a CDA is to understand the relationship between ways of interacting (genre), ways of representing (discourse), and ways of being (style). A CDA can help the analyst, through the processes of description, interpretation, and explanation, see the way in which orders of discourse are configured as networks of practices and consequently start to understand how some meanings get privileged over others.

It is worth reviewing the domains of analysis at this point and interweaving some of the prior, ethnographically based, examples into this explanation. The levels of analysis correspond with the codes presented in Appendix F.

I have coded the level that is concerned with "ways of interacting" (genre) in **bold** in the chart of analysis. The elements of this order of discourse include cohesive devices (e.g., repetition), metaphors, wording, information focus, turn taking structures, and participant structures.

The next level of analysis is the "ways of representing" or the "discourse." This level includes the way people understand institutions and societal narratives and from which perspective they represent them. This order of discourse is underlined in the chart. Discourse is the order of discourse concerned with societal meta-narratives such as the discourse of deficits as well as how these perspectives are set forth. This domain assumes that people represent the institutions they speak from in particular ways that are represented as Discourses. This may mean either how individuals understand their social roles, played out in institutional situations as evidenced in their talk, or how institutions are constructed through discourse. That is, we understand the institutions of the school, church, and local government because of the texts, both oral and written, that are produced from these institutions and that we consume.

For example, in previous chapters, we came to understand how June perceived her role with her children's schools. She was involved in the literacy work at home as well as being involved with the school through meetings and regularly "dropping by" the school. June's understanding of the institution of the school is revealed in how she talked about her own and her daughter's current experiences within these institutions: for instance, the reccurring metaphors of talking about reading as an individual endeavor, as a skill that needed to be practiced, and as something measured and defined by tests that demonstrate if they have "come up" or "gone down" in their literacy development. So, through both June's language and her practices, we learn how June understood the institution of the school and her role within it. This domain of analysis requires attention paid to how institutions are defined and illustrated through texts, both oral and written. That is, how do individuals take up certain social roles? Often, at this level of analysis we can see how social roles are distributed and maintained through discourse, part of the third domain of analysis (Goffman, 1971).

The third order of discourse is style, or "ways of being" that are associated with identity affiliations. Interactions and phrase units that signal people's ways of being in the social world are *italicized* in the chart. At this level of analysis I coded for pronoun use, verb tense, modality, transivity, and passive and active voice.

As the analyst looks across orders of discourse (genre, discourse, and style) and across discursive contexts (e.g., discourse of mothering, discourse of schooling), there may be networks of practice that are conflicting and some that are in alignment. One prominent example of this, which I demonstrate in the following analysis, is the intersection of the discursive context of "schooling" and that of "mothering." June's silence in the CSE meeting is, on one hand, a consequence of the efficiency and formal nature of the meeting. However, there was also something deeper and more substantive happening in the meeting. I argue her silence illustrates her conflicting subjectivities, which included her past experiences with school, the negotiation over her daughter's school, and a strong commitment to being a "good" mother. The point of this analysis is to empirically demonstrate the relationship between genres, discourses, and styles within and across discursive contexts.

As Fig. 6.2 demonstrates, "context" and "orders of discourse" are in a dialectical relationship. The analyst may choose to foreground context (local, institutional, and societal) or orders of discourse (genre, discourse, and style). The work of the analyst in conducting a CDA, what Fairclough (1995) referred to as "description," "interpretation," and "explanation," informs both orders of discourse and context in the conceptual framework I have presented. I argue in the conclusions that it is necessary to attend to both orders of discourse and context in a CDA.

In order to point to instances in text, either in stretches of talk, in writing, through a transcript, or in another written artifact, I looked for indexes such as how phrases work together (or not) in order to construct, undermine or resist social positions. Within this domain, I attended to the ways in which subjectivities are constructed through discourse. In the following section, I present four sets of interactions that occurred during the CSE meeting as a way of representing the different and yet overlapping paradigms repre-sented at the meeting table. I selected this section of the meeting because it is a representative example of the turn-taking style in the meeting as well as representative of the interplay between orders of discourse. I present these interactions (see Table 6.1) and walk through my analysis of the orders of discourse. The literacy event I begin my analysis with is the introduction of the meeting and I stop the analysis when June made the decision ("If she have to go into it, she can go into it, into special ed") during the meeting (transcript, 6/18/98).

Genre of the CSE Meeting. At the interactional level, there is a predict-able set of events that occur in the meeting. This is the structure that binds the meeting together. Looking through the entire transcript of the CSE meeting (see Appendix G), the sequence of events includes the opening of the meeting and ending discussion about the programs available at the middle school for the following year. The opening of the meeting, which included introducing the attendees and stating the purpose of the meeting, was orchestrated by the DT, chair of the committee (lines 1–27). Next, the psychologist (AB) began the identification of Vicky's problem (lines 28–185). Then, the speech therapist (SS) reviewed her test results (lines 186–248). In lines 249–421, there were a series of interactions between the members of the committee and myself. I refer to this section as "questioning the evidence." From here (lines 422–454), DT "reviewed the available support" for Vicky within the district. In lines 455–457, June publicly stated her consent to Vicky's placement in special education, saying, "If she have to go into it" (line 455). Next, in lines 458–844, the longest stretch of the meeting, there were a series of negotiations and discussions about the different programs Vicky would be involved in the next year. This section I refer to as "enabling," because it is the discursive context where the school officials evoked June's role as a mother (who clearly wanted her daughter to have support) and showed June all of the resources that would be available to Vicky the following year. In lines 847–871, "the label" is introduced and supported. In this set of interactions, SL, with the help of DT *and* AB announced the constraining aspects of receiving the support—Vicky needed to be assigned a label. In line 872, there was a last-minute rebuttal on my behalf. I asked, "How is that different than learning disabled?" (line 872). "Signing the papers" occurs in lines 883–922. Lines 924–1124, "the specif-ics of the placement," reflect peripheral questions, coming mainly from me, about the specifics of Vicky's placement. In lines 1125–1145, the meeting is brought to a close, initiated in line 1125 by AB.

The meeting, though longer than most CSE meetings, was highly orches-trated and followed a routine sequence of events. It was significant to note

Table 6.1
Chart of CDA in the CSE meeting

Participants	Orders of Disclosure		Dialogue in Message Units
Chair of the	**Genre:**	15	DT: *Upon receiving the referral,*
Committee (DT)	Ways of interacting	16	*we* asked *our* school psychologist
	Topic selection	17	to do complete evaluation,
	Opening	18	observations
	Turn taking	19	and also MM (Speech therapist)
	Discourse:	20	*our* speech and language therapist
	Ways of representing	21	to do *some* testing.
	Testing	22	So **I'm going to start with**
	Institutional positions		[psychologist]
	Style:	23	to review *her* evaluation
	Ways of being	24	**and then [speech therapist],**
if you don't mind.
Psychologist	**Genre:**	76	AB: *She often* had difficulty
(AB)	Identifying the		understanding directions,
	"problem"¹	77	*she would often* ask for clarification
		78	when *I would give her* a direction.
	Discourse:	79	Um, Vicky's performance on the
	Access to records		intelligence test
	Testing paradigm	80	is within in the well-below-average range
	Discourse of deficits	81	compared to other children her age.
		82	Um, *she's* demonstrating *significant*
	Style:		deficits
	Pronoun use	83	in *her* verbal
	Modality	84	and *her* nonverbal,
	Passive/active	85	excuse me [clears throat],
	construction	86	*her* nonverbal reasoning ability
		87	When a lot of interpretation is
required,
		88	*I think* the difficulty
		89	that *she* has
		90	with *her* language development
		91	*really* interfere
		92	with *her* performance.
		120	*She* has difficulty understanding
		121	and interpreting the language
		122	that is used in word problems.
		123	In spelling
		124	*she* scored low average
		125	and similar to a late-fourth-grade level.
		126	However, *her* word-decoding skills
		127	scored at a second-grade level
		128	and *are considered* below average
		129	for her grade.

Table 6.1 (continued)

Participants	Orders of Disclosure		Dialogue in Message Units
		130	Um, *I think* when *she* is decoding words
		131	*she* will look at the <u>first letter</u> or so
		132	and <u>guess the word</u>.
		137	*Her* <u>reading comprehension</u> is <u>below average</u>,
		138	around a <u>third-grade level</u>.
		143	Vicky *received* <u>a below-average rating</u>
		144	on *her* <u>writing sample</u>
		145	*that was taken* during <u>testing</u>.
Speech and Language Therapist (SS)	**Genre:** "Speech and language deficits" Pronoun use/ distancing Discourse: Testing paradigm Production/ consumption of information about Vicky Discourse of deficits *Style:*	187	SS: I gave Vicky <u>three different tests</u>.
		188	The first <u>test</u> was <u>understanding the words</u> *she hears*
		189	It is *just* a <u>one-word test of receptive vocabulary</u>.
		190	*She* <u>had a lot of difficulty</u>
		191	*just even* <u>understanding vocabulary</u>.
		192	Um, then *I gave her* <u>a test</u>
		193	<u>that tested</u> both *her*
		194	<u>understanding of language</u>
		195	and then *her* <u>use of language</u>.
		196	*Her* <u>receptive</u>
		197	and *her* <u>expressive language skills</u>.
		198	And *she* did have *some* <u>difficulty</u>
		199	<u>understanding</u>
		200	<u>and processing</u> *some* information
		201	but *even her* <u>expressive skills</u>
		202	were <u>even lower</u>.
		207	It's not that *she* <u>can't communicate with people</u>.
		208	It's just that *she's* <u>not using</u>
		209	the <u>types of sentences</u>
		210	that *she should*
		211	and <u>the vocabulary</u>
		212	that *she should*
		213	for <u>a child of *her*</u> age.
		214	So *she* really <u>has</u>,
		215	you know,
		216	<u>a deficit</u> in *her* <u>language skills</u>
		217	which is affecting *her* <u>academic performance</u>
		218	in <u>math</u>
		219	<u>and in reading</u>. Um,

Table 6.1 (continued)

Participants	Orders of Disclosure	Dialogue in Message Units
Researcher/ **Literacy Teacher**	**Genre:** Asking for permission to take a turn; reference to third-person pronouns	249 BR: *Can I ask a question?*
		250 DT: Sure.
		251 BR: When you said,
		252 um, that *she* was <u>at the second grade in decoding</u>,
		253 what <u>is that based on?</u>
	Discourse: Remedial reading	254 Is that consistent
		255 with *her* <u>remedial reading reports</u>
	Decoding at a second-grade level	256 as well?
	third- and fourth-grade level	296 BR: *The reason I ask*
		297 is that when I work with *her*
		298 throughout the year
	Style:	299 *she* has been <u>reading</u>
	Critique of Discourse of deficits and inconsistencies	300 between a *<u>third- and a fourth-grade level</u>*
		301 when *she* is <u>reading authentic books</u>.
		302 *I'm not sure* how *her* <u>decoding is isolation</u>
		303 because *I don't do that*
		304 with *her.*
Chair of **Committee** **Psychologist (DT)**	**Genre:** Review of available "support" Future tense	422 DT: *I think* when we look at *our* <u>in-district programs</u>
		423 *we* always start at the <u>least restrictive</u>
		424 which *would* be a <u>resource room for support</u>
	Discourse: In-district programs	425 but with *her* um,
		426 <u>reading being almost</u>
	Least-restrictive environment	427 <u>3 years below grade level</u>,
	Resource room	428 *I think* at this point
	Grade level	429 almost a <u>smaller classroom setting</u>
		430 *would be* appropriate for *her*
	Style:	435 So *we could* <u>develop</u>
	Enabling and constraining	436 a <u>program</u> where *she would*,
		437 have <u>15 students</u>
		438 <u>in a class</u> with a <u>teacher</u>
		439 and a <u>teacher's assistant</u>
		453 (to June) And you have had time to think about that.
		454 What are your thoughts?

Table 6.1 (continued)

Participants	Orders of Disclosure	Dialogue in Message Units
June	Decision In this context June's relationship to schooling rather than mothering is evoked.	455 J: ////*If she* have to go into <u>it</u>, 456 *she* can go into it. 457 into <u>special ed</u>.

not only the sequence of the events, but the subtleties of the sequencing and how this adds to the legitimacy of the process. For example, the "review of available support" (lines 422–454) was done *before* the decision was made by June (line 455) and before the educational handicap and label were introduced (lines 847–871). That is, the committee let June know about all of the additional resources available given Vicky's "problem." They based the review of this support on the AB's statements that Vicky needs "intensive support." This signifies how the structure or the pattern/form of the meeting is established. That is, important decisions are not made in unimportant ways.

Furthermore, all of the people present at the meeting were members of the discourse community of the CSE, except for June, myself, and Shauna. The officials of the school shared a set of discourse practices that included labeling procedures, the structure of the meeting itself including the turn-taking procedure, and references to tests and available instructional resources. Institutional meetings such as the CSE meeting name students as less capable or less important in a public forum. In this case, the labels used to describe Vicky informed the entire community, the parent representative, the psychologist, June, her daughter, and myself, that Vicky, and June by virtue of being Vicky's mother, were less able and deficient.

Overall, June had only nine turns through out this 50-minute meeting. She was virtually silent throughout the meeting. This stood in stark contrast to her voice as described in previous chapters, specifically in the context of her home and community. June's turn takes included such responses as, "Where you work at?" (directed to the speech therapist); "She can take it" (referring to a foreign language); "I don't know" (with regard to whether Vicky liked Spanish); "Who her teacher goin' to be for next year?"; and "if she have to go into it, she can go into it. Into special ed." Using Mehan's (1996) terms of analysis, most of June's turns were *elicited* from her, rather than instances of her *presenting* information to the committee. In contrast, the psychologist or the speech therapist presented information to the committee.

WAYS OF REPRESENTING AND WAYS OF BEING: DISCOURSE AND STYLE

Having presented an overall look at the meeting and the interactional elements that comprised the CSE meeting, I now turn to "discourse" and "style," "ways of representing" and "ways of being," as outlined in Table 6.3. I present the analysis by turns taken by each of the participants in the meeting. I describe, interpret, and explain the relationship between genre, discourse, and style in each of the turns. I begin the analysis with lines 15–25. The chair of the committee (DT) started the meeting by laying out the procedures for the meeting. She articulated the participant structure (genre) in lines 22–24 when she stated, "I'm going to start with the psychologist to review *her* evaluation and then the speech therapist."

DT explained what had been done after the initial referral. She did so with a passive construction (style), "upon receiving the referral" (line 15). There was no reference to where the referral came from, namely the classroom and reading teacher, neither of whom were present for this meeting. DT also used the pronouns "we" and "our" to mark a community between members of the special-education referral team (style). She did this in line 16, "we asked our school psychologist," and again in line 20, "our speech and language therapist." DT's use of the pronouns "we" and "our" functions in two complementary ways in this order of discourse. First, it marks who was involved with what Wenger (1998) referred to as a "legitimate" participant in the special-education referral discourse. Second, it functions as a community-building strategy, that is, building collectivity around the issues of placement that rhetorically was a decision left to the parents.

In this set of interactions, DT called on the language of the institution, of school, referenced through the different social roles and procedures done within the school (discourse). For instance, in line 15, she referred to "the referral." In lines 16–25, she referred to the "school psychologist," the "complete evaluation" and "observations," the "speech and language therapist," "testing," the "psychologist," and the "evaluation" (discourse). These roles and procedures defined the institution of the school as objective, official, and complete. For instance, the school did not just do *an* evaluation; they did a "complete evaluation." It was not conducted by ordinary classroom teachers but by highly trained specialists such as the psychologist and the speech and language therapist. These indexes in language establish the validity of the institution, and thus the reports made from within the institution.

DT outlined the participant structure of the meeting (genre). She then referenced the special-education Discourse by referring to tests and school officials, which is intended to objectify the testing process (discourse). She marked the community of decision makers through the use of the pronouns "we" and "our," which served to establish a community of which June and I were not members (style).

As the psychologist (AB) spoke, other members of the committee listened. Amid a shuffling of papers and notecards, I wrote down what she was saying. June, sitting to my left, listened to AB speak. Shauna, sitting in the chair to the right of me, played with a Mr. Potato Head doll she had gotten from the lobby downstairs (fieldnotes, 6/18/98).

The Psychologist. DT set up the participant framework with AB following her introduction, expressly to review the results of the psychological tests. In lines 76–92 and 120–145, AB "identified the problem" (genre) through her presentation of test results (discourse).

In the domain of Discourses or "ways of representing," the school officials had access to formal records. Indeed, this was the mode through which they represented Vicky. AB had Vicky's permanent file in front of her and she read Vicky's background information from this file. This information included Vicky's date of birth, the schools she attended until the third grade, and that she wore glasses. Similarly, each of the other school representatives, with the exception of the parent representative, had a stack of manila folders and papers in front of them. They were knowledgeable and informed about Vicky as a student, from a "schooled literacy" perspective. They spoke from official documents. June, when she spoke, spoke from memory rather than "official" knowledge (Mehan, 1996). The school was defined through a testing paradigm. I have underlined the sections that refer to "ways of representing" in the transcript. This discourse suggests an adherence to the objectivity and positivism of a testing paradigm that suggests reliability of evidence. For example, AB referred to "the direction" in line 78. In lines 79–81, Vicky's "performance" suggested the criteria for evaluation on the "intelligence test." This test was a performance that indexed, or was specific, to the institution of the school.

AB also referred to the various other tests administered to Vicky. Along with the intelligence test there was a Wechsler Intelligence Scale for Children (3rd ed.; WISC-III), Wechsler Individual Achievement Test (WIAT), Basic Academic Skills Individual Screener, Adaptive Behavior Evaluation Scales, and Developmental Test of Visual Motor Integration. Performance on the intelligence test suggested that her scores fell in the "well below average range compared to other children her age." Vicky was compared normatively to other peers her age, an important comparison in the functioning of the school. Furthermore, the cultural beliefs of age-level comparisons perpetuate behaviorists' views of learning and development that posit sequential learning of skills rather than nonlinear growth and development (Gipps, 1994; Shepard, 1997)

In line 86, AB's description of the institution of the school was referenced through Vicky's "nonverbal reasoning ability." In line 90, "language development" and in line 92 "performance" were also markers of the institution and individual deficits within the institution. The institution was constructed through a discourse of objectivity and scientific rhetoric in order to convey that the representation of Vicky was accurate. In this case, the institution was defined as objective and valid thus ensuring that Vicky's designation as "multiply disabled" was accurate.

A larger discourse of deficits operated that defined Vicky from a deficit perspective. Aside from being a contradictory portrait of what we saw of Vicky in chapter 4, this discourse defined her *solely* from a deficit perspective: for instance, the claim that Vicky decoded at a second-grade level (line 127), that her reading comprehension was "below average" (line 137), and that she "received a below-averge rating on her writing sample" (lines 143–144). There was no mention of what Vicky *could* do, nor of the instructional contexts where she was proficient.

AB represented Vicky from a deficit perspective. A close analysis of the "ways of being," or the style, helps to further illuminate the relationship between orders of discourse. An analysis of the pronoun use, referenced in the transcript in italics, highlights how Vicky, a 12-year old adolescent girl, was removed from the conversation. Vicky was referred to as "she" and "her" repeatedly through the transcript (e.g., lines 76, 77, 82–89, 188, 208, 210, and 436). The third-person pronoun served to distance and objectify Vicky from the decision being made and from the reconstruction of her identity from that of a student experiencing difficulty and who has "low achievement in reading and math" to that of a student who is "multiply disabled." This, in part, reflected the relationship the evaluators had with Vicky. They did not know her outside of the testing situation.

A deficit statement followed each third-person pronoun: for example, in line 76, "she often had difficulty understanding directions"; lines 82–86, "she's demonstrating significant deficits in her verbal and her nonverbal reasoning abilities"; and line 120, "she has difficulty understanding." The important point to make is the way in which discourse (ways of representing) and style (ways of being) work together to construct a privileged understanding of Vicky's abilities and "disabilities."

In addition to the third-person pronoun serving to objectify rather than personalize the review of assessments, AB often positioned her own role as a psychologist as active and Vicky as passive. The discourse of disability implicated Vicky into the role of a passive agent as she was talked *about* through third-person pronouns, objectified through the testing paradigm, and encoded in a discourse of deficits. For example, in lines 143–145 AB stated, "Vicky received a below-average rating on her writing that was taken during testing." Here, Vicky *received* a rating from an unnamed administrator during testing. Though Vicky was positioned as a passive recipient of the testing process, the psychologist used the cognitive statements of "I think" in order to make her point. An analysis of transitivity—or how individuals position themselves in relation to the verb—was an important part of understanding their "ways of being." For example, in line 88 the psychologist states, "I think the difficulty" and in line 130, "I think when she is decoding words." These cognitive statements combined with the objectivity of the test scores and Vicky positioned as a passive recipient function to construct a coherent view of the plausibility of the test results and the label of "multiply disabled." It is clear in this analysis that language functions across orders of discourse—ways of interacting, representing, and being— in order to privilege some meanings over others.

The layers of contradiction in terms of assessment, learning, literacy, and development in this stretch of interaction are almost too many to point out. First, if we are to accept that Vicky is indeed decoding at a second-grade level, we have to overlook three very important pieces of data[4]. The first was that this descriptor defied the evidence I had collected on Vicky as a reader over the course of the year as she participated in a book group wherein she chose and read literature around a fourth-grade instructional level. Second, it contradicted the evidence Mrs. Matthews told both June and I in our October meeting, presented in chapter 2. That is, that Vicky was reading "level b of a fourth grade level." Furthermore, the reading teacher commented on Vicky's report card, "Vicky is reading and understanding at about a fourth-grade level. She is diligent and neat about her work." Third, this information also contradicted one of the documents the psychologist had in front of her, which stated that Vicky was reading at a fourth-grade level with assistance. If we are to overlook these three contradictory pieces of evidence, and accept Vicky's "decoding at a second-grade level," then it seemed reasonable and highly appropriate that Vicky would receive additional reading instruction in her middle school placement. However, this was not a part of Vicky's IEP (individual education plan) and she received no addition reading support at the middle school.

Speech Therapist. When AB was done talking, the speech therapist (SS) began, as DT had suggested in her opening of the meeting (genre). A similar pattern across orders of discourse can be seen in the SS's talk in lines 186–248. Here, in the discourse domain, SS also had access to the records and spoke from a file producing the information rather than, as June did, consuming it. As she outlined how she administered tests of receptive vocabulary and expressive language, she called on a highly specialized discourse of "receptive vocabulary" (line 189) and "expressive language skills" (line 197). Again, the school was de.ned through how SS produced this knowledge and through a testing paradigm. In SS's case, she did not administer only one test; she "gave Vicky three different tests" (line 187). She referred to Vicky's deficits through "the types of sentences" (line 209), "the vocabulary" (line 211), and her "academic performance in math and reading" (lines 217–219). This reference to Vicky's weak vocabulary skills resonated with June because June had already identified herself as having weak vocabulary and reading skills.

Also within the "discourse" domain, a discourse of disability operated. This discourse of disability was referenced through such terms as below a "child of her age" (line 213) or "a de.cit in her language skills" (line 216). Although it was contradictory to Vicky's engagements with literacy and language at home and in her community (e.g., the interviews, explaining the process of and receiving WIC, and the book discussions) it resonated with June because of how she perceived herself as a reader and writer. These views, as I have pointed out, stemmed from her experience and knowledge of tests as well as her past and current experiences with school. When the officials of the institution mentioned these things, along with the way the meeting was set up (genre), the use of official tests, and the presentation of material (discourse), the discourse of disability (style) made sense. Even if June did not believe it, with what tools would she disagree?

In this interaction, discourse and style work together. An analysis of the pronoun use, active/passive construction, modality, and transitivity of this stretch of interaction reveals many of the same patterns as when AB spoke. Vicky was again referred to mainly as "she" and "her" (lines 188, 190, 193–196, 201, 207–208, 210–214); that is, in almost every line Vicky is referred to with a third-person pronoun. In addition, each of these third-person pronouns is followed by a deficit statement (discourse): for example, line 198, "she did have some difficulty understanding"; line 201–202, "her expressive skills were even lower"; line 208–209, "she's not using the types of sentences"; and lines 214–216, "she really has a deficit." SS, unlike AB, included qualifiers in her discussion of Vicky: for example, line 190, "a lot of difficulty"; line 191, "just even understanding"; line 198, "some difficulty"; and line 214, "really has." These qualifiers function to either intensify or diminish the effects of the deficit statements. SS also qualified her statement by using a negative construction at the beginning of a sentence in lines 207–210: "It's not that she can't communicate with people. It's just that she's not using the types of sentences she should." Though she pointed out what Vicky was not doing, she did not make reference to what Vicky *was* doing. Nor did she address the limited nature of the communicative interactions embedded within a speech and language test.

SS also used the modal "should" to compare Vicky to other peers. When, in lines 208–213, she stated, "she's not using the types of sentences that she should and the vocabulary she should for a child her age." Analyzing the "types of sentences" Vicky was using during a closed-ended communicative interaction such as a speech and language test does not address what Vicky *could* do in authentic communicative interactions. Furthermore, "types of sentences" is another way of discussing the syntactic construction of language. Vicky and June both speak a well-developed variety of African American Vernacular English, which historically has been discriminated against in testing situations (Harry & Anderson, 1994).

In summary, SS, like AB, stepped into the predictable organizational structure of the CSE meeting (genre). She made reference to the official nature of the test and positioned Vicky within a discourse of deficits (discourse). This "way of representing" Vicky works in relation with "ways of being" within an institution. Vicky is referred to with third-person pronouns, effectively distanced from the conversation and seen as deficient. The speech therapist also used qualifiers and negative constructions (style) that appear to soften the blow of her presentation of Vicky's deficits, yet the results clearly state Vicky had a "deficit in her language skills" (line 216). Orders of discourse, genre, discourse, and style work together in a network of practices in order to construct an interpretation of Vicky as disabled.

Researcher/Literacy Teacher. I interrupt the proceedings of the committee meeting in line 249 and ask, "Can I ask a question?" Here, I am asking permission to interrupt the otherwise already-established genre of the committee meeting. Like June, I have not been asked to speak, nor is it assumed I have anything to contribute to the proceedings, despite that the committee members know I am a teacher and a literacy researcher. I challenge the discourse of deficits that has permeated the meeting, specifically using their language—line 252, "second grade in decoding"—to ask if this was consistent with her remedial reading reports (discourse). I knew from speaking with Vicky's reading teacher that she was around a third-grade level in remedial reading. I justified the reason I was asking, which served as a hedging comment. Rather than assuming I had the legitimacy to talk and to challenge the evidence that was presented, I justified why I questioned the evidence (style). In line 296, I stated, "The reason I ask." I also presented counterevidence (discourse) of her reading level when she is reading authentic texts. My response to the committee was not responded to, nor was it integrated into the proceedings of the meeting. I return to an analysis of my participation in the meeting at the close of this chapter and also in Appendix H on the role of the researcher.

Chair of the Committee. Turning to the next stretch of interactions excerpted for this analysis, in lines 422–439 DT, "reviewed the available support." In terms of ways of interacting, DT pulled the results that have been presented thus far back into the framework of decision making (genre). At the domain of discourse or "ways of representing," again, the school is constructed through a series of terms including: line 422, "in-district program"; line 423, "least restrictive"; line 424, "resource room with support"; line 427, "three years below grade level"; line 436, "a program"; lines 437–438, "15 students in a class"; and lines 438–439, "teacher" and the "teacher's assistant." In terms of ways of being, two aspects of language are compelling in this stretch of interaction. First, the chair of the committee, like the psychologist, used cognitive statements of "I think" (e.g., lines 422, 428).

DT used the modal "would" (line 424) to first suggest the possibility of a "resource room with support" (style). She then went on to say that with her "reading being almost 3 years below grade level," a "smaller classroom setting would be more appropriate for her" (lines 429–430). Here, smaller classroom setting means a self-contained classroom, but she chose not to use the construct of a self-contained classroom. She asked June to make her decision based on the fact that the committee would "develop a program" (lines 435–436). This statement implied that the school would create a program specifically for Vicky, rather than place her in a preexisting self-contained classroom. She elaborated on this by stating the ratio of teacher to students—"15 students in a class with a teacher and a teacher's assistant" (lines 437–439)—to make the "program" sound attractive to June, that is, fewer students with more support from the teacher. DT, after presenting this option, then immediately turned the decision over to June in lines 453–454. June responded in lines 455–457, "If she have to go into it, she can go into it, into special ed."

DISCURSIVE CONTRADICTIONS

The labeling and naming of programs indexed relations of power as officials of the institution named and allocated the resources that were available to Vicky. Despite being a public forum wherein Vicky's educational identity was being cemented, the rhetoric of "special education" was hidden from June. It is significant to note that nowhere in the meeting, other than in lines 455–457 where June said "she can go into special education," are the words "special education" mentioned. Furthermore, even though it was stated that Vicky would go into a smaller classroom setting, nowhere in the meeting did the school officials say that Vicky would be in a "self-contained classroom." Thus, the labels of "special education" and "self-contained" classroom were cloaked with other terms. A CDA helps analysts to look for invisible as well as visible aspects of discourse.

In this set of interactions, the notion of contradictory subjectivities embedded within discourse was apparent. In lines 456–457, June stated, "she can go into it, into special ed." This statement by itself, however, does not reflect the five solid reasons June reported as evidence why Vicky should not go into special education, which were listed earlier. To reiterate, these are:

First, June said Vicky was not slow. Second, June stated that once a person goes into special education they never come out and therefore they must not teach anything in special-education classrooms. Third, Vicky would not learn anything from a special-education teacher that she could not learn from a regular-education teacher. Fourth, June cited specific areas of improvement she had observed at home. Fifth, June stated, "I didn't ever go in one so why should she go in one?"

Of most immediate relevance to this meeting are June's first, second, and third assertions juxtaposed against the rhetoric of this meeting. First, June asserted that Vicky was not slow. In the cataloguing of Vicky's deficits, apparent most readily in lines 28–248, June did not say anything. This is not because she fully believed in the school's claims but because she was conflicted over what was best for Vicky: provide more support of her daughter's strengths (discursive context of mothering) or continue in her belief in the authority of the school (discursive context of schooling). However, whereas June said nothing about Vicky's strengths, I did. In lines 249–256; 296–304, 332–343, 345–391, and 398–416, I specifically pointed out what Vicky's strengths were with regard to reading and writing. I disputed the evidence presented that reported Vicky was decoding at a second-grade level.

June's second and third assertions are similar in terms of the quality of instruction available in special-education programs. Her points are addressed most specifically in the meeting when there is conversation about the different programs and resources available to Vicky (see Appendix H for the full transcript, specifically lines 458–844 and lines 918–1123). Though June did not raise these issues in the meeting, I did, knowing that they were issues June had spoken to me about. For example, in lines 482–483, 515–521, 576–578, 605, 654–656, 669, 755–756, 763–764, 812, 872, 924–926, 980–981, 1000–1009, 1028–1029, 1076–1081, and 1099–1100, I questioned the specifics of Vicky's instructional program at the middle school.

In analyzing my interactions in this meeting it becomes clear that many of the questions I asked during the meeting are in line with June's assertions (see chap. 5). That is, even if June did not raise these issues in the meeting, I did. Regardless, they were discarded from the meeting. Though June's silence represented her conflicting subjectivities of mothering and deferral of authority to schooling, my presence and interaction in the meeting are also highly indicative of my own contradictory subjectivities—an issue I explore in the final section of this chapter and in Appendix H.

In order for Vicky to get the resources that would enable her to "achieve better" in a classroom, she needed to have the constraining effects of a self-contained classroom. Vicky would be placed in a smaller classroom setting with 15 other students, a teacher, and a teacher's assistant. This meeting effectively evoked June's role as a mother to get what is best for her daughter while at the same time insisting she remember her own deficiencies with "schooled literacy."

In this meeting, Vicky's identity moved from what Mehan (1996) referred to as the "ambiguity of everyday life" to the social construction of a label. Her academic identity moved from concerns about her "low achievement in reading and math" (transcript, CSE report, referral forms) to a child that is "multiply disabled." Vicky's identity, as it had been constructed through the psychologist (AB), the chair of the committee (DT), and the speech and language therapist (SS), was quite different than what I presented in chapter 4. As I mentioned in an earlier section, there were a number of contradictions folded into the layers of paperwork, meetings, and assessments that comprised this CSE meeting.

In the meeting, SS stated about Vicky's communication, "I mean she can communicate. Very well. It's not that she can't communicate with people" (lines 205–206). She used this statement to qualify her previous statement about the deficits in Vicky's expressive and receptive language skills. These comments, set side by side with listening to Vicky explain to me the process of applying for and receiving WIC (chap. 4), represent the web of inaccuracy in this meeting. Furthermore, these comments, set side by side with listening to Vicky as she told me a different interpretation of the newspaper article about her sister, demonstrate the narrow range of evidence that counts as relevant and credible in Vicky's case. And finally, these comments, set side by side Vicky's interviewing and talking about the "everyday heroes" in her life, demonstrate the severe consequences of looking at only the school's definition of achievement.

In terms of the discrepancy in evidence, AB stated that Vicky's "word decoding skills scores at a second-grade level and are considered below average for her grade" (lines 126–129). When I pushed and asked, "When you said, um, that she was at a second grade in decoding, what is that based on because is that consistent with her remedial reading as well?"

AB responded:

It is consistent with what her reading teacher is seeing as well. That's based on the test that I have her, the standardized test that I have her. That is the grade-equivalent score that came off of the test and she was required to just decode words in isolation on that test. Um, and that is where that grade equivalent came off of. That's basically where her classroom teachers are indicating that she is functioning. Mrs. Matthews was going to be coming. Let me look at the referral form, she may have a grade listed here. . .(looking through the papers ///). Yeah there is . . . well, reading at about a fourth-grade level with assistance, and um, ///. She has some grade-level 2 materials that she is still making errors on. So, I think, um, with the support in the classroom that she received she is able to read at somewhat a higher level but this is an independent without no support whatsoever. I am not allowed to help her at all with the testing. This is where her decoding scores are falling (transcript, 6/18/98, lines 257–291).

As she responded to me, she was unsure where she had gotten this evidence. I asked AB to cross-check the information. I was aware of the inconsistencies presented about Vicky through the lens of "objective" tests. Her first reaction to me was "it is consistent with what her reading teacher is seeing" (line 257–258). AB defended the second-grade decoding scores by repeating the word *test* four times in the next two statements (lines 260–265). She then wavered and stated that's "basically" where her classroom teachers indicate she is functioning. Then, AB made reference to the reading teacher, Mrs. Matthews, who "was going to be coming" (line 271). Still not certain about how to answer and receiving no support from the other committee members, AB returned to the referral forms sitting in front of her. A 3-second pause filled the room with silence as AB looked through the papers. Based on her hesitancy, AB seemed uncertain about reading the information she found on the referral form, but did: "Well, reading at about a fourth-grade level with assistance" (lines 277–279). She admitted that within an instructional context, Vicky was reading fourth-grade material. She *admitted* the contradiction embedded in her test results.

I responded to her, "The reason I ask is that when I work with her throughout the year she has been reading between a third- and a fourth-grade level when she is reading authentic books. I'm not sure how her decoding works in isolation because I don't do that with her" (lines 296–304). Again, AB stated, defending her initial statement, "The test, the test is going to give somewhat different results again because you are not allowed to assist, it is not a teaching situation. It's basically she is asked to perform and that's it" (lines 305–314).

Here, AB referenced the test and the invalid results that are received about how a child can read when it is within a teaching situation. In lines 282–287, she stated, "[so, I think, um, with the support in the classroom that she received she is able to read at somewhat a higher level but this is an independent without no support whatsoever." She failed to recognize the social conditions always embedded within the tests from the production and the consumption to the administration (Johnston, 1998; Moss, 1998). Her reliance on the validity of the tests as an objective measure of what Vicky can do independently failed to recognize that assessment is always a social enterprise.

The third contradiction embedded in this meeting is the insistence on parent involvement but a structuring of the circumstances in a manner whereby the parent cannot help but consent with the logic of the institution. June was surprised by the term "educational handicap." I was surprised when they decided to label her as "multiply disabled." This is exemplified in her statement "a what?" (line 845). Once, when I looked over at June in this meeting, tears ran down her face. She was asked to sign a set of forms agreeing to the educational label and to Vicky's placement in a self-contained classroom beginning with the next year. DT got up from the end of the table and walked over to June, setting the papers down in front of her. As DT handed June the paperwork, she stated:

> Because without your written permission, we cannot provide this program. I can, I hand wrote out a permission if you would like to sign it today, and then I can put her on a class list. That's up to you . . . Basically all this says is that we're going to identify her as multiply disabled realizing that she has learning needs and speech needs, recommending a smaller class and mainstreaming for math. And these are your due process rights. Without your signed permission we can't provide the program (transcript, 6/18/98, lines 907 –922).

DT reminded June that without her written permission Vicky would not be "enabled" to get all of the extra resources they had discussed during the meeting. AB evoked June's responsibilities as a "good" mother, concerned with the education of her children. DT then reminded June, "that's up to you," meaning the decision. This interaction marked the first time June was informed by the school that she had *rights*. Furthermore, the manual on special education was given to June at the conclusion of this meeting rather than at the start of the process. June looked at the papers, momentarily, and then signed her name and the date to the form, as she had with so many other forms that year. Here, June's decision-making power, as a parent, was used as a means to go along with the decision of the school.

The interactions I presented herein (from the opening of the CSE meeting to the decision) occurred before the label of "multiply disabled" was introduced. I argue that by looking at the orders of discourse in the domains of genre, discourse, and style combined with an ethnographic approach to literacy and learning, it is possible to see how Vicky's label was constructed. However, we are still left with the question of why June conceded to the logic of the institution when she apparently believed something quite different about her daughter.

A discourse analysis of the relationship between genre, discourse, and style within this CSE meeting has illuminated the way in which discourse operates to effectively shut people out of the discussion as well as to legitimize the labeling of a student as "multiply disabled." I want to suggest, though, that there is more going on within this meeting than what a discourse analysis of just this meeting alone can provide us. In the following section I suggest that the CSE meeting evoked two sets of conflicting subjectivities from June, that of mothering and that of schooling. June brings her "histories of participation"[5] within each discursive context into her participation in this CSE meeting.

EVOKING SUBJECTIVITIES

At the beginning of this chapter, I argued that this meeting demonstrated how power and discourse are mutually constituted. I have shown this to be the case in my analysis. By looking at the relationship between genres (ways of interacting), discourses (ways of representing), and styles (ways of being), it is possible to see the ways in which people take on the authority of institutions and it is communicated through language in formal settings. However, I also argued that this CSE meeting did not represent a complete picture of the decision to place Vicky in special education. June's silence in this meeting is not representative of an uninvolved parent, nor a parent who believed that her child was unable and "multiply disabled." Her silence represented what Key (1998) claimed was a "literacy shutdown." June's silent resistance in this meeting suggests the interrelatedness of social distancing to people in power. June's passion about her daughter, evident in chapter 5 was lost in the shuffle of papers, the reminder of disability, and her continued and prolonged trust of people in power. This is similar to the research of Goldstein, et. al. (1980) and Meyers & Blacher (1987), who demonstrated that even parents who express severe criticism of the school in interviews nevertheless conceded to the decision of the school in terms of placement within special-education programs. Furthermore, June was also reminded that she was not a literate person. June was, instead, a person with literate failure. These contradictions come more clearly into focus by juxtaposing June's statement in the CSE meeting, "If she have to go in it, she can go into it, into special ed," to her active resistance to this placement (chap. 5) and her fragile literate identity (chap. 3).

Studies of discourse in institutional settings (e.g., Fairclough, 1995; Fairclough & Wodak, 1997; Mehan, 1996) have demonstrated that one of the defining characteristics of institutional language is that it exhibits constraints on what participants can relevantly say. Furthermore, within institutional talk, which identities are relevant is constructed through a combination of turn-taking and interactional patterns, the way in which the institution is discursively organized, and the subjectivities that are evoked (e.g., Fairclough, 1995). Therefore, we might expect June to take a submissive stance in the meeting based on the formalized register of the meeting. However, June's decision to place Vicky in the special-education classroom is more complex because it calls on her history of participation with literacy, one with commitments to herself as a student *and* to her role as a mother.

The tight control of information in the meeting coupled with the efficiency of turn taking and presentation of data facilitates the discursive role June is implicitly asked to play in this meeting. In this discursive context, June's role as a mother and as a student with literate failure are evoked at the expense of her desire *not* to have Vicky placed in a special-education classroom. Because June accepted the ideology behind the authority of external evaluators determining learning and achievement, normative comparisons, grade-level equivalents, and deficit orientations in relation to her own history with schooling, it made sense to her with regard to Vicky's education, as seen in the Discourse of Schooling. June's view of her relationship to schooled literacy was through a deficit lens: "It [reading] was a problem" ; "I was down to a one in readin'"; "I couldn't read. . .I couldn't read that good." Thus, when assertions were made about the deficits of her daughter couched in the rhetoric of deficits and of standardized tests, both of which resonate with what school and literacy mean for her, the statements make sense to her and evoke her past failures within the institution of school.

At the same time the institution called on the Discourse of deficits, a linguistic framework with which June is familiar, it also called on her role as a mother and her commitment to making the best educational decision for her daughter. Thus, June's belief about what is right for her daughter were effectively suspended because the institution thought something different about the educational needs of her daughter.

Although the meeting evokes June's history as a student with literate failure, it also insists on her responsibilities as a mother—responsibilities that she takes very strongly—as seen in the prior section (Discourse of Mothering). As stated previously, special education is a process that insists on parent involvement through due process and yet structures the institutional circumstances in a manner whereby the parents cannot help but consent with the logic of the institution (Mehan, 1996). However, in order to enable their child, they need to constrain them with a handicapping condition (Allan, Brown, & Riddell, 1998).

Indeed, the school officials requested June's permission at all stages of the special-education process. Despite this, the officials in the school did not give June any information on that process until the end of the CSE meeting after the label for her daughter had been finalized. At this point in the meeting, the psychologist handed June a copy of A Parent's Guide to Special Education and stated, "This will give you a little more information on how the process will proceed" (transcript, 6/18/98).

Within this Discourse, Vicky's *needs* are construed throughout the meeting in such a way that asks the parent to make a decision based on what is right for their child, given few alternatives. For example, following the identification of the problem, the psychologist turned to the chair of the CSE in order to review the available support for a student with Vicky's needs (lines 422-454). The chair of the committee explained that with the severity of Vicky's deficits, "her reading being almost 3 years below grade level," a smaller classroom setting would be a better option for her.

The school officials present at the meeting called on the Discourse of deficits, a set of terms that June was familiar with from her own experiences with school, in order to make the case for her daughter's special educational needs. There was also a move to create a consensus of voices in the process. This can be seen in the following excerpt when the psychologist said to June, "We spoke at the parent conference about identifying, um, identifying Vicky with an educational handicap in order for her to get the program?. . .[a]nd um, I think [this label] would·lend itself to provide her with the more extensive services that we're looking at" (transcript, 6/18/98). The psychologist calls on the use of "we" as a discursive marker that suggests affiliation with all of the participants in the meeting. Again there exists the theme of enabling a student to get certain educational resources but having to constrain them in order to do so. Embedded in this statement is the assumption that June will agree to this label, perhaps already does, despite June's statement, "she will not go in no special ed" (transcript, 3/26/98), that which she said not only in her home but in informal meetings with Vicky's teachers as well.

Thus, the meeting evoked two contradictory subjectivities from June: her history of participation as a student with literacy failure within the same school district where her daughter attended, and her role as a mother determined to provide the best educational opportunities for her children. In this case it is precisely because the values and beliefs of the discourses of the home and the school are in alignment that June acquiesced to Vicky's placement in a self-contained classroom. As I have demonstrated in earlier chapters, June believed in, indeed valued, the logic of the school. She wanted both herself and her children to do well within the institution of school. It is precisely this belief in the logic of the school that caused her to conclude that she and her daughter were not competent. Indeed, June brought her history of participation with schooled literacy to this meeting, a history etched with unending belief in the system and yet scarred with traces of also believing she is not capable within the system. When the officials of the school use test scores to demonstrate Vicky is disabled, June is torn between believing her daughter is not disabled and believing in the logic of the school.

The meeting also evokes the discourse of mothering. It is clear from previous chapters that June is an advocate for her family and children. She wants the best educational opportunities for her children. Thus, when Vicky's placement in a self-contained special-education classroom is framed as allowing Vicky to get additional support from teachers within a smaller classroom setting, June is convinced this is a logical decision. June is faced with constraining her daughter in a self-contained classroom in order to enable to her get additional help. The meeting effectively evokes June's contradictory subjectivities of mother and of student with past literacy failure. Working together, June concedes to the logic of the school. A discourse analysis of genre, discourse, and style alone would not have allowed me insight into alternative explanations of *why* June conceded to the placement of her daughter in special education despite her adamant resistance as described in chapter 5. However, ethnographic data from across contexts, over time, allowed me to trace how June's histories of participation are indeed structured through orders of discourse shift and change depending on the discursive context of which she is a part.

I cannot overlook the contradictions or the inconsistencies in the meeting without also looking at my role in the meeting. When I sat in on this meeting, implicated into various linguistic communities as a researcher, a literacy teacher, a friend of the family, and an advocate for Vicky (as June had called upon me to be), I struggled over which language and set of conventions to adopt for this meeting. Part of me (the researcher) wanted to observe and see how the event would unfold and how June would negotiate the system. However, I was ethically unable to do this and my intention, as June and I had discussed going into the meeting, was to advocate for Vicky.

In June of that year, I did not have all of the ethnographic data on Vicky and how she proficiently negotiated texts in her home and community. Even if I had, would they have mattered? I would present more evidence with stronger examples. I would not question my ethical responsibility to intervene in exchange for objectivity. But I didn't then. Instead, I presented examples from the case report I had and listened, almost in disbelief, as the meeting unfolded around me, wrapping June and me in the myths, deceptions, and power of the rhetoric of the institutions. The coherence of the meeting was a surprise to me. Before I knew it, the school personnel had labeled Vicky as "multiply disabled" and suggested this was the appropriate classification in order to get the services she would need, rhetoric that would name June's daughter as multiply disabled and alter the course of her life, certainly the educational component of it. Instead of denying the label, insisting on an examination of the instructional contexts, all I asked was, "How is that different than learning disabled?" and "Will there be reading instruction next year?" I complied, just as June did.

Torn between documenting and advocating, I continued to ask questions until the end of the meeting. After the meeting, June, Shauna, and I walked over to the playground that was on the school grounds. I pushed Shauna in the swing and talked with June. She told me that her sinuses were bothering her in the meeting and that is why her eyes watered. She didn't seem to want to talk about it much after the meeting. It seemed as though she had made her decision in the informal meeting she had with the reading teacher and the psychologist (6/12/98), not during the CSE meeting. The dynamic between silenced and heard voices within the context of the school is complicated in the next chapter as we move into the second CSE meeting after Vicky had been placed in a self-contained room for 1 year.

NOTES

1. Ysseldyke, Algozzine, Richey, and Graden (1986) showed that during CSE meetings, a label depends on whether a psychologist or a speech therapist is on the committee. In this case, both the psychologist and the speech therapist were present. Therefore, Vicky was labeled as "multiply disabled" rather than just "learning disabled" or "speech and language "disabled."
2. DT is the chair of the committee. AB is the psychologist. SS is the speech therapist. BR stands for myself.
3. Chouliaraki and Fairclough (1999) referred to orders of discourse as "genre," "discourse," and "style," following closely the three-part schema in systemic functional linguistics. I refer to order of discourse as genre, discourse, and style, which can be analyzed at the local, instutional, and societal domains of analysis. In addition, each order of discourse and local, institutional, and societal contexts are described, interpreted, and analyzed. Elizabeth Berkes, Glynis O'Garro, Diane Hui and I collaboratively constructed this heuristic during a doctoral seminar I taught on critical discourse analysis.
4. A CDA can help the analyst to understand the relationship between genre, discourse, and style. However, if we were to end the analysis here, we would see a description, interpretation, and explanation of the tight control of turn taking and control of the topic and the participant framework, coupled with a discourse of deficits and the legitimacy of the school, wrapped in third-person pronoun references to Vicky, and passive constructions of Vicky as a learner. I would argue that this analysis is valuable because it helps the analyst to point to the specific places in discourse that operate to maintain or to transform social conditions. However, I believe in the importance of embedding discourse analysis within an ethnographic context so that the analyst can look across discursive contexts in order to support or refute the claims made by the discourse analysis. June, in this meeting, looked like a "silenced" parent. Had we not seen her strength and determination in earlier chapters, we might have been led to think that she believed that her daughter was "multiply disabled." However, I suggest there is a more intricate and complicated story to tell. The nuances of this story can only be fully understood by combining a close attention to language, which a CDA provides, with ethnographic data.

5. I define "histories of participation" as the set of values, beliefs, and networks of practices that people bring with them from their experiences in a range of discursive contexts—including home, community, work, school, and recreational contexts. People have histories of participation that are networks of practices that may either conflict or be in alignment with the network of practices that constitute various contexts.

Through The Eyes Of The Institution[1]

June seemed relieved as she stood in her kitchen that afternoon in March and told Vicky, "Tell Becky what they said to you at school." Vicky began, "They told me I could come up out of special class." June smiled with pride (transcript and fieldnotes, 3/8/99). "What exactly did they say?" I asked. Vicky explained that there was a meeting at the school about her not being in a special-education classroom next year. Vicky stated, "I'm definitely not going to be in special ed" (transcript, 3/8/99). June stated, "She comin' out of special ed class."

June talked about her memories of the beginning of the referral process a little over a year ago and how Vicky did not want to go into a special-education class. June said, "[Vicky] was talkin' about, 'Nah, I don't want to go in no special ed class,' remember that, Becky? I don't want to go in no special ed class. Now she comin' out. She's come a long way. Vicky come a long way" (transcript, 3/8/99). It was interesting for me to hear June tell me that it was Vicky who did not want to be in a special-education class. Although this was certainly the case, such a significant part of June's thinking about the referral process had been her resistance to it. At that moment, as the three of us stood in the kitchen, we all believed in the education system. We believed it was possible for Vicky to have a better educational experience than June. The preceding conversation led us into the second-year CSE meeting with the mind-set that Vicky was going to come out of a special-education classroom for her eighth grade year.

Vicky began her first year at the middle school labeled as "speech impaired" and "multiply disabled." This was the term the psychologist thought "best described" Vicky's "difficulties with visual motor, with speech and language, with cognitive reasoning and with academics" (transcript, 6/18/98).

The general argument presented at the CSE meeting (Year 1) was that Vicky had severe learning disabilities. She needed extensive support. Although the policy on special education suggests the "least restrictive environment" as the best option for the child, the school officials did not see this as the best option for Vicky (transcript, 6/18/98). The psychologist decided that Vicky needed a smaller classroom setting because of the magnitude of her learning disabilities. A self-contained classroom was the best placement for Vicky because it would give her individual attention and more support. The label of "multiply disabled" would allow for Vicky to receive this support. The argument evoked June's multiple subjectivities as a mother who wanted to make the best educational decisions for her daughter and a person who has had literacy failure within the institution of school. Committed to doing what was right for her daughter and reminded of her history with education, June agreed to sign the forms.

As I visited the Treaders' home in the following months, I asked June how things were going for Vicky at the middle school. June repeatedly told me that Vicky was, "doin' real good up there in the middle school." June provided evidence for this by saying that she had not received any telephone calls home from the school about Vicky's work or her behavior. This was in contrast to the end of Vicky's sixth-grade year when June constantly received notes and telephone calls from the school about the special-education referral process. June also showed me science, spelling, and math tests that Vicky brought home with her (fieldnotes, 2/99). These tests were in the 90s and 100s. She associated Vicky doing well with these high marks. June seemed accustomed to Vicky's placement despite her adamant refusal of placing her daughter in special education. She seemed less concerned that Vicky was in a self-contained classroom, and was relieved that Vicky was doing well in school. She did, however, believe it was a temporary placement.

June continued to be involved in the elementary school where Luanne was in the third grade and where Shauna attended kindergarten. The speech therapist commented to me that she saw June all the time around the school. June was even on a fund-raising committee at the school (fieldnotes, 9/99). June noticed differences between the middle school and the elementary school. She told me with frustration that she could not just walk into the classrooms anymore like she had in the past. She had to first check in with the main office and they would page a security guard to escort her to her destination, as they did with all of the other visitors at the school. June also noticed that the teachers never called her and she had to wait until Vicky's report card came home in order to find out how she was doing in her classes. June did not think there was enough involvement between the home and school. In fact, she thought the middle school set up roadblocks so she could not be involved.

Vicky seemed to be well adjusted to her new life in the middle school. What she enjoyed most was coming home and hanging out with her friends "around the corner." Continuing a preadolescent interest in clothes, television shows, hair paraphernalia, and cool hangout spots, Vicky managed to attend to her homework assignments in order not only to get them done but to do reasonably well on them.

THE MEETING

Despite signing the paperwork, June continued to believe that her daughter did not belong in a special-education class. When June did speak with me about Vicky's being in the special-education class, she did so with the belief that she would come out of it before the end of her middle school years. She believed that Vicky's progress in the classroom was evidence that she would be in a "regular" classroom. The point I make in the following sections was that at the second-year review meeting, a different structure and logic was used than at the meeting the first year.

The meeting was held February 19, 1999. At 10:00 a.m. June and I walked into the guidance office. Similar to our first visit to the middle school, June mentioned again that the office was the same as when she was in school here. We were shown into the guidance counselor's office. It was an office that looked out over the circular driveway of the school's main entrance. The walls were covered with a dark paneling, which cast a shadow over the room. There were folding metal chairs set up around the desk. I waited to see where June would sit and then sat down next to her. The guidance counselor engaged us with small chat. After a few minutes the special-education teachers, the teacher's aide, and a student teacher came into the room. They sat in the now-formed semicircle around the desk. Vicky had been given a pass to come to the meeting from her class. After general introductions, Vicky came into the room and sat next to the guidance counselor (fieldnotes, 3/19/99). Recall that Vicky was not at the first CSE meeting.

The meeting lasted for 30 minutes. The people present were: the guidance counselor; Vicky's special-education teachers, Mr. Ethan and Mr. Bradley; a student teacher; a teacher's aide; and June, Vicky and me. Everyone in the meeting sat in a circle on folding chairs. The guidance counselor sat behind his desk. Vicky sat near the door, parallel to the guidance counselor. She was not part of the larger circle of chairs (see Fig. 7.1 for a diagram of the seating arrangement). This was in contrast to the Year 1 CSE meeting where the school officials sat at a formal conference table in a special building designed for special-education meetings.

The meeting began with general introductions, similar to the previous year. In the meeting, the option of Vicky being integrated into mainstream classes rather than staying in a self-contained special-education classroom was brought up. This evidence confirmed my doubt that June and Vicky had been deceived into thinking Vicky would be de-classified. It was not that Vicky was going to come out of special education completely like she and June reported to me in their kitchen but that integration was an option.

Genre of the Second Special-Education Meeting.   The guidance counselor opened and closed the meeting. There was informal talk and then the

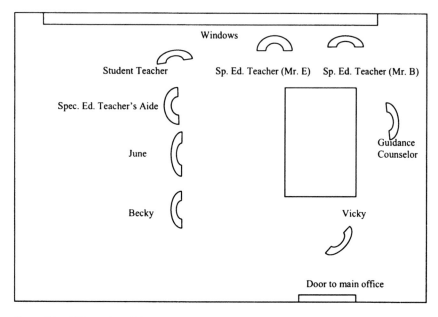

Figure 7.1   CSE meeting 1999.

guidance counselor asked everyone present to introduce themselves to the room. During the introductions Mr. Ethan stated that Vicky was a "star" in his classroom, but that she had difficulty with the math teacher and had missed many math assignments. The topic shifted to a general discussion of "how things are going for Vicky." A recommendation was made by the guidance counselor for Vicky to stay in the self-contained classroom. June asked what type of class this was. Mr. Ethan introduced the idea of an integrated classroom because of Vicky's "ability in math." The student teacher followed and confirmed this idea by stating that Vicky handed in a quality science project, a fact that was announced on the PA system. Mr. Bradley observed that Vicky had gained more confidence since the beginning of the year. There was a general discussion of Vicky's attitude and how it had changed for the better over the course of the year. Mr. Bradley raised the issue that Vicky was not handing in her homework on time. June stated that Vicky was doing her homework at home each night:

> She was doin' it at home. She was doin' it and then when she finish it she put it straight into her book bag. And then I ask her, every day when she come home, do you have homework? She tell me if she have homework or if she don't have homework. And then if she don't have homework I ask her to read a book if she don't have homework to do.

Vicky stated that she thought the teacher lost her homework. Mr. Ethan brought up the point that Vicky was placed in an honors math class by mistake at the beginning of the year, and when this was realized and she was put into a "regular" classroom, she was playing "catch up" through out the year. The guidance counselor posed the critical question of the meeting when he asked, "Do you want us to try for a program where you would be what they call integrated or included into the regular class program but with special-ed follow-up, with somebody following you through the classes?" June immediately responded "yes" and asked if this was for all of her classes. The guidance counselor replied affirmatively. June clarified and asked, "So she still won't be into a special ed next year?" I asked about the possibility of her coming out of special education completely. The guidance counselor responded that the next step would be an integrated program before de-classifying her completely. I asked how many special-education students were in the integrated classroom. There was discussion of the specifics of the integrated program. Mr. Ethan stated how they hated to lose somebody like Vicky because they enjoyed having her in the room. He stated, "You know, you look for students like her." The guidance counselor made reference to wanting to challenge Vicky while at the same time making sure she was successful. June brought up the topic of Vicky talking in class, an issue she often brought up with Vicky herself. The guidance counselor stressed that integrating Vicky into the regular classroom would mean an increase in commitment from her in terms of workload. Mr. Ethan and Mr. Bradley agreed that she would spend more time each night on homework. The guidance counselor asked Vicky what her decision was. He stated, "Well, Vicky, what do you think? You have two options of staying with Mr. Bradley and Mr. Ethan next year for English, Social Studies, Math, and Science or going into a regular classroom where there is going to be probably seven other special-ed students and a teacher who will be helping you guys out." Mr. Bradley stressed that there would be 17 other non special-ed students. Vicky stated, "I want to go with Mr. Ethan and Mr. Bradley." June nodded, affirming Vicky's decision. I asked about the other services that were a part of her IEP. Mr. Bradley stated that she was dropped from speech class because of her "marginal needs." I asked about her language arts and reading instruction. The guidance counselor responded that there was no room with the electives and the block scheduling for her to have extra reading support. I asked Mr. Ethan for evidence about Vicky's reading in his class. He responded, "She is one of the top readers in the class." I handed June the case report I had written on Vicky's progress over the course of the year I had worked with her. June distributed the case report to the rest of the committee. They asked me if I would continue to work with Vicky. I responded that I intended to keep working with Vicky. There was a discussion of after-school programs available to Vicky. June stated she didn't want Vicky to stay after school because she would have to walk home and the streets were not safe. The bell rang and the teachers headed back to their classes.

It is readily apparent that the meeting did not have the structure and sequential topic organization as the first-year meeting. There are other contradictions, too. In the following sections, I address each of the contradictions that became apparent in this meeting through a CDA of the genre, discourse, and style across the two CSE meetings[2]. I address each one of these in turn, relying on the discourse in this meeting and the 2 years of ethnographic data I had collected on June and Vicky and their participation with literacy and social structures in different contexts.

CONTRADICTION 1: RHETORIC OF EVIDENCE

The first set of contradictions embedded within the structure and format of this meeting was that the evidence of Vicky's progress and achievement was called upon differently than in the first year. Whereas the first-year CSE meeting was very formal and highly structured, the second-year CSE was not. Using CDA to look at the turn-taking structure and format of this meeting juxtaposed against the first-year meeting brings these contradictions to light.

It may be argued that the purpose and the intention of the original placement meeting and the annual review were very different. That is, the goal of the original placement meeting was to ensure that Vicky was labeled so that she could receive support, a goal decided on at the start of the referral process (chaps. 4 and 5). The goal of the second meeting was to review Vicky's progress and to see if changes should be made in Vicky's program to ensure the decision was a good placement for Vicky. Each of these goals required different amounts of evidence.

As discussed in the previous chapter, the committee presented evidence from formal, standardized tests. Each member of the committee spoke from formalized records and folders that documented Vicky's deficits with reading, with academics, and with speech and language. There was a formal and structured procedure for the first meeting, complete with turn-taking rules reinforced by the chair of the committee. This procedure ensured the efficiency of the decision-making and labeling process (Mehan, 1996).

Here, the meeting was structured as a bunch of friends talking about Vicky during their free period. Mehan et al. (1986) suggested that the, "relations between voices in public political discourse take the form of a conversation" (p. 135). It is through this "conversation" that ideologies are manufactured that lead to consent. However, the point made by Hennimore (2000) that "educators never just talk" is relevant in this case. Although the meeting lacked the formal structure and evidence, the way in which the instructional arrangements were described to Vicky ultimately led to her decision to stay in the self-contained classroom.

There was no formal evidence presented in the meeting. Both of the teachers spoke from memory of Vicky in their classroom. They referred to Vicky as a "star" but had no achievement data, formal or otherwise, to show the improvement Vicky had made during the year. It was revealed after much discussion that Vicky had been dropped from speech services because of her "marginal speech needs" but there were no formal records of her progress. It appeared from this meeting that Vicky had made progress in the class, progress noted by the classroom teachers, and yet none of this was documented in a manner that established credibility or an impetus for having her placed in the integrated classroom. This lack of evidence made it impossible to demand Vicky's placement in the integrated classroom. The general areas of improvement cited were not documented. Even if Vicky's progress had been documented, the documentary evidence would not have carried the same amount of institutional weight as the formal, standardized evidence presented in the first-year CSE meeting.

CONTRADICTION 2: DEFICIT FRAMEWORK TURNS INTO A STRENGTHS FRAMEWORK

Whereas the logic of the first year's CSE meeting functioned from a discourse of deficits, the second-year meeting operated from a strengths perspective. However, a profound contradiction was that the strengths catalogued in the second meeting were the very same weaknesses that ensured Vicky was labeled as severely speech and language impaired *and* multiply disabled.

The reasons the CSE gave for why Vicky was classified as "multiply disabled" was because she was "decoding at a second grade level," had "severe speech and language needs," and had "weak comprehension skills." However, her seventh-grade special-education classroom teachers considered Vicky to be a "star in the classroom." Vicky's classroom teacher referred to her as "one of the top readers in the class." Furthermore, Mr. Ethan, Vicky's math and science teacher, explained how Vicky handed in a science project that was, "quality work, it's hanging in our room right now as an example of how to do a science project. I mean she got honorable mention at the fair for it. . .it was beyond the call of duty." Vicky won an award for this outstanding project. It was put on display in the library and announced over the loudspeaker.

When I asked about the status of Vicky's speech and language services for the following year, it was revealed that Vicky no longer received speech and language services. None of Vicky's teachers could recall her going to speech classes during her time at the middle school. The guidance counselor informed us that Vicky was, "marginal in terms of her speech needs and so they decided to drop her." Her low reading skills and her speech and language deficits, the very criteria that placed Vicky in a self-contained classroom with a label of multiply disabled, were seen as her strengths the following year. For instance, during the first-year CSE meeting, the speech therapist stated, "I think her delay in language is really affecting her academic skills. She really needs some help in the language area (Speech therapist, 6/18/98, lines 245–248). And, the psychologist said, "I think the difficulty that she has with her language development really interferes with her performance (Psychologist, 6/18/98, lines 88–92).

However, as I pointed out, the strengths reported in Year 2 were not documented in a formal way and thus were not presented as strong enough to ensure Vicky's placement in an integrated classroom (Contradiction 1). Furthermore, the presentation of Vicky's strengths in these classrooms along with the teacher's pride and pleasure of having her in class (Contradiction 3) functioned to persuade Vicky she was welcome and "safe" in the self-contained classroom.

CONTRADICTION 3: CONTINUED CONSENT

June's discourse both at home (3/9/99) and at school (3/18/99) suggested that she wanted Vicky out of special education. Throughout the meeting, June delineated between "regular" and "special education" when she tried to understand the placement for her daughter for the following year.[3] For example, the guidance counselor stated that the recommendation was that Vicky should continue the following year with her teachers Mr. Ethan and Mr. Bradley for the four main subject areas. This was contradictory to both June's and Vicky's interpretations and expectations of what the school's plan was for Vicky for the following year. They both thought, as did I from their reports, that Vicky was coming out of a self-contained classroom because of the progress she had made during her seventh-grade year.

In hearing the recommendation to continue Vicky's placement as was for the following year, June questioned, "What's that? Regular class or?" The guidance counselor avoided her question and instead outlined the parameters of the 15:1 program. This was information June had already heard in the first meeting. Hearing June's concerns, Mr. Ethan, the science and math teacher, stated that one of the goals was to get Vicky out of special education. As he said this, June nodded her head and stated automatically "yeah." Again, later in the meeting, the guidance counselor asked June if she would like them to try for the integrated classroom situation where

Vicky would be in a regular classroom program. Again, June positively affirmed this decision. She then asked, "for everything or just math?" Engaged in the discussion, taking 76 turns as compared to her 9 turns in the previous year, June attempted to clarify the labels that were used.

The school officials referred to a "15:1 program," a "mainstream class-room," an "integrated classroom," a "regular classroom program," and a "special-ed follow-up." Sorting through the various terms being used, June asked, "So she won't be into a special ed next year?" One of the teachers told June that she would still be "special ed but it would be an integrated program." June interrupted him and said, "It's more into a regular class." Their response to her was that it was almost entirely like a "regular" class. The integrated class would be fast-paced, challenging, and the kids would have more homework. Based on June's emphasis on Vicky's placement with "regular" kids, it seemed as though June had learned the "popular" distinction between "regular" and "special" education. Wanting to make sure this would be the case, June asked, "with regular kids?" June still believed her daughter did not belong in a special-education classroom and, indeed, was a "regular" child.

After this stretch of interaction, the special-education teachers agreed that the integrated classroom was an option for Vicky because of her ability and the progress she had made that year. However, they also stated that Vicky was one of the smartest students in their classes, and that they, "hate to lose someone like her" because they really enjoyed having her in the classroom. Mr. Ethan stated, "You know, you look for students like her." Vicky, hearing this, looked up and smiled at Mr. Ethan. At that point the guidance counselor reminded Vicky that her other option would be to stay in the same classroom that she has been in this year. Mr. Bradley, the language arts and social studies teacher, chimed in and added that if Vicky were to choose the integrated classroom, she would be with about 7 other special-education students and 17 regular-education students, extending the distinction between "regular" and "special" education.

Vicky had listened to most of the discussion, infrequently being drawn into participating. Mostly, she was an observer during this discussion about her fate in the school system. The teachers did ask Vicky why she did not turn in her homework in math. Math was the only subject where she was in a mainstream class. As it turned out, at the beginning of the year, the guidance office placed Vicky in an *advanced* math class by mistake. Vicky spent the first half of the year catching up with the rest of the class. After this "error" had been noticed, Vicky was so far behind in math and her esteem so low, the guidance counselor decided to put Vicky in a self-contained classroom for math as well as for the other subject areas.

The guidance counselor asked Vicky what she wanted to do for the following year. Unlike in Year 1, Vicky rather than June made the decision, stating, "I want to go with Mr. Ethan and Mr. Bradley." There was a general shuffle in the room and June laughed, a nervous and relieved laugh, and said, "They gonna be keepin' her in there then if she feel comfortable with it." Vicky saw the possibilities and the potential for what she might become linked to the special-education classroom.

Whereas June was led to believe she had decision-making power in the 1998 CSE meeting, here, Vicky is given the option to make the decision. The team of teachers turned the decision over to Vicky, an adolescent girl. When she decided that she wanted "to stay with Mr. Ethan and Mr. Bradley," there was no question about the *best* instructional placement for her. That is, would Vicky profit from having language arts within an integrated class-room where she would read literature and have support from a resource room teacher? Would the increase in verbal stimulation of being in a classroom with students who may be more proficient with the discourse of school benefit Vicky rather than having her in a self-contained classroom? Here, as in Year 1, the institution set up a restricted set of options from which Vicky and June were allowed to choose. When the school asked Vicky and June to decide on Vicky's placement after structuring the conditions in very particular ways, ways that suited the goals of the dominant class interests (the school), it appeared as if they (Vicky and June), not the institutional webs of discourse, were in control of their fate. Thus, being labeled as "multiply disabled" was not a racist and classist act. It was an instructional decision based on internal deficiencies and individual con-sent. In the end, attending a special-education self-contained classroom, a modern day form of "symbolic violence" (Bourdieu, 1977), was a decision made by the student within the classroom.[4] Bourdieu (1991) aptly described this situation as "telling the child what he is" (p. 52) rather than what they might do and how they might do it.

THEORIZING FROM THIS CASE

Each of the contradictions presented in this case was discursively con-structed within and across the CSE meetings. To understand how social reproduction was maintained through the special-education process, I looked across orders of discourse including ways of interacting (genre), ways of representing (discourse), and ways of being (styles) (orders of discourse) within each meeting and across meetings in order to understand, and possibly interrupt, such processes.

We might assume that a change in turn taking (an aspect of genre) where June spoke more and actively contributed information rather than merely being asked to contribute would democratize the meeting and the decision making. However, the data presented in this chapter demonstrate this was not the case. The meeting in Year 2 was marked by such a change. June had 76 turns compared to 9 turns the previous year. She questioned terms and told the teachers she wanted Vicky placed in a "regular" classroom. The results, however, were the same as for Year 1.

Similarly, the "discourse of deficits" as it appeared in the CSE Year 1 meeting is often critiqued as representing what children cannot do rather than what they can do (discourse). We might predict that when a child is presented from a strengths framework, as Vicky was in the CSE Year 2 meeting, she would be given the opportunity for more challenging instruction. However, a strengths framework (discourse), operating with the changes in ways of interacting in the meeting (genre), served to reinforce that the self-contained special-education class was the best placement for Vicky. Vicky flourished academically in this context and therefore it was a good placement. The consequences of this can be seen within and across the meetings in terms of June's and Vicky's ways of being or the affiliation with special education (styles). Outside of school, in the context of the home, both June and Vicky continued to think Vicky should be moved out of special education. However, in the context of the meeting room, both consented to the placement. June's and Vicky's "ways of being" were in alignment with the school discourse, at least within the context of the meeting room. Each of these discursive practices—genres, discourses, and styles—helps to describe, interpret, and explain the location of social reproduction in the special-education process.

Looking across orders of discourse in the two CSE meetings demonstrated the shift in genres, discourses, and styles. I would have predicted that the orders of discourse would remain the same if in the second meeting Vicky was kept in a self-contained classroom. A close analysis of the ways of interacting, ways of representing, and ways of being demonstrate the shifts in the networks of practice over time in the second CSE meeting. The second-year meeting was characterized by what appeared to be a democratization of the process. That is, the participant framework opened up (genre). Indeed, June had much more of a voice in the second-year meeting. Vicky's strengths rather than her deficits were presented (discourse). Finally, Vicky was given the choice to continue her affiliation (style) with the self-contained classroom for the following year. However, the shifts in the networks of practice did not lead to a democratization of the process. Instead, Vicky "chose" to stay in the self-contained classroom. The shifts in networks of practice (genre, discourse, and style) were possible because the framework had been established the previous year. Whereas June decided in June of 1998, Vicky decided in March of 1999. June decided to label Vicky so she could get extra support. Vicky decided to stay in the classroom because she was doing well and she was comfortable. Each year, I was surprised by the outcomes of the meeting.

It is evident from the discussion in the previous two chapters that the teachers and guidance counselors, as representatives of the institution of schools, chose the narrative that best suited them at the time, within the institutional boundaries from which they were operating. There was a lack of coherence within the special-education system. That is, there were very specific reasons (cited in chap. 6) that caused Vicky to be labeled as "speech impaired" and "multiply disabled." Conversely, her status within the self-contained classroom was maintained through much more vague and abstract reasons.

Recent work in the anthropology of disability (McDermott, 1987; 1996; Mehan, 1996) has focused on locating the source and reproduction of disability as a complex interaction between the individual and the social world (Sternberg & Grigorenko, 1999). Much more work has been conducted on disability as residing within the individual than on how disability gets constructed, maintained, and reproduced, as we have seen in this case. Often when disability is construed as a cognitive phenomenon, the complexity and contradictory nature of the issues involved, including race, class, and gender issues, are masked.

By looking at the intersections of texts, contexts, and subjectivities, we see how these contradictions fit within the scope of what is acceptable. Vicky's placement in the self-contained classroom was not only an educational placement but also a cultural system, a mode of thinking about herself in relation to others. Vicky saw herself as succeeding within this classroom setting and thus it became part of her thinking about herself, or her literate subjectivity (Bourdieu, 1991; Collins, 1993). However, Vicky never believed that her stardom in the classroom was attributable to her as an individual. She believed it was because of her classroom teachers and that they told her she did well. She had internalized the deficits and was not given the time and the space to believe in herself with regard to "schooled" literacy. Like her mother, Vicky did not see her literate proficiencies outside of school as mattering. Also like her mother, Vicky was acquiring a set of ideological relationships to literacy that were shaped both by the school and by her strong connections to her family.

The logic of her sustained placement in a self-contained classroom was not framed as overly deterministic. Indeed, Vicky was given the decision to make. However, like June's decision about Vicky's original placement (Year 1), Vicky's choice to remain in a self-contained classroom was a choice manufactured through consent to the dominant ideology of schooling. Neither June nor Vicky believe they are literate people. Rather, they believe in the authority of the school that causes them to see only one kind of literacy as "counting."

Whereas Vicky stated that she wanted to move out of special education in her kitchen, in the meeting room she consented to the logic of the institution. It is reasonable to extend the argument I presented in chapter 6 about June to Vicky's case as well. We see the complicated web of June's and Vicky's proficiencies in out-of-school contexts, their strong commitment to education, and yet their continued consent to educational decisions that were not in their best interests. Whereas the committee meetings in both years reveal a piece of how June and Vicky learned to see themselves in the eyes of the institution, the more powerful, more deeply embedded logic, occurred in their day-to-day interactions with literacy and language. It is the ideological work done prior to the meeting and after the meeting that allowed for the successful manufacture of consent.

These ideologies about individualism and hard work, about the power of literacy and schooling are framed through commonsense representations. It is though these cultural narratives, such as differential abilities, that individuals and groups realize different social locations. The severe consequences of these decisions are the sets of practices that coincide with them. That is, we learned during Vicky's sixth-grade year that she was defined as "multiply disabled," thus deserving a separate and self-contained classroom where she would not be reading interesting and challenging books. Nor would the goal for Vicky even be to get up to grade level, as I asked during the meeting. Instead, as the chair of the committee informed June and I during the meeting, the goal would be to "increase [Vicky's] fundamental reading skills. Increasing her sight word vocabulary, in terms of English usage, increasing grammatical usage" (lines 1094–1100, transcript, 6/18/98). In other words, Vicky would receive more of the same (lack of) reading instruction that she had during her elementary years. Thus, a seventh grader who, as we have seen, was already reading proficiently was subjected to a basic-skills classroom.

This logic transmits or reproduces not only ways of using literacy but also how Vicky understood her relationship to the social world. It is the informal nature of evidence—the practices that seem everyday—that result in the strongest pieces of ideology and domination.

NOTES

1. An early version of this chapter appeared in Rogers (2002c).
2. I did not audio-record the second-year CSE meeting. I did take detailed fieldnotes during the meeting and wrote up notes immediately after leaving the school. I conducted a CDA on the fieldnotes, which included lines of direct quotations on the second-year meeting. Similar to the first year, I was interested in the relationship across genre (ways of interacting), discourse (ways of representing), and style (ways of being). However, in order to investigate social transformation, over time, I put the two CSE meetings side by side and looked across the orders of discourse; that is, I intertextually analyzed the ways of interacting including turn-taking and participant structure for each of the meetings. I also

analyzed how Vicky was represented and from what perspective in each of the meetings (discourse). Similarly, I looked at the styles (ways of being) across the two meetings, that is, how people were positioned vis-à-vis social structures. I would predict, prior to participating in and analyzing the meeting, that if a child were to be kept in a self-contained classroom, even though both the child and the parent did not want the child in the class, that the structure, the discourse, and the style would be largely the same as in the first-year meeting. In other words, the participant structure would be tightly controlled with scripted roles. The institution would be defined through tests and official procedures and Vicky would be represented through a discourse of deficits, where Vicky was positioned as a passive recipient and the testers as active. However, as I point out through my analysis in this chapter, this prediction was wrong.

3. The word *special* as applied to education implies "separate" educational activities for people who are "different." But as Stangvik (1998) pointed out the distinction serves as a "money-bearing logo in the resource allocation process" (p. 151), which is made to seem fair and legitimate through assessment processes (seen in the last chapter) made through the official "gaze" of the school. In addition, Stangvik found that segregated special-education classrooms had consequences for the identity development of disabled children, including separate and unequal educational practices, social relationships, and motivational orientations. Similarly, Allington & McGill Franzen (1995) pointed out there is no available evidence at the federal, state, or local level in the U.S. that demonstrates the effectiveness of special education practices. Allington & McGill Franzen stress that students placed in special education classes receive less rather than more of the institutional support they need, particularly in accelerative literacy instruction.

4. This coincides with cultural reproduction theory wherein modern power is no longer forceful and omnipotent but rather is exercised through individuals (Foucault, 1977). In the meeting, Vicky was given the choice to move out of the special-education classroom and into an integrated classroom, and yet she chose to stay with her two self-contained classroom teachers. This works in a similar manner as did the decision to place Vicky in special education. The decision was given to June to make either to "enable" Vicky to have more resources available to her so she might succeed academically or to "constrain" her by putting her in a special-education classroom. The logic of the institution is that the placement is indeed enabling rather than constraining. Thus, a solid decision for Vicky.

The Paradox of Literacy

Literacy in the Treaders' lives is paradoxical. Simply stated, literacy is not what it seems or promises to be. In this final chapter, I draw together why the interpretation and analysis I have presented thus far may be considered a trustworthy reading of the Treaders' literate lives. I use the CSE meeting presented in chapter 6 as a frame of reference to draw together the points made thus far. I have chosen this formal meeting as a reference point because many of the issues running through this book—literate subjectivities, discursive practices, and social structures—intersect during this meeting. June's participation in this meeting illustrates the complexity of her social and literate lives and how these positions influenced Vicky's participation within the same institutions.

CRITICAL DISCOURSE THEORY

The claims and foundations on which critical discourse theory and analysis are based are an important starting point for this discussion. Critical discourse theory, the theoretical anchor of this research, assumes that language is both a reflection and a construction of the social world, riddled with relations of power and privilege. Critical theorists often ask how dominant power relations are understood, transmitted, and reproduced in the social world. Often, these relations are seen as natural and common sense. Indeed, in chapter 1, I asked the following question: What are the processes through which literate practices lead to (or thwart) the attainment of social resources?

Throughout the book, I have presented analyses that reveal these processes. For example, recall the interactions in the CSE meeting room presented in chapter 6. Remember the precision of the turn taking, the objectivity of the language, and the careful orchestration of CSE membership. Also, remember June's almost complete silence and then her consent to put Vicky in a special-education classroom. Bear in mind also my questions to the committee, but also my ultimate consent to Vicky's placement. Similarly, in chapter 6 I noted the contradictions embedded in my role in the meeting. Each of these interactions point to the significance of subjectivities trapped within institutional webs of discourse.

Returning to the cultural mismatch hypothesis I presented in chapter 1, research in New Literacy Studies has demonstrated that parents of working-class and minority children do value education and school and are involved with their children's education. I want to suggest that it is precisely because of this belief and involvement that working-class and minority families' efforts are thwarted within the institution. June wanted to do what was best for her daughter. It was because of her involvement with the school, both in terms of her own education and her daughter's, and her belief in the current model of education as a means of upward social mobility that caused her to concede to the logic of the school.

In this book, I have illustrated that there are several ways in which critical theory addresses disempowerment and inequity, especially in relation to studies of literacy, in both formal and informal settings. First, it provides a framework from which to reject the commonsense assertion that simply *more* literacy or *more* literate competence would lead to different results for June and Vicky. That is, the decision made to label Vicky as "multiply disabled" with "severe speech and language needs" and June's silence in the meeting were not contingent on the sole existence of more literacy or literate competence. There has been a wide range of literacy programs and research efforts under the umbrella of family literacy conducted with such assumptions (e.g., Morrow, 1995; Sticht & McDonald, 1989). This study (especially in chaps. 3 & 4) shows how within the Treaders' lives the absence of literacy or literate competence is not the issue. June negotiated a petition for traffic conditions, Vicky critically read the newspaper, and June resisted special education. Both June and Vicky not only "have" literacy but they are extremely proficient with the literacies in their daily lives. An active questioning of the assumption that more literacy is better literacy is one of the tenets of critical discourse theory.

Second, critical social theory also undermines the notion that the "problem" is that there is merely a mismatch between literacies or discursive practices. Starting with the assumption that all literacies are ideological, critical discourse theory assumes unequal relations between various systems of Discourse (Gee, 1996). From this perspective, success in school often follows having the "right" type of literacy—namely "schooled" literacy. Again, in the field of family literacy there have been a number of research studies conducted with the premise of a cultural or linguistic mismatch (e.g., Heath, 1983; Moll et. al, 1992; Purcell-Gates, 1995). Although this explanation holds some ground in the present case, it does not explain the existence of schooled literacy in the Treaders' home, nor their belief and value in the institution of the school and their failure to move from literate capital to social profit. Neither of the commonsense narratives—not enough literacy (or literate incompetence) in the Treaders' home, nor the wrong kind of literacy (not schooled literacy)—fully explains why it is that despite all of their efforts the Treaders' failed to capitalize on social resources. Rather, I argue that what keeps the Treaders in their place is their quite complete acquisition of the ideology behind "schooled literacy." The central problem that CDA helps to reveal is that the Treaders have come to see themselves through the eyes of the institution. The use of CDA in this study has illuminated June's and Vicky's subjectivities in and across contexts. However, CDA does not do a good job of showing us how individuals *learn* to see themselves through the eyes of the institution.

A third explanation for June's ultimate consent in the CSE meeting and Vicky's acquisition of the "multiply disabled" label lies in the distinction critical discourse theory makes between structure and agency. Critical social theory often claims that ideology is imposed on individuals through more powerful and dominant social structures. Therefore, another possible way of explaining the decisions made in this meeting would be that the school, as more powerful, imposed its decision on June and Vicky. Instead of an overly deterministic view of social life or an overly optimistic view of human agency, critical discourse theory and analysis holds the potential for movement back and forth between structure and agency.

Ideology, the commonsense assumptions that bind individuals to their social worlds, is a thread running through this book. This is a concept widely utilized in critical discourse studies because it assumes the presence of contradictions within the social world (e.g., the ethos of competitive individualism and equality). The concept of ideology is an important one in understanding the paradox of literacy in the Treaders' lives because it is the assumptions below the surface of the amount (is this enough literacy?) and type (is this the right kind?) of literacy that matter. Ideology is powerful because it operates from within—it is the internalization of structures and relationships—a way of viewing the world and oneself. Ideologies, as I have shown in this book, operate most effectively through split and contradictory subjectivities. What is important, as we have seen herein, is *which* subjectivity (literate competence, literacy as enabling/women's work) is evoked in which circumstance.

CRITICAL DISCOURSE ANALYSIS

The use of the case study method (Merriam, 1997), as I promised in chapter 2, has allowed for the investigation of bounded social phenomena. In holding empirical data up to preexisting theoretical frameworks such as critical social theory, spaces appear where the data address the gaps in theory or cause new ruptures (Burawoy, 1991). The investigation of literacy in the Treaders' lives through a critical approach to discourse studies has allowed me to reconceptualize discourse theory and analysis in a number of ways. I address these in a later section of this concluding chapter.

A longitudinal ethnographic case study across contexts shows the places where June and Vicky negotiated language and literacy in different contexts and how they thought about themselves as literate in the process. In these cases, CDA allowed me to see the broad patterns with regard to uses of literacy and to speculate on why it was that individuals are unable to turn social and literate capital into social profits.

In the following sections, I highlight the conceptual and analytic strengths of CDA using the CSE meeting as a point of reference as well as drawing on other peripheral examples from this book. I also suggest that a CDA of formalized instances of power and language also is not enough to account for the paradoxes and contradictory subjectivities that insisted on this particular ordering of social relations.

A CDA of this meeting clearly shows how power was embedded and communicated through discourse. What is not apparent is the way in which the context of the meeting brought a particular subjectivity to the foreground of June's decision, and how it is that these literate and contradictory subjectivities are acquired.

Conceptual Strengths. CDA brings a number of theories, specifically social theory and linguistic analysis, into alignment. CDA highlights the configurations of social practices through genres, discourses, and styles. In the CSE meeting, for example, I called on the turn-taking procedures, the presentation of information, and the use of pronouns as examples of the genre of the CSE meeting. In terms of discourse, I highlighted the way in which members of the special-education committee constructed their understanding of the institution of the school through discourse. I gave examples that illustrated how the school personnel used technical terms and indicators of accuracy embedded in formal reports to define social roles and the institution itself. In the domain of style, or ways of being, I demonstrated how the meeting called on two contradictory subjectivities. The first was June's history as a person with literate failure within the institution and the second was her strong connection to mothering within which she wanted to provide the best for her children. Looking at these domains, or orders of discourse, it is easier to see the way in which social narratives and subject positions intersect and are mutually constructed. CDA allows for a means of pointing at configurations of discourse in social practice. Nonetheless, as I show in my critique of CDA, an understanding of the history and contradictory nature of subjectivities may be understood only by looking at individuals in different contexts—an approach not often taken in studies using CDA.

This method of analysis is also an apt tool for highlighting contradictions in the data. If we are to believe the assumption noted previously that social life is bound by contradictions, then it makes analytic sense to formulate a method of describing and analyzing these relations. The use of CDA helped me to see the contradictions between the first and second CSE meetings (chaps. 6 and 7). Analyzing for genre allowed me to see that the format of the meeting from Year 1 to Year 2 was different in terms of politeness conventions, turn-taking sequence, and degree of orchestration. Also, in chapters 5 and 6 I highlighted the "I" statements made by June as she resisted the special-education placement (style). Furthermore, I showed how she delineated four concrete reasons why her daughter should not be placed in special education. The surprise or contradiction is found in the meeting that occurred a week later in which June is silent (chap. 6). The conceptual rigor of orders of discourse allowed me to look across the dimensions in order to hypothesize about the existence of power in language, across contexts.

CDA also allowed for surprises. In going back and forth between the theory and the data, I was able to see that it was neither in the meeting (chap. 6), nor at the initial point in the referral process (chap. 5) that the school personnel made the decision about Vicky's placement. Neither was it just the institution of the school carried more institutional weight than did the home (e.g., Mehan, 1996). What is important is how different institutional contexts evoke specific literate subjectivities.

The "orders of discourse" I have presented through CDA (genre, discourse, and style) are a process-oriented means of analyzing the relationship between texts and social structures. This analysis assumes change and overlap between texts, institutional contexts, and societal positions. In this study, the domain concerned with subject positions (style) in connection with cultural narratives has provided a way of locating the intersection of contradictory literate identities in relation to various texts.

Methodological Strengths. Many of the methodological strengths of CDA overlap with the conceptual strengths of the analytic tool. First, as I mentioned earlier, using CDA to look across texts allows for, in fact insists on, surprises in data. Fairclough (1992) discussed the usefulness of using instances of "cruces" or moments of tension in the data to illuminate the commonsense nature of power and language. Second, CDA calls on a multifocal view of texts. This means that not only different texts (oral and written) but different genres of texts (e.g., newspaper articles, spoken broadcasts, interviews, and conversations) are useful analytic points for CDA. Also, CDA is an appropriate tool for investigating local literacies because it assumes a range of discourse practices (e.g., face-to-face, face-to-text, and text-to-text).

Third, because of the conceptual richness of the framework, there is a great deal of flexibility in the application of CDA. For example, as I point out in chapters 2 and 6, I adopted Fairclough's (1989) orders of discourse to describe, interpret, and explain genre, discourse, and style at local, institutional, and societal domains. The critical feature is not the label of the levels, but a clear definition and justification of what each of the levels assumes and expects of discourse.

Methodological Weaknesses. CDA would not be a critical tool if it were not subject to ongoing critique of its dimensions (Blommaert, 2001; Flowerdew, 1999; van Dijk, 1993, 1998; Toolan, 1997; Widdowson, 1998). The present study has pushed the boundaries of CDA as a methodological tool in four primary ways. First, more attention should be paid to the most useful contexts in which to call upon CDA. That is, I used CDA throughout the book, even in places where it did not become represented through the orders of discourse (as in chap. 6). The limitation of this was that it did not allow me to go beyond the power present in the text or the interaction of that specific event. For example, analysis of the community petition (chap. 3) demonstrated a number of things. First, CDA indicated the places where June's words were encoded into the text (genre, local). Second, it showed how June constructed the institutions she referred to (e.g., city hall and the adult literacy center) (discourse, institutional level) and how this set of practices was a part of two intersecting discourses of at-risk (e.g., poor city streets) and proficiency with literacy (style, societal level). However, without looking at how these examples fit in with the larger picture of June's life, my analysis would have focused on the ways June was active with literacy in her life. Although this is a significant piece of who June Treader is, it did not represent the broader pattern of struggle in her life. It did not show why June's attempts to turn social and literate capital into social profits were thwarted. In other words, why, despite June's substantive efforts, did she not get the stoplight? The money she deserved from social services? An equitable education for her daughter?

Furthermore, CDA did not give me analytic leverage on how June understood and internalized her relationship with her social world. That is, with just an analysis of the petition, I might have overlooked the larger themes of practice this represented. That is, June initiated the petition for a stoplight not because she was practicing her literacy skills (subjectivity as a literacy student), but because she was concerned about the safety of her children on the street (subjectivity as a mother). This event combined with the others in chapter 3 (the fair hearing, the preschool records) describe

June's literate life as active but they also point to a pattern of the context in which she is literate and what internal resource she calls on in order to engage with these events. I return to this aspect of CDA in the next section— for I believe it suggests conceptual limits as well as analytic limits of CDA.

Second, more attention needs to be paid to the areas of social cognition including affect, emotions, attitudes, and beliefs. Though I found CDA to be useful in analyzing a range of written artifacts, including transcripts, newspaper reports, written documents, and face-to-face interactions, each set of analyseis demanded a different set of assumptions and a different relationship with the data.

The instances of employing CDA that I found to be most useful, and the places where I believe my argument was strongest for identifying the connections between texts and contexts, were interactions that involved June or Vicky with either a text or with a representative of a social institution. This was probably because I had over 2 years of data on the way in which they interacted with various social institutions and how they viewed themselves in different contexts in relationship to literacy. And, it was the nature of their literate subjectivities (including their emotions and re-sponses to codes such as the red stripe on the wall at the middle school) in various social institutions that made these analyses so rich. CDA is not able to handle issues of emotion well (e.g., June crying as she told me about her reading, and again in the guidance counselor's office).

Third, part of the problem with any coding system designed for analyzing data is that the codes lose the theoretical richness that is embedded in the original frameworks. This is also the case for CDA. For instance, a review of the definitions I laid out in chapter 6 (see Appendix E) for each of my levels of analyses indicates the difficulty of making a clear connection between these codes and my levels of interpretation. For instance, given these definitions, what separates or distinguishes the interpersonal domain from the ideational domain of analysis? One could argue that the institutions are in fact part of society. However, the "ways of being" (style) domain of analysis refers to a higher level of abstraction of meaning making, such as those connected with "mothering" or "schooling" as well as subjectivities. In order to understand that, one also needs to understand how individuals make sense from and operate within these sets of "meta-narratives." Each level presumes a familiarity with a set of social assumptions that are steeped in a tradition of critical social theory.

Therefore, if I were to ask another individual, not learned in the social assumptions underlying a critical approach to language and literacy, to code a transcript, it is a fair bet that neither the coding nor the interpretation would look the same. I do not believe that is a fault of the codes themselves. What it does suggest is that interpreting research entails more than building codes from the "ground up" or "training" other researchers to "see" the data in the same way. What it also suggests is the need for systematic ways of thinking about the relationships between texts and social structures and *what it means to teach others how to do this.* I am not suggesting a stabilization of CDA, but rather, a justification of the theoretical arguments guiding CDA.

Conceptual Weaknesses.   Whereas CDA accounts for subjectivities within orders of discourse—at the societal level—often neither the theoretical nor the methodological tool has been used to locate subjectivities within histories of participation and within various social contexts. Gee (1999) wrote the following about discursive histories:

> Words have histories. They have been in other people's mouths and on other people's pens. They have circulated through other Discourses and within other institutions. They have been part of specific historical events and episodes. Words bring with them as potential situated meanings all the situated meanings they have picked up in history and in other settings and Discourses (p. 54).

As we saw in chapters 5 and 6, this history of discursive events is important for understanding how it was that June moved from resisting to consenting to her daughter's placement in special education. It is not just that power and ideology are translated through formalized settings (e.g., medical exam, an interview, or a CSE meeting). It was that within the formal setting of the institution, June's subjectivity as a literacy student, a literacy student who was unsuccessful in the eyes of the institution, was evoked. This is juxtaposed with June's strong and resilient voice and interactions with literacy, where literacy was attached to mothering, rather than schooling. Though CDA often looks at these instances of formalized power, what I argue here is the need to consider how power is translated and acquired through ideology in everyday, informal situations such as in a family's literacy practices.

Presently, CDA is not often used to locate subjectivities in different contexts that would provide a visible way of locating contradictions over time. One of the themes of this case study has been the significance of June's history of participation with the school. Individuals' participation within Discourses have histories that extend beyond the traces an analyst can pick up on in one textual analysis. What seems pressing then, given what we know about differential values placed on discourses, is how individuals and groups of individuals learn to think about themselves and to imagine possible identities through these discourse systems, that is, a theory for conceptualizing learning through power and unequal social relations.

CRITICAL SOCIAL THEORY AND LEARNING

To this point, I have argued that critical discourse theory allows social analysts to undermine commonsense assumptions about literate ability and participation. Therefore, it is not possible to turn to descriptions or a catalogue of the Treaders' literacy practices in order to understand why, despite all of their efforts, the assumptions (both the Treaders' and those representatives of social institutions) often remain in place. Nor can we turn to discursive mismatch theories that highlight the distinctions between communities of practice. Theories of power that highlight deterministic structures at the expense of agency are also incomplete explanatory frameworks. As I demonstrated in chapters 5, 6 and 7, June and Vicky believed in the logic of the institution. Within the context of the school, the Treaders believed they were unable, disabled, and did not count as literate individuals. In order to understand how this happened, despite their proficiencies, we need to consider how individuals acquire counterproductive ideologies.

Commonsense assumptions are embedded in ideologies, transmitted through discourse, in formal and informal situations. The CSE meeting presented in chapter 6 is a frame of reference to show the effectiveness of language and power. I showed the strengths of CDA to provide an explanatory framework for the intersection of texts and contexts, individual subjectivities and institutional contexts. I also illustrated how a CDA framework must be combined with a theory of how it is that individuals learn and acquire ideology. Fairclough (1989, 1992, 1995, 2000) did not address this in CDA. Other discourse analysts have though. Gee (1996) provided a conceptual model of learning and acquisition through the concept of primary and secondary Discourses.

As I have pointed out in this study, there is no clear split between the Treaders' primary and secondary Discourses. Gee (1996) recognized this boundary crossing of Discourses when he stated that there is room for Discourses to "jostle up against each other" (p. 13). He also said that Discourses "cannot have discrete boundaries" (1997, p. xv). Of membership within Discourses, Gee (1993) wrote, "People can be members of many, even conflicting Discourses, can give relatively pure or mixed performances within their Discourses in different contexts, can borrow from one another, can confuse them, can give them up, actively resist them or take overt pride in them." (Gee, 1993, p. 344). Gee (1996) argued that individuals *acquire* their primary Discourse. Primary Discourse, as I pointed out in chapter 1, is generally related to the family and community. Through exposure, immersion, and practice, individuals *acquire* their home and community language and also ways of believing, practicing, and performing literacy. Individuals *learn* their secondary Discourses generally through public sphere institutions such as schools, social service and government agencies, banks, and shops.

Gee (1996) provided definitions of learning and acquisition:

> Learning is a process that involves conscious knowledge gained through teaching (though not specifically from someone officially designated as a teacher) or through certain life-experiences that trigger conscious reflection. This teaching or reflection involves explanation and analysis, that in breaking down the thing to be learned into its analytic parts. It inherently involves attaining, along with the matter being taught, some degree of meta-knowledge about the matter.

> Acquisition is a process of acquiring something (usually, subconsciously) by exposure to models, a process of trial and error, and practice within social groups, without formal teaching. It happens in natural settings which are meaningful and functional in the sense that acquirers know that they need to acquire the thing they are exposed to in order to function and they in fact want so to function. This is how people come to control their first language (p. 138).

In this book I have demonstrated that there is often little distinction between the Treaders' primary and secondary Discourse systems. Furthermore, I have illustrated that the boundaries between learning and acquisition, especially the contexts in which these occur, are fluid and dynamic. I have shown in this book that the primary Discourse of family literacy is structured by institutional practices. The two primary institutional sources of literacy and language in the Treaders' home were schooled literacy and the forms and documents from various social service agencies. In chapter 3, I highlighted the institutional nature of the Treaders' family literacy practices. Because family literacy practices stem from social institutions and reflect larger societal narratives (e.g., ability, disability, dependent) and also are acquired, I argue that the Treaders are also acquiring how to think about themselves in relation to their social world.

June's and Vicky's relationship to literacy through "schooled literacy," and to their work as a woman, a mother, and an adolescent girl, are two themes in this study. First, the Treaders' family literacy practices were structured by the presence of schooled literacy at home. Schooled literacy, as I point out in chapter 2, is defined by de-contextualized skills, individual mastery, practice of skills, and evaluation that occurs through external authorities. As the children interacted with schooled literacy at home and at school, they were learning how to think about what literacy means. Furthermore, because within the context of the school both June and Vicky have learned to see themselves as not literate and unable, they have acquired sets of assumptions about themselves in relation to this schooled literacy. That is, within this institutional context they have learned that they were not literate people. They see themselves as people with literate failure. This constitutes one piece of the acquisition of ideology in the context of the home and the school.

According to Gee (1996), "it is of course a great advantage when any particular secondary Discourse is compatible (in words, deeds and values) with your primary ones" (p. 142). This may be the case for individuals who have learned to see themselves as successful through the eyes of the school, but as we have seen with June (chap. 3) she had not. Therefore, investigation into the *context* where acquisition and learning occurs is important. In the Treaders' case, the Discourse of the school was their secondary Discourse. However, they interacted with it both at school and at home. At school, they learned schooled literacy but they also acquired subjectivities about themselves as not literate or proficient. Because schooled literacy and literacy from various public sphere institutions were also a large part of the Treaders' primary Discourse, as they interacted with these literacies, they also acquired a set of relationships that assumed gendered and class relationships (chaps. 3 and 4). The point here is that in learning literacy the Treaders' also acquired sets of relationships with their social worlds. As I have demonstrated, these relationships (schooled literacy/not able and family literacy/relationship to family and children) were often at odds with each other.

The second theme that is relevant to the Treaders' case is the negotiation of literacy as women's work within the context of the home. In chapter 3 I drew on Luttrell's (1997) analysis where she pointed out the strong relationship between working-class women and schooling. I demonstrated the ways in which June's literacy practices within the home were closely aligned with two societal narratives—that of the school and that of mothering. Through family literacy practices June learned that literacy is women's work and always connected to her role as a mother. This is contradictory, because even though June is less proficient with schooled literacy than her husband, it is she who managed most of the literate demands of the household. What June acquired through this set of social relationships is the concept that literacy was women's work. Second, literacy was done in conjunction with her role as a mother. That is, all of June's interactions with literacy (chaps. 3, 5, 6, and 7) were connected to her children. Third, June acquired the belief that the literacy that was a part of her life did not matter. It did not matter because it was not counted or valued by various social institutions. Indeed, following the institutional ideology, June did not define these accomplishments as literacy. They were, in a sense, invisible to her. I suggest that in these daily negotiations with language and literacy, June acquired—and embodied—two contradictory subjectivities. One was a strong relationship to schooled literacy and the other to mothering. Each of these subjectivities was evoked in different contexts.

Through apprenticeship, Vicky also acquired these sets of social relations and assumptions in her daily interactions with literacy. Thus, Gee's (1996) statements about the difference between learning and acquisition make sense in this context. As he said, "we are better at performing what we acquire, but we consciously know more about what we learn" (p. 139). What he left out of his analysis of the distinction between learning in secondary Discourse communities and acquiring in primary Discourse communities is that in the process of *learning* their secondary discourse, individuals are *acquiring* the ideological relationships and concepts of their secondary discourse.

A salient point to be taken from this is that through participation in systems of Discourse, individuals often acquire partial and split subjectivities. June's resilient use of literacy in conjunction with her role as a mother and the counterpoint of her fragile relationship to the school suggests the boundaries of these subjectivities. In this regard, this study supports Wenger's (1998) analysis of participation and negotiability in terms of discourse communities and gender:

> Indeed, learning within a community does not necessarily lead to an increased level of negotiability in a broader context. An internal reconfiguration may reflect our new identities, understandings, perspectives and skills. Yet once we have seen our own practices as located in broader economies of meanings (up against institutional definitions of ability, achievement and progress) we may come to the conclusion that the meanings we learn to produce locally have little currency in the wider scheme of things (p. 220).

That is, June acquired a set of assumptions that the literacy work of her daily life—that of family literacy practices—had little value and meaning in the eyes of social institutions. It was not recognized or valued, and furthermore both her and her daughter were seen as low literate and unable. In terms of the stronghold of ideology, these concepts were acquired rather than learned, so that they were essentially preconscious, and not readily resisted.

One of the major paradoxes in this study has been the presence and value of schooled literacy in the Treaders' home. Besides a library room, a time and place allocated for homework, and the other aspects of schooled literacy I pointed out in chapters 3 and 4, there was also the belief and value of education as a means of upward mobility. The Treaders' have internalized the ideology of the school. The "conflict" between discourse communities resides more in the fragmented subjectivities between "mothering" and "schooling" that were apparent in the literacy work June does for herself and her children. The Treaders strongly related to the values, beliefs, and actions of the school. However, through the school June and Vicky had learned that reading and literacy were individual endeavors. So, even though reading was something done by an individual, it was measured and valued by someone outside of the individual. That is, their progress was not in their own control. Through these external measures, both June and Vicky learned that they were unable and disabled within the eyes of the institution—the same institution they believed in and worked hard to achieve within. Because a salient piece of what literacy means to June is done in conjunction with her children, a slice of her literate subjectivity is centered on the demands of "mothering."

In June's desire to be what Lareau (1989) referred to as the "ideal mother" in the eyes of her children and the school, she adopted many middle-class values and stances toward literacy and her participation within the school. Though June supplemented the school curriculum at home and did not seem to be intimidated by the teachers, she was unable to resist *within* the institution of the school. As I demonstrated in chapter 5, her resistance or "talking back" to the school occurred within the domain of the home, not the school. Convinced that special-education was in Vicky's best interest, the school evoked both June's attachments to mothering and to schooling in the special education meeting presented in chapter 6. June's partial subjectivities rested in part on mothering and partly on her own past and present experiences with school. The division of June's identification with literacy allowed for the ideology of the school to be set more firmly in place. As a result, both June's and Vicky's fragile literate identities were reinforced, as I demonstrated in chapters 6 and 7. Therefore, this book has illuminated that family literacy practices are institutional and therefore ideological. Because the literacy work of the household is structured by two narratives—that of mothering and that of schooling—June and Vicky acquired problematic ideologies that did not allow them to see themselves as literate, in spite of their literate competencies.

Furthermore, the notion of subjectivities across contexts is a powerful means through which to recognize the places where parents, women, and children are likely to feel comfortable speaking back to or against institutions. For, as the Treaders' case indicates, June's speaking against the institution occurred within the context of the home, not the school. A question that must be asked is what are the sorts of institutional arrangements that would allow for her resilient voice and her literate competence?

WAYS FORWARD

The educational implications of this work are also important. This book brings to light the questionable assumptions and intentions behind current efforts aimed at children's and families' literacy "needs." Using this case, I have demonstrated that a simple lack of literacy or literate competence was not the entire reason that the Treaders' efforts were constantly thwarted by institutional discursive practices. In particular contexts, June and Vicky were proficient with literacy and language and demonstrated considerable knowledge of institutional structures and social organizations. A more equitable schooling would make space for the recognition of these literacies in the school and the classroom. Because of the power of discourse in constraining individuals' destinies, amply demonstrated in this study, a liberating education must include a reflexive awareness of discursive environments.

Along with the theoretical issues just raised, this study also illuminates practical and pedagogical challenges. The issue of subjectivities in contexts has practical implications for the lives of children and teachers in schools. As I demonstrated in this study, schools are one site where subjectivities are cultivated. As children learn literacy, they also acquire a set of relationships to their social worlds. They learn how to think about what it means to do literacy, what counts as literacy, and to whom. People like June and Vicky often learn to define themselves in problematic ways as a result of this acquisition. This hidden curriculum results in a stronghold of relations because of the common sense of the logic.

There are some practical things that teachers, as the primary agent of establishing the discursive environment of the classroom, might do to allow for the construction of productive subjectivities. First, it is important for teachers to be aware of aspects of the hidden curriculum. That is, as we teach, what is being acquired? In order to ask these questions, though, it is necessary that teachers are aware of their own subjectivities. That is, what historical, economic, and social processes have shaped their relationships to literacy and to social structures such as the school? Awareness of these influences through critical language awareness highlights the transparent nature of values attached to literacy learning.

In problematizing aspects of the hidden curriculum, children and teachers can unravel the language of instruction in order to sort out different positions for themselves. A primary concern must be how to arrange for schooling to leave less scar tissue on individuals' subjectivities. The study suggests some of the dimensions of the discourse of schooling responsible for producing the subjectivities that hold June and Vicky in place. The question is how to change the discourse of the school, particularly when it is reified in so many institutional practices.

Of importance in the present study is the continued value of the literacies and funds of knowledge children and families bring into the classroom, not only as an "add-on" but as a site of curriculum development. From these authentic and purposeful connections, teachers might listen for the connections children make between texts (whatever these texts may look like) and their social worlds. Teachers can guide children with authentic questions to theorize about these connections and why they seem natural or commonsensical. In doing this, educators can capitalize on children's sense of injustice and their "healthy skepticism" of institutions often learned within their primary Discourse. These local literacies can become a scaffold to the literacies of power. This is not to imply that educators use local literacies solely as a bridge or to replace local literacies with schooled literacy. Rather, local literacies and critical language awareness may be responsive at both a personal and a social level.

One space for continued teacher development is within the university. Within teacher education courses, a critical ethnographic lens might be constructed so that teachers and teacher educators continue to theorize about the connections between their lives and the often contradictory relations of power we find ourselves in our own institutions. A central piece of this learning and unlearning involves a conscious effort to make the familiar strange. This involves an active questioning of the acquisition of ideologies that guarantees peoples' places in the social system. Through these processes it is possible to open up more productive subjectivities in the college classroom. In doing so, universities, schools, and community agencies might work to form effective forms of dialogue across differences, across sites.

To conclude, this book has explicated how language is central in contemporary social life, and central to the struggle over meaning and power. Therefore, any ways forward must include people's increasing control over the direction of their own social circumstances. This involves, foremost, an understanding of how language figures within these changes.

A Brief History of Education in Albany

A HISTORY OF EDUCATIONAL AND CIVIL RIGHTS

Marian Hughes (1998), in her book *Refusing Ignorance: The Struggle to Educate Black Children in Albany, New York 1816–1873*, outlined the details of the historical relations between the African American community and the local school systems. This account chronicles the history of Black parents and activists, long before the abolition of slavery in the United States, and their fight for an education for their children. Parents and other Black leaders' initiatives were responsible for the creation of the first school for "children of color" in 1816, a segregated and sporadically funded school called the Wilberforce School. Hughes also documented the continuation of segregated schools lasting in Albany until 1873, when civil rights legislation, drafted and advocated for by an uneducated Black parent, deemed it unconstitutional to segregate children on the basis of color.

In 1863, after the Emancipation Proclamation, the issue of equal schooling became more of a pressing issue in the city as elsewhere around the nation. As Hughes (1998) wrote, "Black Albanians continued to press for the rights that had been granted to them on paper but had not translated into tangible improvements in their lives" (p. 63). In order to recognize these conditions, Black leaders held a public meeting on January 5, 1863, to ratify the Emancipation Proclamation, with Frederick Douglass as the guest speaker.

Black parents continued to be active in their fight for equal and safe education for their children. In 1866, the Board of Public Instruction was authorized to pay for the expenses needed to make repairs to the Wilberforce School. This funding authorization was made in response to a complaint by seven Black parents who were concerned about the unsanitary conditions of the school. The petitioners also requested that an additional teacher be assigned to the school. At the time there were 56 students in attendance daily with two teachers present, one of whom was Thomas Paul, the principal and a Black activist and educator. The board reported the following: "the building in a dirty, musty condition. . .in a rotten and dilapidated state; the privies small and in a condition too filthy to be entered for examination of the vaults. . . piles of coal ashes were found in the yard" (p. 60). Although the funding for repairs to the school was allocated, the conditions at the school were deemed a result of "neglect on part of the Principal, whose duty we deem it to keep or see that the same is kept well ventilated, and in a clean wholesome condition" (Hughes, 1998, p. 60). Paul was soon replaced. The board, however, did not supply any additional teachers, asserting that they were "unable to see the particular force" (p. 61) of the parents' arguments.

In 1873 William Henry Johnson, a barber and parent of Wilberforce students as well as head janitor at the New York State Senate, authored a draft of the state civil rights bill of 1873. This bill prohibited school officials from denying Black children entrance into public schools. Johnson had no formal education, yet became a well-known spokesperson and advocate for racial equality in New York State. From his position at the New York State Senate, Johnson lobbied the legislature with his draft of a civil rights bill. On April 9, 1873, lawmakers acted on the bill. Central to the law was the provision that Black children could not be excluded from any public school.

When the Wilberforce School closed in 1873 as a result of this legislation, many of the teachers of color were not offered positions at other public schools. In spite of the growth of professional teacher-training programs in the city of Albany, this pattern of exclusion remained until the middle of the 20th century. For instance, few Black graduates from programs such as those at the State Normal School, established in 1844 and then in 1914 designated as the New York State College for Teachers, and the Albany school district's Teachers' Training School, established in 1883, were hired by the Albany public school system. Most of these teachers were advised to seek employment in the South.

Albany has always had a rich history of parents advocating for the rights of their children to have an equitable education. These parents were not only involved in but were central to establishing legislation that ensured the desegregation of schools. However, the admission of Black children into the public schools did not ensure that Black teachers or parents were welcomed into the school. Indeed, June Treader and her family are connected to the local courage of the people in her community who came before her and who frame the long tradition of the struggle for equity in the inner city of Albany.

The history of struggle continues to the present day and is confounded by the presence of other social, economic, and political inequalities that exist in the city. As Hughes (1998) stated, "The indignation of the Black parents over the treatment of their children by the Albany public school system did not end with the building of a better schoolhouse or the appointment of an experienced principal such as Thomas Paul. Indeed, the issue of equal school rights grew more heated in Albany following the Civil War" (p. 76).

The history of oppression in Albany is not unlike its history elsewhere, intersecting around points of race, class, and gender. Indeed, it is impossible to separate the history of struggle, oppression, and triumphs and the present research from the intertwined issues of race, class, and gender. One of the ways in which people have communicated about education within the city has been through the news media. In 1842, Stephen Myers, one of Albany's most vocal Black citizens, founded two newspapers, *Northern Star* and *Freedom's Advocate*, and used these publications to tackle, among others, the issue of education. The following is from one of Myers' articles:

> The subject of education is so frequently discussed that it is almost worn threadbare; and yet the very fact that it is so discussed, [shows] it is very far from having produced all the results which philanthropy seeks to obtain.
>
> Education is indeed a prolific theme. Its mode of operation, the powers, mental and even physical, it enlarges: the moral, social and political training which it effects, are fruitful topics, and would require the pen of inspiration to do them justice.
>
> We look around us and find a distinct race of people, different in many respects from their fellows, who are degraded by condition, by habits of servitude, by poverty, and much by legislative enactments.
>
> It is not our intention at this time, to say where is outland of promise, or how our condition is to be permanently changed. It is a subject which at present is beyond our ken; but what we mean to say is, that while this state of things lasts, it is more necessary than ever that just notions of education should prevail among us. (Myers, 1842, as quoted in Hughes, 1998, p. 33)

Myers was born a slave in 1800 in Rensselaer County. As a Black advocate, his home was a station along the Underground Railroad. His wife, Hughes (1998) noted, was said to be the "skilled hand who transformed his editorials into acceptable prose for publication" (p. 33).

It has been more than 150 years since Myers wrote the preceding article yet the phrases "threadbare subject of education" and people . . . "degraded by condition, by habits of servitude, by poverty and much by legislative enactments" still resonate. This should cause a pensive halt as well as a critical interrogation of current-day conditions.

Data Collection Timetable

Data Source	Year	Domain
Fieldnotes	1996–1997	ABE classroom
	1997–1998	ABE classroom, elementary language arts classroom, and remedial reading classroom Treaders' home Community Assemblies, recognition ceremonies, graduations at the elementary school CSE meeting
	1998–1999	ABE classroom, middle school science and math classroom Treaders' home Community Assemblies, recognition ceremonies, graduations at the preschool, elementary school, and middle school
Interviews Formal Semistructured	1996–1997	ABE classroom teacher June Treader
	1997–1998	June Treader Vicky Treader Lester Treader Vicky's language arts and remedial reading Teacher Alderman Reverend President of the PTA Barber Priest Worker at Community Coalition
	1998–1999	June Treader Vicky Treader Vicky's special-education teacher Action research interviews

Data Source	Year	Domain
Reading group	1997–1998	Once a week in Treaders' home
	1998–1999	Once a week in Treaders' home
Document collection	1996–1997	ABE classroom and school Census information
	1997–1998	Treaders' home, school, and community
	1998–1999	Treaders' home, school, and community
Photographs	1997–1998	Treaders' home, school, and community
	1998–1999	Treaders' home, school, and community
Researcher journal	1996–1997 1997–1998 1998–1999	I wrote in my researcher journal following every field visit

Fieldnote Chart

Date:

Time:

LITERACY EVENTS AND ACTIVITIES	INTERACTIONS	REQUESTS FOR LITERACY	INVOLVEMENT WITH SCHOOL

Document Summary Form

- Name or description of the document
- Where the document was located
- Date received
- Institution to which the document is connected
- Brief summary of the contents
- What issues or themes arise from the document?
- What do I need to follow up on?

Chart of Critical Discourse Analysis Definitions and Codes

QUESTIONS TO ASK IN EACH (AND ACROSS) DOMAIN OF ANALYSIS

Fairclough (1992a) suggested selecting "cruces" or moments of crisis in the data as an entry point into the analysis. These are moments in the discourse when it is evident something is going wrong. Fairclough wrote, "such moments of crisis make visible aspects of practices which might normally be naturalized, and therefore difficult to notice; but they also show change in process, the actual ways in which people deal with the problematization of practices" (p. 230).

I. Genres/Textual

Ways of interacting
   The object of this domain of analysis is to describe the organizational properties of interactions. What are the ways of interacting that comprise the genre?

Microlinguistic analysis:
   What are the microlinguistic aspects of this text?

Analysis in this domain includes:
   Thematic structure of the text
   Information focus
   Cohesion devices (parallel structure, repetition)
   Wording
   Metaphors
   Turn taking

II. Discourses/Interpersonal:

Ways of representing
   The object of this domain is to describe how knowledge is represented and from what perspective. What are the processes by which the text is

produced, consumed, and distributed? How is meaning made in the text? What links are made to other texts?

Production:
> Who are the author(s) of the text? What voices are represented?
> Manifest intertextuality and interdiscursivity ("smooth" and "bumpy" intertextuality)
> What is the intended message?
> Does the text draw on more than one genre? If so, what are they?
> Are there discernable stages of production?
> Is the text produced individually or collectively?

Distribution:
> Specify the distribution of a type of discourse by showing the intertextual chains it enters into.
> Are there signs that the text produced anticipates more than one type of audience?

Consumption:
> What are the possible interpretations of this text?
> Who are the possible audiences?
> What resistant readings are possible?

III. Style/Ideational:

Ways of being
The purpose of this domain of analysis is to specify the social structures and processes and how people are drawn into such processes. This domain includes: systems of knowledge and belief; social relations; and social identities. The analyst may ask:

> What are the sociohistorical relations governing these processes? Are the intertextual chains stable or are they shifting and contested?

Analysis in this domain includes:
- Pronouns
- Active and passive voice
- Politeness conventions
- Modality (tense, affinity); Often associated with modal verbs (*must, may, can, should*) and adverbs (*probably, possibly*)
- Transitivity—Transitivity is a property of language that enables humans to build a mental picture of reality, to make sense of their world and the "goings on" of doing, happening, feeling, and believing. These goings on are sorted out in the semantic system of language, and expressed through the grammar of the clause. The reflective, experien-

tial aspects of meaning is the system of transivity. Transivity specifies the different types of processes that are recognized in the language and the structures by which they are expressed.

- Action

  Action with dialogue
  Action passive
  Action active
  Physical or cognitive action (*or* lack of action)
  Modal construction

- Affective—statement of want, desire, like, or need (deficit affective)
- State—statement of physical or mental being

  had

- Ability—internal characteristic of something he can or cannot do

  (lack of ability)
  Have, got, am, get

- Cognitive—think, thought, believe, remember statements

(See Gee, 1999, appendix; Fairclough, 1992a, chapter 8; and Halliday & Hasan, 1989.)

Snapshot of Vicky's Remedial Reading Lesson

1/20/98 Observation Remedial Reading
9:45–10:45 a.m.

Remedial reading time started with decoding practice and then students took their individual lesson plans and worked from workbooks. They were not allowed to move to the next section until they got a certain number right from the workbook. The reading teacher stated that they would read books as a group when they had time. The following transcript shows how the books were introduced and vocabulary words discussed. The books were introduced through vocabulary words similar to the event recounted in the following dialogue. Here, the teacher is flashing vocabulary cards at the students from the story *To the Top!*

T:	Very quickly, let's do it. Let's do it. Come on, come on, try it.
ST1:	Oxygen
Vicky:	Oxygen tanks
ST1:	Meshner
T:	No mesh. Not mesh. Look at this. What's this?
Vicky:	Mess
T:	No. What's this?
Vicky:	Mess
T:	Mess. Spell ess. Spell ess.
Vicky:	e-s-s
T:	That's right. Spell mess.
Vicky:	M-e-s-s
T:	Yulp. Spell ner.
ST2:	n-e-r
T:	What's his name?
Vicky:	Reinhold Messner.
T:	How many parts in Mesner?

Vicky:	Two
ST2:	= two
T:	Two. Look at it. Say Messner.
ST2:	Messner
T:	Perfect. Say it again but don't say mess.
ST2:	Ner.
T:	Spell it.
ST2:	n-e-r
T:	Say Messner
Vicky:	Messner.
Vicky:	Mess
T:	Spell mess.
Vicky:	M-e-s-s

Before the class read a book together, each student worked from their individualized folder. In the folders, each student had a workbook that the reading teacher had determined was on an appropriate level for them determined by the amount of errors they made. An example of one of the workbooks in Vicky's folder is *Discovering Science Through Cloze*. Each cloze section opened with a model paragraph followed by practice paragraphs wherein the student would fill in the blanks. If there was time the students would read together, aloud, as a group.

Committee on Special Education Meeting Transcript

1	DT:	And June,
2		Vicky's mom,
3		is here with us today.
4		The purpose of our meeting, um
5		we have received
6		your referral
7		and there were concerns
8		about Vicky's classroom, um,
9		well actually
10		the classroom
11		and the remedial reading teacher
12		are concerned about her achievement
13		in reading and in math
14		and also her weak speech and language skills.
15		Upon receiving the referral,
16		we asked our school psychologist
17		to do complete evaluation,
18		observations
19		and also,
20		our speech and language therapist
21		to do some testing.
22		So I'm going to start with [the psychologist]
23		to review her evaluation
24		and then [speech therapist],
25		if you don't mind,
26		and anyone can feel free to jump in at any time
27		if you have questions.
28	AB:	Okay, um,
29		In looking over Vicky's school records
30		I know she attended Sherman Hollows school
31		for Pre K through third grade
32		and she had received remedial reading help
33		while she was in [name of community].
34		Looking at her report cards
35		her teachers were indicating
36		that she was having difficulty

37	with the work.
38	Um, she then transferred to [school]
39	and she had remedial reading
40	and math
41	during the fourth and fifth grade.
42	When you look at her group achievement tests
43	over the years
44	they have been consistently low in reading.
45	Um, her attendance has been good.
46	This year she is in sixth grade
47	and getting remedial reading
48	and math
49	and also receiving private tutorial instruction.
50	Um, Vicky's classroom teacher
51	and remedial reading teacher,
52	who I believe is on her way now,
53	have reported that her reading skills are very low
54	and this affects her progress in all levels academically.
55	The only health issue is that she wears glasses.
56	She is near-sighted
57	but generally doesn't wear glasses in school,
58	I should say.
59	Um, when I went into the classroom
60	to observe Vicky I could see
61	that she required a great deal of support
62	from her teacher
63	and from other students in the room.
64	She was often asking questions
65	about how to do the assignment,
66	often raising her hand to get some assistance,
67	very willing to ask for help
68	when she needed it.
69	In testing with me,
70	Vicky was very attentive,
71	she usually persisted when the work was difficult for her,
72	she oftentimes needed a great,
73	an extended period of time to process information
74	and I could see in relating to her
75	that her verbal skills were very weak.
76	She often had difficulty understanding directions,
77	she would often ask for clarification
78	when I would give her a direction.
79	Um, Vicky's performance on the intelligence test
80	is within in the well-below-average range
81	compared to other children her age.
82	Um, she's demonstrating significant deficits
83	in her verbal

84		and her nonverbal,
85		excuse me (clears throat),
86		her nonverbal reasoning ability
87		When a lot of interpretation is required,
88		I think the difficulty
89		that she has
90		with her language development
91		really interfere
92		with her performance.
93		Um, she displays adaptive skills
94		with the average range
95		and her visual-motor skills
96		are scored below average.
97	Liaison:	Were her glasses worn for the visual-motor testing?
98	AB:	She's near-sighted
99		and no,
100		she reads fine,
101		she was fine on all of the perceptual tests
102		without them.
103		I think at this point in time,
104		they are broken are lost,
105		I don't know where they are,
106		her glasses. ///
107		Her academic skills
108		scored very strong
109		in math computation.
110		When you give her some math problems to do
111		and she is not required to interpret any language
112		um she scored high average
113		at about a high-eighth-grade level.
114		Um, she's is able to multiply and divide fractions
115		so that is a real strength for her.
116		However, when she works on word problems
117		or applied math
118		her skills are significantly lower
119		and are, um, in the below average range.
120		She has difficulty understanding
121		and interpreting the language
122		that is used in word problems.
123		In spelling
124		she scored low average
125		and similar to a late-year fourth-grade level.
126		However, her word-decoding skills
127		scored at a second-grade level
128		and are considered below average
129		for her grade.
130		Um, I think when she is decoding words

131		she oftentimes will look at the first letter or so
132		and guess the word.
133		Whereas when she is spelling
134		she is forced to kind of give a more
135		thorough analysis of the word
136		and so she tends to do better.
137		Her reading comprehension is below average, um
138		around a beginning-third-grade level.
139		And I think difficulties
140		with language comprehension
141		are interfering with her reading comprehension
142		as well as difficulties with decoding.
143		Vicky received a below-average rating
144		on a writing sample
145		that was taken during the testing.
146		She has excellent penmanship
147		and is able to communicate ideas in writing.
148		However, she doesn't elaborate
149		and doesn't use the vocabulary
150		that you would expect of a child her age.
151		And again that is tied to the weaknesses
152		in her language development.
153		Um, when Vicky's mom and I met the other day
154		with [reading teacher] at [school],
155		we talked about Vicky entering the seventh grade next year
156		and that she would need some pretty intensive support
157		given that her decoding skills are at a second-grade level
158		in order to make progress
159		in areas like social studies
160		and science
161		where she is going to be reading textbooks
162		and where she is going to have to be interpreting information
163		and do writing assignments
164		and doing things of that nature.
165		I feel that her strong performance in math
166		lends itself to her
167		being in a mainstream situation
168		for mathematics.
169		In most other areas I feel she will need some really intensive
170		support.
171	Liaison:	[name] do you have an overall math grade equivalent from the
172		testing?
173	AB:	
174		[No because the scores were so disparate.
175		It would just be an average.
176		It wouldn't really make sense.
177	Liaison:	[Okay. Right.

178		[Okay.
179	AB:	Again
180		it is the language that interferes.
181		And she is doing interpretation,
182		if she is doing word problems,
183		she will need someone to help her interpret.
184		And I think [speech therapist],
185		that you had pretty similar test results.
186	SS:	Yes, I did.
187		I gave Vicky three different tests.
188		The first test was understanding the words that she hears.
189		It is just a one-word test of receptive vocabulary.
190		She had a lot of difficulty
191		just even understanding vocabulary.
192		Um, then I gave her a test
193		that tested both her
194		understanding of language
195		and then her use of language.
196		Her receptive
197		and her expressive language skills.
198		And she did have some difficulty
199		understanding
200		and processing some information
201		but even her expressive skills
202		were even lower.
203		She has,
204		she uses,
205		I mean she can communicate.
206		Very well.
207		It's not that she can't communicate with people.
208		It's just that she's not using
209		the types of sentences
210		that she should
211		and the vocabulary
212		that she should
213		for a child of her age.
214		So she really has,
215		you know,
216		a deficit in her language skills
217		which is affecting her academic performance
218		in math
219		and in reading. Um,
220	Liaison:	[speech name] do you
221		have some of those test scores?
222	AB:	Oh, right here. (Passes the test to her)
223	Liaison:	Sorry (inaud)
224	SS:	That's okay,

225		that's okay.
226		One of the tests that I gave her /
227		was because I wanted to see
228		how she more specifically dealt
229		with her expressive language
230		was called the word test
231		and that deals with synonyms
232		and you give them
233		a silly sentence
234		and you have to fix it,
235		and opposites
236		and word definitions
237		and multiple meanings.
238		And she really had a difficult time
239		with those skills.
240		Um, and again it was her ability to interpret
241		these types of things
242		because first you have to understand it
243		and then you have to answer.
244		Anyway, so, overall language,
245		I think her delay in language
246		is really affecting her academic skills.
247		She really needs some help
248		in the language area.
249	Becky:	Can I ask a question?
250	DT:	Sure.
251	Becky:	When you said,
252		um, that she was at the second grade in decoding,
253		what is that based on?
254		Is that consistent
255		with her remedial reading reports
256		as well?
257	AB:	It is consistent
258		with what her reading teacher
259		is seeing as well.
260		Um, that's based on the test that I gave her,
261		the standardized test that I gave her.
262		That is the grade-equivalent score
263		that came off of that test
264		and she was required to just decode words
265		in isolation on that test.
266		Um, and that is where
267		that grade equivalent came off of.
268		That's basically
269		where her classroom teachers
270		are indicating that she is functioning.
271		Mrs. Matthews was going to be coming.

272		Let me look at this referral form
273		she may have a grade listed on here. . .(looking through the
274		papers///). Yeah there is. . .
275	SS:	[On the first
276		page, the CSE referral, oh wait, no,
277	AB:	Well reading at about
278		a fourth-grade level
279		with assistance, and um, (pause///).
280		She has some Grade 2 materials
281		that she is still making errors on.
282		So I think, um
283		with the support in the classroom
284		that she receives she is able to read
285		at a somewhat higher level
286		but this is independent
287		without no support whatsoever,
288		I am not allowed to help her at all
289		with the testing.
290		This is where her decoding scores
291		are falling.
292		Um, and again
293		her comprehension is slightly higher
294		so she may be able to understand
295		third-grade-level material.
296	Becky:	The reason I ask
297		is that when I work with her
298		throughout the year
299		she has been reading
300		between a third- and a fourth-grade level
301		when she is reading authentic books.
302		I'm not sure how her decoding is isolation
303		because I don't do that
304		with her.
305	AB:	The test,
306		the test
307		is going to give
308		somewhat different results
309		again
310		because you are not allowed to assist,
311		it is not a teaching situation.
312		It's basically
313		she is asked to perform
314		and that's it.
315		And that is where her skills topped out.
316		And grade-equivalent scores
317		are not the most reliable scores
318		that are used.

319		If you look at the standard scores,
320		those are the scores
321		that are going to really tell you
322		where she really functions
323		compared to other children her age
324		and that is within
325		the below-average range.
326		There is a significant deficit there.
327	DT:	Do you want to share any information,
328		I know that you have been working
329		with her on a regular basis
330		and that would be helpful.
331		If you would like to share any. . .
332	Becky:	Well I actually have a report here
333		that I wanted to submit to, um,
334		I talked to Mrs. Matthews [reading teacher]
335		and she said
336		that it would probably
337		go to her teacher next year
338		and I've given a copy to June
339		and I just thought that if it,
340		the reading teacher
341		or whoever she was with
342		has as much information
343		as possible it would be helpful.
344	DT:	Sure.
345	Becky:	But some of the strong points
346		that I've noticed working with Vicky,
347		I've worked with her since September
348		until currently
349		and she has increased
350		a grade level
351		in her reading.
352		She is reading
353		around a fourth-grade-level text.
354		That is based on running records
355		and an ongoing assessment
356		of what she has been doing.
357		The records show
358		that Vicky's exhibiting a lot more,
359		self-monitoring behaviors,
360		she's checking her meaning
361		more and more,
362		reading for meaning,
363		especially in books that she likes
364		and can connect to
365		like Rosa Parks

366		and Maya Angelou.
367		Vicky has more and more
368		self-corrections, um,
369		not just based on initial visual cues.
370		She is doing a more
371		thorough analysis of the entire word.
372		She has better retellings
373		of the stories,
374		and again
375		these are books
376		like *The Box Car Children*
377		a biography of *Rosa Parks*
378		and um, things like that,
379		that are not cloze passages
380		but reading from authentic books.
381		But I have noticed
382		a lot of improvement
383		and more risk taking in her reading
384		and also another strong
385	DT:	[Uh hm, Uh hm
386	Becky:	point is in her writing.
387		She seems to really likes to write.
388		And I have gotten
389		a lot of really long writing samples from her.
390		Um, so that can be used
391		a lot in connection with her reading.
392	AB:	She is proud of her penmanship.
393	Becky:	Yeah.
394	DT:	When you mention writing,
395		she uses proper capitalization,
396		punctuation, grammar,
397		things like that?
398	Becky:	She has a lot of conventions
399		and she has quite good expression.
400		I've included two writing samples
401		in this case study.
402		Um, one from the beginning of the year
403		which is fairly short
404		and I point out the conventions
405		she has and then
406		toward the end of the year
407		that is much longer
408		and a lot of conventions
409		as far as capitalization,
410		of proper, proper nouns
411		and things like that
412		but also the expression

413		and the language
414		which was pretty impressive compared
415		to the beginning of the year.
416		So I've seen her make some real progress.
417	DT:	Will she be continuing with you through the summer?
418	Becky:	Yup, yup.
419		
420	AB:	How about next year also?
421	Becky:	Yup.
422	DT:	I think when we look at our in-district programs
423		we always start at the least restrictive
424		which would be a resource room for support
425		but with her um,
426		reading being almost
427		3 years below grade level,
428		I think at this point
429		almost a smaller classroom setting
430		would be appropriate for her,
431		but we would encourage
432		that she would be mainstreamed
433		for the math
434		because that definitely her strength.
435		So we could develop
436		a program where she would,
437		um have 15 students
438		in a class with a teacher
439		and a teacher's assistant
440		doing most of the academics
441		but her schedule will allowed
442		her to be mainstreamed for the math.
443	AB:	And we discussed that, Mrs. Treader,
444		when you
445		and I met
446		and talked about having
447		Vicky receive
448		a lot of support
449		for most of the day
450		and then be able
451		to go out
452		and do math within a larger classroom.
453		And you have had time to think about that.
454		What are your thoughts?
455	June:	(Pause////) If she have to go into it,
456		she can go into it.
457		Into special ed.
458	DT:	And what we can do
459		is closely monitor her progress

460		and every year
461		you would be invited into a meeting and um,
462		do new testing
463		is her reading level
464		has come up,
465		if you know,
466		if she continue to make nice increases
467		like she has with you this year,
468		here is always the opportunity
469		for more mainstreaming.
470		And she would actually be mainstreamed
471		for art, music, gym
472		and library and computers
473		and all of those subjects and the math.
474		Also it would be basically
475		social studies,
476		science,
477		and English that she would have a smaller setting.
478		And they would modify the curriculum.
479		they would do seventh-grade curriculum
480		but they would modify
481		the work to her level.
482	Becky:	How do they modify it,
483		what do they do?
484	Liaison:	Oftentimes
485		they will use a different text,
486		a test,
487		some of the publishers
488		that we have used have been Steck Vaughn,
489		high interest
490		and um, and um,
491		the concepts are seventh-grade concepts
492		but the readability
493		might be at a lower level.
494		And I don't know specifically
495		what that teacher
496		may have ordered
497		but generally
498		we use those type of publishers
499		and as I said the readability
500		of the material tends
501		to be at a third- or fourth-grade level
502		but the concepts taught
503		are at a seventh-grade level.
504		They modify them.
505	DT:	And as far as the homework assignments,
506		instead of if she was in a regular seventh-grade

507		social studies classroom
508		they may have her read a whole chapter,
509		whereas in this classroom
510		they may read it aloud to her
511		or they have her read one page
512		and then they read the next page
513		so they would make modifications
514		throughout the day on her lessons.
515	Becky:	What are the possibilities,
516		June and I talked about having her
517		in a resource room
518		to begin with
519		and then reevaluating her after 6 months
520		and see if she would need to go into a basic-skills classroom?
521		What do you think about that?
522	AB:	Um, I think that the deficits
523		that we see right now
524		that it makes sense
525		to have her start right away
526		with the intensive support
527		as soon as possible.
528		Um, [reading teacher] has been working
529		with her pretty intensely
530		and you have as well
531		and looking at her testing right now
532		she still has this significant deficit.
533		Um, I think that it would be unrealistic
534		to think in the next 2 months
535		over the summer time
536		that she's going to make up enough progress
537		to be able to function um,
538		well, and I don't want her
539		to suffer any of the consequences
540		of poor self-esteem
541		and all of the other thing
542		that happen when you are real frustrated.
543		It is going to be a new environment for her,
544		with a lot of new things going on,
545		a lot of new expectations for her.
546		Um and I think it would be extremely difficult
547		for her with just resource room. //
548		I would guess,
549		I guess I would flip flop
550		that and say let's start
551		with the more intensive
552		and get her where she needs to be
553		and then lessen the services

554		to the resource room.
555	Liaison:	[I'll say this too.
556		Resource room in the middle school level
557		is different than the resource room
558		at the elementary school.
559		It tends to be more of a support program
560		not a direct instructional program
561		so the time is used
562		to help the kids complete the academics
563		in the regular-ed classroom
564		and it doesn't take place
565		on a daily basis
566		because of the rotating schedules
567		at the middle school.
568		It would be like every other day support.
569		And given what we're hearing
570		at the table with her needs,
571		I'm not too sure that
572		that would give her enough support
573		on a consistent basis
574		to be successful
575		in those regular classes.
576	Becky:	Is there any remedial reading programs
577		at the middle school level
578		that she can get additional reading instruction?
579	DT:	What they do at [middle school] is, um,
580		about 2 years ago
581		they changed their scheduling
582		so they work on what is called a block schedule
583		and um, like [name of school]
584		or a regular school
585		that doesn't have a block schedule system,
586		you normally go to school
587		and have first-period English,
588		second-period math,
589		third-period gym
590		and it's that way every day.
591		[name of school] rotates
592		and first period on Monday may be English,
593		you may not get English again until Wednesday sixth period.
594		And they are 59-minute periods.
595		Within her schedule that allows students
596		more opportunities
597		for different types of classes.
598		They have electives.
599		So remedial reading
600		or reading component

601		can be one component
602		that can be put into her schedule
603		when she works with the guidance counselor
604		and develops her schedule.
605	Becky:	So they do have a remedial reading program?
606	DT:	I think it's called reading lab
607		or you know
608		and I think all of the students get that.
609	Liaison:	So [name of chair], it's 59,
610		every period is like 59-minute period.
611	DT:	Yes.
612	Liaison:	OK, I didn't realize that.
613	DT:	And you recommend speech?
614	SS:	Yeah I recommended speech.
615	DT:	Why don't we say two times per week for speech
616	SS:	Yeah because I had put the 40 thinking of [school], I don't
617		know.
618	DT:	Yeah.
619	June:	Where you work at?
620	SS:	I'm at [name of school]
621		but I used to be at [name of school]
622		and [name of school]
623		I'm at [name of school] this year.
624		And I was thinking
625		of their 40-minute slot two times,
626	DT:	I don't know how the therapist over there does it,
627		if they take them for part of their regular class,
628		why don't we,
629		we normally do 30 minutes
630		of speech,
631		why don't we do that
632		and if it takes longer that is fine.
633	SS:	Yeah.
634	Liaison:	In the math, um, mainstreaming,
635		how long is the period of math,
636		would you say 59 minutes?
637	DT:	I believe they are 59-minute periods.
638		You have to say how long?
639	Liaison:	Yeah we do.
640		I'm going to put one times 45 per day
641		and if it is longer. . .
642	DT:	It's every other day though because it's longer.
643		Oh, I see what you're doing.
644		The subjects are every other day
645		instead of every day
646		at the same time.
647		The subjects,

648		that way they can get more subjects in
649		and they have more time instead of 42 minutes
650		and the bell rings,
651		they have more time
652		for teachers
653		to really expand on their lessons.
654	Becky:	Is the reading instruction component
655		separate than the English
656		or the language arts?
657	DT:	Yes.
658	Becky:	It is.
659		So can that be written in too
660		that she should be getting the extra reading instruction?
661	Liaison:	That wouldn't be a special-ed program
662		and our responsibility
663		in developing a program
664		is to recommend the special-ed component of it.
665	DT:	That
666		wouldn't be done by a special-education teacher.
667		That would have to be scheduled
668		by her guidance counselor.
669	Becky:	But she can get that?
670	DT:	I believe all the students
671		at [middle school] get it.
672		I'm almost sure that the majority of them do.
673		It's right in their schedule.
674	Becky:	But it's not remedial reading.
675		Right? Like, right now
676		she sees [reading teacher] sees twice or three tines a week.
677	DT:	It's the middle school's version of remedial reading.
678		It's the middle school's version.
679		They work it right into their schedule.
680		Where she is probably pulled out of something
681		to go to remedial,
682		they try to work right into their daily schedules.
683	SS:	And then with her speech and language therapy
684		she would be working on a lot of vocabulary and grammar,
685		and you know,
686		the things that would help her
687		with reading and writing.
688		You know it isn't her speech per se,
689		it is her language skills.
690		So following directions,
691		working on,
692		in fact,
693		most of the time we just incorporate
694		whatever vocabulary she has for whatever subject area,

695		you know to reinforce that
696		so it's another support
697		and reinforcement for everything
698		that she is doing throughout the day.
699	Liaison:	I would like to recommend to the committee
700		that we, um,
701		exempt her from foreign language
702		given the difficulties
703		with language and regular English.
704	SS:	Yes.
705		Liaison:
		It wouldn't make sense
706		to necessarily to have her struggle
707		with a foreign language.
708	DT:	Every student at the middle school
709		takes French or Spanish.
710		So, are you, unless that is something
711		that you feel like she may enjoy,
712		we, you know.
713	June:	For what?
714	DT:	For her to take a foreign language.
715		Every student in middle school
716		when she makes out her schedule
717		they take Spanish or French.
718	June:	[She can
719		take it.
720	DT:	You want her to take it?
721		June nods her head.
722	Liaison:	You know,
723		I would just throw out,
724		I mean she certainly can,
725		she has every right to take it,
726		but as, um as a special education teacher
727		and given her difficulties
728		with English language,
729		understanding and expressive language,
730		um, it might be difficult
731		for her to also try to approach a foreign language.
732		But she certainly has a right to it,
733		but I would recommend exemption.
734	DT:	But just to play devil's advocate,
735		um, a lot of students
736		who are nonreaders
737		sometimes do well with a foreign-language
738		so why don't we see how she does
739		with it and in the event

740		that she is really frustrated,
741		you will know.
742		You know, let us know that Spanish
743		is really over her head
744		and she can't keep up,
745		she keeps getting frustrated
746		and she would rather have that time
747		to work and build her basic skills,
748		then we can exempt her from it.
749		If you want to have her give it a shot,
750		if you think it is something
751		that she really likes
752		and enjoys.
753	Becky:	Can I ask another question?
754	DT:	Sure.
755	Becky:	Will she be receiving credit for regular education
756		or for special education?
757	DT:	She will be receiving credit
758		for regular education
759		at this point.
760		We are still going to put down
761		that she is working
762		toward a local diploma.
763	Becky:	Does she need a foreign-language requirement for that
764		diploma?
765	Liaison:	A student who is identified as special needs,
766		a special-education student,
767		can have that foreign-language requirement waived.
768		She wouldn't get a regular diploma.
769		It is within the regulations
770		that we can exempt her from that.
771	DT:	And that can be done anytime,
772		you know,
773		well be meeting on a regular basis
774		now so you know,
775		she does a year
776		of it and it feels you know
777		that it wasn't really successful experience
778		for her we can exempt her in the years to come.
779	Liaison:	Do they take the language for the entire year or for half the
780		year?
781	SS:	At [middle school] they used to do half a year
782		for the language
783		and half for computers,
784		something, I don't remember.
785	Spec ed:	I think you may right. I think it is half a year.
786	SS:	I now she takes Spanish at [elementary school].

787	DT:	She does take it now?
788	SS:	Yeah they have Spanish there,
789		but I don't know,
790		you see because I don't work
791		with her I just do the evaluation
792		so I'm not really sure.
793	DT:	Does she like the Spanish?
794	June:	I don't know.
795	DT:	Yeah, okay.
796		Are you comfortable
797		with the smaller classroom setting to start,
798		with mainstreaming for math,
799		it's basically
800		during those three academic periods,
801		like I said, science, social studies
802		and English that she would have the smaller class setting
803		with modified instruction.
804		And we would also add
805		some testing modification on to her IEP.
806		She needs extra time to take her test,
807		or if she needs questions read to her,
808		or directions read,
809		we can add those modifications,
810		so she can be
811		more successful in the program.///
812	Becky:	For the, what, it is the social studies, science?
813	DT:	English.
814	Becky:	And, that's it.
815	SS:	Mainstreamed for math.
816	DT:	Anything that involves a lot of reading,
817		we would look at
818		having her in the smaller setting.
819	Becky:	Do you know
820		what the language arts
821		or the English class looks like
822		and what books
823		she will be reading?
824	DT:	I'm. . .
825	Liaison:	I'm not sure
826	DT:	Yeah.
827	DT:	You know you're welcome to talk to the staff at [middle
828		school]
829		and you know
830	June:	Who is her teacher goin' to be for next year?
831	Liaison:	We have two teachers that team teach this program
832		and I'm not sure how this is going to work next year
833		but Mr. E [name] and Mr. B [name]

834		have been teaching this program.
835		One does the social studies and math,
836		and I believe
837		and the other does the science and English
838		so they, you know,
839		she will still change classes
840		even among that program.
841		Um, in order to provide the program
842		we need to identify
843		her with a disabling condition
844		and um, [psychologist]
845	June:	A what? [to special education liaison]
846	DT:	Pardon me? [to June]
847	AB:	[We talked [to June]
848		at the parent conference
849		about identifying, um,
850		identifying Vicky with a educational handicap
851		in order for her to get program?
852		And I discussed both speech impaired [to committee]
853		and multiply disabled with,
854		um, Vicky's mom.
855		In my opinion,
856		multiply disabled
857		is a more accurate term.
858		It describes her difficulties
859		with visual motor,
860		with speech
861		and language,
862		with cognitive reasoning
863		and with academics.
864		And um, I think it would lend itself
865		to provide her with the more extensive services
866		that we're looking at.
867		We're not looking at
868		just giving her speech
869		and language therapy
870		although that is one of her deficits.
871		Um, so that would be my recommendation.
872	Becky:	How is that different than learning disabled?
873	AB:	A learning disabled child
874		would generally have average cognitive skills,
875		whereas Vicky is functioning well-below average
876		in her IQ score.
877		A learning disabled child
878		would have average IQ
879		and below-average achievement
880		and that is not the profile

881		that we are seeing here.
882		We are seeing multiple disabilities.
883	DT:	////If you're interested, um,
884		in this program,
885		I can have you sign permission today
886		and I can go ahead
887		and put her on the class list
888		so she'll be all set for September,
889		if you need time to think about it,
890		I certainly understand that,
891		and you would receive a whole packet
892		in the mail probably
893		in about 3 weeks
894		with what is called an IEP,
895		Individual Education Program,
896		and on that IEP will have her specific goals
897		in social studies,
898		science,
899		and in English areas
900		as well as in speech
901		and language goals.
902		It will have a permission slip
903		for you to sign
904		and get back to us
905		and it will have your due-process rights
906		as a parent.
907		Because without your written permission,
908		we cannot provide this program.
909		I can, I hand wrote out a permission
910		if you would like to sign it today,
911		and then I can put her right on a class list.
912		That's up to you. [brings paper over to June]
913	DT:	[stands over June; paper is on table] Basically
914		all this says is
915		that we're going to identify her as multiply disabled,
916		realizing that she has learning needs
917		and speech needs,
918		recommending a smaller class
919		and mainstreaming for math.
920		And these are your due-process rights.
921		Without your signed permission,
922		we can't provide the program.
923		///
924	Becky:	Can she get a copy of all the referrals
925		and all the forms
926		and recommendations?
927	DT:	She will get a copy of the IEP

928		in the mail, um,
929		it will detail
930		what we have detailed
931		what we discussed
932		at this meeting
933		what the recommendations are
934		and it's the goals
935		and objectives
936		for the program
937		for next year.
938		And that should be
939		within a month,
940		month and half.
941		We'll be able to send it out.
942	AB:	And she does have the psych report.
943		SS And I just gave her speech, a copy of the speech report.
944	DT:	Okay?
945	Becky:	I have one other question
946		if you don't mind,
947		just as far as the reading instruction
948		just because that is what I am most concerned about,
949		what should we do to find out what kind of,
950		how she can get that remedial reading instruction
951		for next year.
952	DT:	What I would do is talk to her guidance counselor.
953		I don't know who she will have.
954		[names of two guidance counselors]
955		at [school].
956		Right in the beginning of the year
957		if not sooner,
958		I believe they are even working
959		the last two weeks in August,
960		you can call [name of middle school]
961		and that you would like to talk to, explain that she will be in the 15:1 program,
962		with Mr. E [name] and Mr. B [name]
963		and that you would like to talk
964		to the remedial reading teacher,
965		and I think that is a great idea
966		so you can do a lot of consistency
967		and carry over among the two programs.
968		And also you it's good for you to talk
972		to the two teachers.
973		But [guidance counselor] would know
974		who her guidance counselor would be
975		at the end of August
976		and um, make sure that is put right into her schedule.

977		I think that would be very helpful for her.
978		Do you want the number at [school]?
979		Do you have it?
980	Becky:	Um, yeah that would be great. [gets up and gets the number]
981	Becky:	(To June) Is that the teacher's name?
982	June:	I don't know. [looking at papers]
983	SS:	You went over there?
984	DT:	And the guidance department is [number]
985	Becky:	(To speech therapist) We visited one of the resource rooms.
986		We met two of the teachers
987		who teach resource room.
988	DT:	These will be different.
989		They do, I mean I was in on it at [name of middle school]
990		but the way it works
991		out at the middle school program
992		is really nice.
993		he kids are just blended in with everybody,
994		you know,
995		or the entire day.
996	Becky:	What is the model called, it's not. . .
997	AB:	It's a 15:1
998	Becky:	That's what it is called
999	DT:	Any more questions?
1000	Becky:	June had mentioned to me
1001		that when she spoke with you
1002		and [reading teacher]
1003		at the school
1004		that you had said
1005		that there might be a way
1006		to assess if this program
1007		is the right decision for Vicky
1008		before the end of the year
1009		to see how she is doing.
1010	AB:	Before the next school year?
1011	Becky:	Before the end of the next school year.
1012	AB:	There will be an annual review every year
1013		in which her program will be reviewed
1014		and we will discuss
1015		whether or not
1016		the program that we decided was successful.
1017		If not
1018		what do we need to change about it
1019		and that will happen every year.
1020		She'll have a triennial evaluation
1021		which is a more thorough evaluation
1022		which involves the psychologist,
1023		the special-education teachers,

1024		um, every 3 years
1025		so it would be 3 years from today,
1026		3 years from the evaluation that I just did.
1027		That she would have a thorough assessment.
1028	Becky:	Is it possible to get an evaluation done before the annual
1029		review?
1030	DT:	They would do achievement testing.
1031	AB:	They are going to do achievement testing
1032		every year
1033		as part of the annual review process.
1034		She is not going to be given
1035		an IQ test every year.
1036		That wouldn't be a valid thing to do anyway.
1037	DT:	So they'll be measuring,
1038		I think usually the test that they use
1039		is the Woodcock Johnson achievement test
1040		and they would be doing spring testing
1041		every year to show growth
1042		so it is really a benchmark for us too
1043		in terms of whether or not
1044		the program has been effective.
1045	June:	Stop, Shauna.
1046	SS:	Yeah the annual reviews start anywhere from
1047		what, January from May.
1048	Liaison:	January through May, or April anyway.
1049	DT:	If you want to review progress
1050		in this program
1051		you can certainly make have a parent conference
1052		with those teachers anytime
1053		throughout the year though.
1054		You just have to contact them.
1055		Yes. And if you need to come back
1056		to the committee we remain available,
1057		all you need to do is call
1058		and request a full CSE meeting
1059		or a subcommittee meeting
1060		that would take place right at the school.
1061	Becky:	Okay.
1062	DT:	June, all right? [gives June the *Parent's Guide to Special*
1063		*Education*]
1064	June:	I got that already.
1065	DT:	You do, okay.
1066		Um, there should be an updated version
1067		coming out because they do have
1068		a new IDEA that was recently,
1069		it was a year now,
1070		reauthorized,

1071		I keep on saying new,
1072		for the next 5 years.
1073		So they will be updating that.
1074		But that will give you a little more information
1075		to how the process will proceed.
1076	Becky:	And what,
1077		as far as the objectives on the IEP,
1078		how will they specify,
1079		what will they say.
1080		What we've gone over today
1081		or how will the goals be met for her IEP?
1082	DT:	Well speech,
1083	SS:	I already did mine,
1084		I couldn't tell you exactly
1085		what they were.
1086	DT:	There will be goals
1087		and objective met
1088		and one of them
1089		will probably be in terms of the English class
1090		to improve reading skills
1091		to improve written language skills.
1092		No there won't be math goals
1093		because she is not
1094		going to get service for math.
1095		There will be science goals
1096		and social studies goals on there.
1097		And they will get what benchmarks
1098		and what objectives we want her to meet.
1099	Becky:	And what is the goal
1100		in terms of the reading and language arts?
1101		Is it to get her on a grade level,
1102		is it to get her to grade level.
1103	DT:	No it would be um,
1104		looking at increasing
1105		her fundamental reading skills.
1106		Increasing her sight word vocabulary,
1107		um, in terms of English,
1108		increasing grammatical usage,
1109		increasing comprehension,
1110		developing strategies for comprehension,
1111		increasing the ability to make inferences
1112		to make written material,
1113		increase sentence meaning.
1114	AB:	Comprehension.
1115	Becky:	Is it specified how that is accomplished
1116		or is that up to the teacher?
1117	DT:	Usually what the teacher uses

1118		are a variety of other standardized tests
1119		to measure day-to-day classroom work,
1120		results of classroom testing
1121		and observations,
1122		informal assessment.
1123		Okay?
1124		Any questions, Mrs. Treader? [addresses June directly]
1125	AB:	Thank you for coming in, Mrs. Treader.
1126	SS:	Thank you.
1127	Becky:	Should I give this to you? [the report]
1128		Will this get in to her teacher?
1129		Or I should I give it to the teacher?
1130	Liaison:	You should put it
1131		in the permanent record folder.
1132		Because that folder at [name of school]
1133		will go right on
1134		with her to the middle school.
1135	DT:	But better yet
1136		if you're going to be meeting
1137		with the guidance counselor
1138		and talking with them
1139		it might be appropriate
1140		just to bring it in the end of August
1141		and then share it
1142		with the remedial reading person.
1143		I think handing it to them directly
1144		would be the best way to get it there.
1145	SS:	[about Shauna] She looks like Vicky a little.

Role of the Researcher

The night I asked June, Lester, and Vicky for permission to publish my work with them with LEA was a hot summer night, a year after the research had formally ended. A dozen people sat outside of the apartment building, scattered across the stoop and in plastic folding chairs on the sidewalk. June's youngest child was in her lap, rubbing his eyes and trying to find a comfortable place to take a nap; the rest of her children and the neighborhood children were dumping the water from an inflatable pool onto the sidewalk. June and I discussed how Vicky was doing in school. June said she was doin' real good at the high school, staying out of trouble. June looked at me and smiled. "Remember that meeting we went to?" she asked me. "I do," I replied. She shook her head, "They didn't even let me talk in that meeting." "I wrote about that." "You did?" I nodded my head. "I also wrote about how you did not want Vicky in a special-education class and how she got put in there. I looked at the language in that meeting to show why you weren't allowed to speak—or why I wasn't allowed to speak." Evan got off of June's lap and came over to mine. He crawled into my lap where the top of his head rested under my chin. He played with my watch, unhooking it and then fastening it again. "I was hurtin' that day. My sinuses were killing me." I knew June was thinking about the day in the CSE room when she started to cry. "I think you were also hurt because Vicky was placed in a special-education class and you didn't want her to be." June, looking down the street at the kids lifting the half-empty inflatable pool in the air, said, "Uh huh."

I thought about the visit to the middle school counselor when June had started crying as she said, "I just don't want her in special ed." My heart broke when this happened. I thought about how in June's own life school had been connected with painful experiences. She relived those experiences through her children. As I asked June about her experiences with and history with reading, she would often cry. I wondered if my presence in her and her children's life had caused more pain through my endless questioning, observations, interviews, and interventions. Oftentimes, it seemed like June did not want to talk about school and reading. Who could blame her? I was a reminder of her desire for upward mobility through education and even I had failed her. And yet, when she introduces me to people in her family network, she will say, "This is Becky. She worked with Vicky and with me on my reading. She did real good. The kids love her." It makes me feel good to hear her say these things and yet I find them hard to believe.

As June realized that, in spite of my working with her daughter, Vicky would still be classified as multiply disabled and put into a special-education classroom that would track her through high school, I wonder if she lost further hope that there could be a difference for her children. June went above and beyond as an involved parent. She accessed resources, including myself as a researcher and literacy teacher trained in reading methodology. Still this was not enough. Will it make a difference for her other children?

I think about June's reaction to my asking her for her consent to publish this book. I asked her, Lester, and Vicky to sign LEA consent forms. I was uncomfortable at the thought of asking them to sign yet another institutional form. I was surprised at how readily they gave their consent. After they had signed, I told them I would pay them half of whatever royalties I made on the book. As Lester said when I explained to him about the book, "You've done a good job here and I don't see any big deal about this book." But it is a big deal. It is a big deal to let other researchers and educators know about this case study so we can learn better research, teaching, and advocacy methodologies in hopes that this story can be interrupted in different places for other families. However, Lester's statement there is the disturbing repetition of a theme that has run through out this book. The Treaders do not see the big deal with publishing their literate lives because they do not see their narratives, their literacies, and their interactions with the school as valuable. I see them as valuable. The research community sees local literacies as valuable. Yet, the Treaders still do not see their local literacies as valuable.

REFLEXIVITY

To extend the overarching claim of this book, I shift the lens in this section to demonstrate how I am also implicated in the stronghold of institutional ideologies. First, I address three points concerning reflexivity—or the examination of the relationship between the researcher and participants. I explore, in detail, how my interactions and ultimate consent in the CSE meeting, similar to June, were a result of my history of participation and ideological relationship to the school.

In the disciplines of anthropology, sociology, and feminist studies, the concept of participant-observation is often problematized through the notion of researcher subjectivity or through the notion of "consequential presence" (Emerson, et al., 1995). Often missing from this discussion is the turning of the analytic frame back on the researchers and their lives.

Lather (1991) raised three points concerning the concept of reflexivity, which I introduced in chapter 2. First is the idea of understanding the worldview of the participants, that is, that research should be based in the participants' worldviews, desires, concerns, and fears. This means that the researcher involves the participants in the structure of the research. In this study, I involved the Treaders in the design and planning of the research. I explained my research proposal to them. I asked them if they would like to add anything or have anything removed. There were also several points where we sat down and discussed future directions for the tutoring sessions as well as the research. From the onset of the study, June called on my role as a literacy teacher, insisting that I work with her daughter as well as be a researcher when I was at their house. In this study I worked to gain an emic—or an insider perspective—in a number of ways. First, I immersed myself in the context of the research, over time. Second, I focused my data collection at the beginning of the study on observing the broad context and then focusing on literacy events and practices. In doing this, my intention was to better understand the social context.

Reciprocity and dialogue is the second central component of a reflexive research. This notion is that the researcher and the participants are involved in learning from each other. Dialogue between myself and the Treaders was the central place for learning. Though I was designated as a researcher (through my work at the university) and as a literacy teacher (by June), and thus carried an institutional authority, the Treaders were the authority of their home and community. Whereas I brought books and knowledge of teaching reading, they taught me the social, cultural, linguistic, and political aspects of what it means to teaching reading. As an ethnographer I was interested in observing, participating, and learning about the Treaders' social world. Whereas this did occur throughout the study, I was aware that the Treaders also observed and analyzed my actions. This phenomenon is evident in chapter 4 in the discussions about the WIC form. In this interaction I did not know about the process of applying for and receiving WIC. Vicky, who has observed her mother, explained it to me. In this interaction, she was the teacher, not I. It is clear that mutual learning occurred.

Reciprocity, in critical social literacy, needs to extend beyond just learning in dialogue. That is, there needs to also be a commitment to material and economic changes of those with whom we work. As a graduate student conducting the research, I was not able to provide the Treaders a substantial stipend. They did, however, keep the many books we read over the 2 years. I was painfully aware that a large part of my own academic success hinged on the lives of June and her children. Now that I have a book contract with LEA, I have promised the Treaders onehalf of all of the royalties I receive on this book. Whereas I move to another state to start my career, June and her children remain on Rosemont Street in Sherman Hollows. That is not to say one is better than the other—but there needs to be a way of ensuring continued and sustained action for those we work with once we have left the research site. Part of this means problematizing the confines of institutional work spaces that make it difficult to sustain relationships between universities and other public-sphere institutions—an issue I come back to in the final section of this chapter.

The third example of reflexivity that is important for this study is the idea that research should include critical analysis and sustained action (e.g., Bourdieu & Wacquant, 1992; Burawoy, 1991; Fairclough, 1989). In research, this might include adopting a critical theoretical approach (Fairclough, 1989, 1995, 1997) committed to social critique and change. In this study, sustained action took place in the transformation of the literature discussion groups to the community interviews, wherein the adolescents initiated a project in which they interviewed people in their own community in order to learn more about social issues. Here, learning moved from the context of literature to the context of the youth social worlds as they engaged with what Freire and Macedo (1987) referred to as "reading the word and the world" (p. 32).

A related example of critical analysis is the need to turn the analytic framework back on the researcher. That is, in what ways can the CDA framework illuminate my role as a researcher and as a teacher? In Rogers (2000b), I described, interpreted, and explained my role facilitating the literature discussion group with Vicky and other adolescents. The intention of the discussion group was to accelerate Vicky and the other students as readers through the process of engaging in literature that was at an instructional level and that would stimulate discussion around critical social issues. In this article, I argued that engaging the students either in resistant readings of the text structure or in discussion about critical social issues even in spaces that were meant to be "critical", was oftentimes less than critical. I demonstrated how my interactions, visible through orders of discourse, were in spite of my conscious efforts often less than emancipatory.

This reflexivity can frequently lead to change in practice. For example, my analysis helped me realize the closed nature of my research questions (genre). That is, I asked the adolescents for definitions of concepts such as "oppression" and I clearly already had a response to in my mind (Discourse). As a result, I changed the way I participated as a researcher and as a literacy teacher.

It may be that there are multiple levels of reflexivity. That is, in writing the fieldnotes, analyzing the discussion groups and my role in them, and planning for subsequent sessions, I modified a number of my actions. However, this reflexive theory and practice is not always possible, especially in the complexity of minute-to-minute interactions that characterize interpretive research. Some reflexivity may only be possible with distance. As an example, in the following section, I return to two excerpts from the

CSE meeting, this time focusing my analysis on my interactions, rather than those of the psychologist, June, the chair, or the speech therapist.

Interaction 1.

249	Becky:	Can *I* ask a question?
250	DS:	Sure.
251	Becky:	When you said,
252		um, that *she* was at the <u>second grade in decoding</u>,
253		what is that based on?
254		Is that consistent
255		with *her* <u>remedial reading reports</u>
256		as well?

Interaction 2.

296	Becky:	<u>The reason *I* ask</u>
297		is that when *I* <u>work with her</u>
298		throughout the year
299		*she* has been <u>reading</u>
300		between a <u>third- and a fourth-grade level</u>
301		when *she* is <u>reading authentic books.</u>
302		*I'm not sure* how *her* <u>decoding is isolation</u>
303		because *I* don't do that
304		with *her*.

I asked for permission to interrupt the flow of conversation in the meeting (line 249). This signaled my position within this meeting as an outsider. It is important to note that in this interaction, as in some of the others in the meeting, I also referred to Vicky as "her" rather than by her name, as in lines 252, 255, 297, 301, 302, and 304. This is the same domain of discourse that I argued the school officials used to depersonalize the results of the testing.

In lines 254–255, I was aware that there was a discrepancy between the psychological report, the reading teacher report, and my own observations and assessments of Vicky reading literature. Instead of stating, "Those scores are not an accurate indicator of Vicky's reading," I asked politely (style), "Is that consistent with her remedial reading reports as well?" Still in the domain of style or "ways of being," this politeness convention of asking, rather than stating what I know to be true, allowed the psychologist to confirm her test results. In addition, after the psychologist had reiterated her position, in lines 296–297 I explained why I was asking the question. That is, I did not make the assumption that because I am present I may speak and may question the report. Instead, I let them know my intention in questioning them. These three interactions, my asking for permission to speak, asking a question rather than stating evidence, and explaining why I am questioning their assertions all indicate my role as an outsider in *this particular* discourse community (genre, discourse, style). My awareness of a discrepancy, however, clearly showed that I was a member in the Discourse of the school. Though I am knowledgeable about the differences between sources of evidence and am also aware of other ways of representing Vicky, I did not demand that these be heard.

I did, however, signify my identification with the school community by reference to "second-grade decoding" (line 252), "remedial reading re-ports" (line 255), "third- and fourth-grade level" (line 300), "reading authentic books" (line 301), and "decoding in isolation" (line 302). Through this interaction I defined myself as part of the institutional language.

I was implicated into the Discourse of Deficits, just as June was, as the rhetoric of the meeting unfolded around us. The meeting evoked my developing subjectivities as a literacy educator, researcher, and critical social theorist as I heard the way in which Vicky was described in deficit terms. Even if I did not know Vicky, the portrayal of any child in these terms is severely problematic (Mehan, 1986; Taylor, Coughlin, & Marasco, 1997). Although these subjectivities emerged throughout the meeting (e.g., lines 249, 256, 296–304), it was clear that my participation in the meeting was silenced, as was June's.

This evidence of consent in my interactions in the meeting, even when I knew how to break into the discourse, extends the overarching theme of this book. Indeed, ideology manufactures consent through histories of partici-pation within institutions (i.e., family, school, community) and split and partial subjectivities (Luke & Gore, 1993; Morgan, 1999).

HISTORIES OF PARTICIPATION

My participation in the CSE meeting and in conducting the research in general is etched with my own history of participation with the institution of school. My histories of participation in schools have taught me about my role within the institution that allowed for, in fact insisted, on this silencing within the meeting. My past experiences are etched with markers of being a "good student." Now, stepping into professionalism, I have chosen a career in education, a field, like many others, that is occupied mainly by women but controlled by men (Lagemann, 2001). This raises a number of issues about the social conditions and institutional practices that provide the conditions for certain groups of people to engage in this work, often at the expense of others (e.g., Evans, 1995; C. Luke & Gore, 1992; Stanley, 1995).

As a working/middle-class woman, my attachments to and value in education run deep, as do the contradictions I have learned from the same institution. It may be that my experience as a literacy educator and a critical social theorist do not have roots as deep as my past experiences with school. I, like June, learned that school officials are authorities. We learn from them; we do not challenge them. These values and beliefs arise from my history of participation with school and other social and cultural institutions.

I was raised in an all-White community of fewer than 1,000 people. The community was working/middle-class. Education, as a means of upward social mobility, was stressed in my working/middle-class family. My family's lineage is from Poland and England (Paternal side) and Holland (Maternal side). I was not taught about my family's genealogical roots as I was growing up. I was raised in a semistrict Catholic home, attending religious services on Sundays and church school on Saturdays. My mother read to me every night from the time I was an infant. I learned to read before attending kindergarten. Books were often given as holiday gifts and my sisters and I were rewarded with money when we earned good grades in school. I won spelling bees, got all A's in schools, started a school newspaper, wrote for a local paper, in other words grew up in a literate world, a world that was defined mainly by schooled literacy. My sisters and I were constantly reminded to get a good education so we would have good jobs. I earned a bachelor's degree in English from the same institution from which I earned a PhD 5 years later.

During one of my early years in college I joined Literacy Volunteers and was trained as a literacy tutor for literacy volunteers. I worked 1:1 and in small groups with adults who were considered to be low-literate. It was here that I first started to see the power of literacy in people's lives and the privileges of literacy I had taken for granted. I was amazed at how much the adults could teach me and in many ways I felt inadequate because I knew how to break into the code of the written word but they had life experiences that I could not even begin to understand. In my work as a literacy tutor I continued to think of literacy in school-defined ways. I began running family literacy workshops and conducted sessions where I modeled reading aloud to children with working-class and minority parents who had children who attended Head Start. Although the parents attended and seemed to take something from the workshops, I sensed that something was missing. I thought back to the adults I had worked with and learned so much from and started to ask the mothers who were in the family literacy programs what types of literacies they interacted with outside of school. This was a turning point for me as I stepped away from school-defined types of literacies to building on local literacies. In reflecting on my own literacy timeline, I learned to see literacy from a point of privilege. My mother had time to read to me every night. There were plenty of books in the house. Indeed, literacy was seen as schooled literacy but also as a part of the fabric of our everyday lives. These early literacy experiences and my successes within the institution of the school shaped how I viewed what counted as literacy and to whom.

I have learned the rules but also acquired a set of ideological relationships within these rules. It is often the invisible and contradictory aspects of this acquisition (e.g., gender and schooling) that make it difficult to challenge these institutional webs of discourse in moments where the orchestration of the meeting unfolded with precision and efficiency. It is similar to Rockhill's (1987) study in which she articulated women's contradictory reality as an educational dilemma. In Rockhill's study, the knowledge and power that became available to the women as a result of their education resulted in split and contradictory subject positions. As Rockhill put it, "It is precisely because education holds out this promise for women that it also poses a threat to them in their everyday lives" (p. 315).

In my own educational experiences, I am aware of this threat and tension with regard to the "promise of education" in my own life. The tension between my own personal and social commitments and my commitment to the university for a degree that recognizes and values intellectual capital, but not always the social and political commitments I have demonstrated in this book, is a reality in my own life. I am aware of these tensions as I think about my future intellectual work within academia. A point of divergence is that the literacy work I have done in this study—the theoretical and analytic work—has been valued. The 3 years of collecting, analyzing, and writing this research have *not* gone unrecognized. I have been awarded several grants, a scholarship, have published and presented aspects of this work, and have been hired at a reputable university. However, whereas the theoretical and outwardly intellectual aspects of the work have been recognized, there has been less recognition of my role as a literacy teacher or the time I spent in community agencies gaining credibility in the community. These aspects, the teaching and the helping aspects of literacy work, have traditionally been and continue to be seen as "women's work" within the university. They are not counted and valued nearly as much as is being published when it comes to tenure, promotion, and raises (Luttrell, 1996; Park, 1996). Therefore, the issue of women's work, who does the literacy work, what is recognized, and by whom, does not concern just June and her family. It permeates all levels of educational institutions and poses significant dilemmas for people with commitments to social justice who are yet bound by institutional regulations and the meritocratic ideologies of "being someone."

I, like June, am implicated in the paradox of education. I believe that knowledge is power—but it is a double-edged kind of power (Stuckey, 1991). For in recognizing the conditions that hold us in place, it is often difficult to break out of these conditions. Though I have a commitment to social critique and change, my working/middle-class roots force me to commit to ensuring I have a good job, health insurance, and a retirement plan. The ethos of a capitalistic society is deeply ingrained in my efforts to "get ahead" in a competitive, meritocratic society. I continue to exert a strong belief that, through education, through meeting academic require-ments (i.e., course work, the dissertation, research projects, securing grants, conference presentations, tenure), I will also "move up." When I hear June's commitment to "move up" to the GED room, I empathize with her commitment to education and to progress—even if defined by the school.

SHIFTING ROLES OF THE RESEARCHER AND PARTICIPANTS

As would be expected, my role in the research changed, as did the Treaders' role. I have documented this shift in my teacher-research role in Rogers (2002b). As a White researcher looking at literacy in a working-poor and minority community, I continually faced a healthy tension characterized by liberation and resistance theories (Delpit, 1988). On the one hand, the reason I started the project was to learn how a woman who was labeled as low-literate could negotiate the literate demands of her and her children's lives in a multiliterate society. I began the research by document-ing the literate events and practices that existed in the Treaders' home and community. I learned that there were multiple uses of literacy, but I also learned that schooled literacy was one of the dominant forms of literacy in the Treaders' out-of-school literacy lives. Though I wanted to value and recognize the Treaders' local literacies, their acts of resistance, and the activism that characterized their day-to-day literacy lives, ethically I had an obligation to try the best I could to make sure I accelerated both June and Vicky as readers and writers. I documented both of their progress. Indeed, Vicky made progress through multiple levels of texts and also in terms of how she talked about literature, made good book choices, and made connections between texts. I ultimately stopped working with June because she told me I should work with the children as they needed it more. This was around the same time she dropped out of her own ABE program. She seemed to have lost hope in herself making progress with schooled literacy. The Treaders expanded my vision of what counted as literacy. I learned how schooled literacy was an intimate part of the fabric of their lives and yet they had never had successful experiences with school. I continually struggled with exploring situated literacies (Barton, 1994; Barton, Hamilton, & Ivanic, 2000; Gee, 1996; Street, 1995) and the Treaders' vision of who I was as a broker of more traditional literacies attached to the institution of schools.

Though in theory I resisted the emphasis placed on written literacy because of the false premise (e.g., Goody, 1987; Olson, 1977) that literacy leads to cognitive and social advancement, in practice I continued to work within a written language model because that is what the Treaders needed in order to move ahead in the social world. In doing so, I continued to challenge the constructed belief of what literacy can achieve—however, it is hard to do that when, being White and literate, I am perceived by the Treaders as "successful" and as an "authority," indeed, as the "literacy teacher." I can afford to critique what access to written literacy can and cannot afford because I am in a position to do so. However, it has not been literacy alone that has allowed me to engage in such criticisms, as proponents of the autonomous model of literacy would suggest (e.g., Goody, 1987), but rather my engagement with literacy and resources within institutions. Literacy and education were necessary but not sufficient. I continue to be cognizant, though, of the danger in privileging the written over the spoken, in my theorizing and in the examples I have presented in this book. This is a serious issue because of my focus on discourse. The study of Discourse studies has its roots in linguistics, the scientific study of language, a discipline built on privileging written texts over oral, a phenomenon that Street (1984) referred to as "written language bias" (WLB). Written and oral texts pose different dilemmas for critical discourse analysts. A frequent criticism of CDA is that it is often conducted on written texts (e.g. political speeches, newspaper texts) rather than on interactional texts (for examples of analyses done on interactional texts, see Chouliaraki, 1998; Lewis, 2001; Moje, 1997; Peyton-Young, 1999; Stevens, 2001). Given this long-standing tension of the privileging of written over oral texts, I worried that, because of the cultural model I was socialized into, I would continue to place an emphasis on written over oral language.

Along the way the Treaders' and my relationship to each other and to literacy changed. I was more comfortable asking questions to which I did not know the answer (e.g., about WIC in chap. 4). The Treaders seemed to be more apt to answer my questions and to step into the role of an authority explaining the texts and interactions that were a part of their lives. However, at first I sensed a skepticism from them. They did not understand why a White woman, who they perceived as having money and being educated, (a) did not know the answer to some of the questions I was asking, and (b) would want to know in the first place. I continually reminded June that I was interested in how she interacted with the texts that came home from school and from other agencies because I wanted to learn from her. At first she was reluctant to share with me, but over time she would show me the documents that came home from various institutions. She taught me what she knew about the documents and the institutions from which they came and I asked questions that may have caused her to think about the institutions in a different way.

I continued to think seriously about the role of power and privilege in the research, especially because I was researching the topic of literacy with a family considered to be low-literate. Even though I have complicated the construct of literacy in this book, literacy levels as traditionally defined played a role in my research process. The Treaders were not interested in reading copies of articles I prepared in order to respond to them and offer criticism, or even to make sure that I got it "right." June would always take the manuscript or the case study and say, "I'll give this to Lester to read." When I asked Lester if he had read it, he would say I was doing a good job with Vicky and to keep doing what I was doing. Throughout the project, Lester was supportive of my presence in the home. His quiet parental involvement—making sure the children were home to do their homework, asking them how they were doing in school, and telling them to "read a book"—is typical of many parents. Though June did most of the literacy work in the home, for example, signing papers, helping the children study for spelling tests, agitating for petitions, and WIC support, Lester was also involved. Most of the final decisions were made by June and Lester together. An example of this was when they decided to have Vicky tested because Lester thought it would be good to "learn more about her." Ironically, I assumed that, because June took an extremely active role in the education and literacy work of the home and challenged many of my beliefs about the scope and nature of literacy, Lester was not involved. However, this is the same logic that teachers and schools often use against parents who do not appear to be involved in traditionally defined ways. That is, if parents do not read books with their children, show up at school functions, and sign and return papers, teachers often assume parents are not involved. June Treader demonstrated all of the traditional types of parent involvement. She went beyond them though, and used literacy in active and strategic ways to ensure the health and safety of her family. Lester, too, was involved and I needed to continue to remind myself of this.

Lester was generally in the living room when I was at the Treaders' house. He physically was not a part of the landscape and therefore is absent from many of my fieldnotes. I want to emphasize, however, that his absence, is not a reflection of his lack of interest in his children or his value of education, but rather, reflects my relationship with Lester. Whereas June was responsible for most of the literate demands of the household, Lester believed and espoused the importance of school and education for his children. He attended Vicky's sixth-grade graduation and Shauna's graduation from her preschool class. He shared his worries about Vicky with me. He told me that he wanted to see the children in the house earlier in the evening so they could get ready for school. My interviews with Lester and observations of his participation in events revealed that he did care about his children's education. I also learned that he valued my role in the home and community. Whereas initially I had feared he would perceive me as a threat to his family, I learned that he believed I had done a good job with his children. He thanked me for working with his children and with his wife. He expressed uncertainty about what would happen when I was no longer their tutor.

Often when I presented this research at conference or when I sent an article out for review, a reviewer would ask me about Lester's role in the family. Though it is "true" that he was less engaged than June, to say that he was uninvolved continues to reinforce the harmful model that I am trying to break away from, that is, that there is only one type of involvement. Isn't it possible to say that Lester was involved with his children in terms of going to work, asking about their school and to see their report cards, and continuing to reinforce my presence in the home as a literacy tutor? Furthermore, he had his own set of "local literacies," ways of using resources, strategies, and networks that I was unfamiliar with because I did not investigate them ethnographically. A critical absence in the research was not learning more about Lester's local literacies.

I worried about issues of power and privilege in terms of publishing the Treaders' words, indeed, their lives, for all to read. Ironically, the narrative I have told in this book is of great importance to a community of educators because we learn from their stories. When I asked June, however, what her thoughts were on publishing her stories and my research in a book with Lawrence Erlbaum, she looked at me with surprise and said, "Why do they want my stories?" I explained to her that through her stories I had learned about her role in her children's education, her participation with her children's school and with her own, that deficit models of parent involvement and lack of literacy at home were false.

I wonder if sometimes we have to suspend our belief in what we envision as equity for a moment in order to understand how people create ethno-theories of themselves and their social worlds. These ethno-theories include a representation of educators and researchers into this theory where we become part of the hierarchy. Lester saw me as part of the social structure that he wanted for his family. I wanted him to be involved in the literacy education of his children because he was the more competent of the two adults. This recognition meant that I put my faith back into a schooled model of literacy and saw Lester as breaking away from this. My cultural model that "literacy is women's work" was reinforced in this situation. Lester saw the literacy work as the work that both his wife and myself were engaged in. However, neither of us tried to get him into this conversation to the extent we might have.

If we actively suspend out beliefs in equity so that we can understand how people we work with view us, then we can work with, challenge, critique and transform these relations. In this book I have conducted CDA, or, in other words, studied the relationship between ways of interacting, ways of representing, and ways of being across written texts, interviews, and meetings. I have demonstrated how orders of discourse combined with attention to context, both within and across various contexts, can lead to a description, interpretation, and explanation of the relationship between literacies, subjectivities, and social practices. My hope is that, in reading the book other literacy researchers, teachers, and advocates will interrupt, challenge, and transform the literacy and language practices that lift people up and hold them in their place. Again, I ask, as I did at the start of this study, what counts as literacy and to whom?

References

Allan, J., Brown, S., & Riddell, S. (1998). Permission to speak?: Theorizing special education inside the classroom. In C. Clark, A. Dyson, & A. Millward (Eds.), *Theorizing Special Education* (pp. 23–31). New York: Routledge.

Allington, R., & McGill-Franzen, A. (1995). Placing children at risk: Schools respond to reading problems. *At-Risk Students. Portraits, Policies, Programs and Practices* (197–217). Albany, NY: SUNY Press.

Althusser, P. (1971). *Lenin and philosophy and other essays.* London: New Left Books.

Anderson, A. & Stoakes, S. (1984). Social and institutional contexts of literacy. In H. Goelman, A. Oberg, & F. Smiths (Eds.), *Awakening to literacy* (pp. 24–37). NH: Heinemann.

Anderson, A. B., Teale, W. B., & Estrada, E. (1980). Low-income children's preschool literary experiences: Some naturalistic observations. *The Quarterly Newsletter of the Laboratory of Comparative Human Cognition*, 2(3), 59–65.

Anderson, J. D. (1988). *The education of Blacks in the South: 1860–1935.* Chapel Hill, NC: University of North Carolina.

Apple, M. (1993) *Official knowledge. Democratic education in a conservative age.* New York: Routledge.

Barton, D. (1994). *Literacy. An introduction to the ecology of written language.* Oxford, England: Blackwell.

Barton, D., & Hamilton, M. (1988). *Local literacies. Reading and writing in one community.* New York: Routledge.

Barton, D., Hamilton, M., & Ivanic, R. (Eds.). (2000). *Situated literacies: Reading and writing in context.* London: Routledge.

Baugh, J. (1999). *Out of the mouths of slaves: African American language and educational malpractice.* Austin: University of Texas Press.

Belenky, M., McVicker-Clinchy, B. Goldberger, N., & Mattuck-Tarule, J. (1986). *Women's ways of knowing: The development of self, voice, and mind.* New York: Basic Books.

Bergvall, V., & Remlinger, K. (1996). Reproduction, resistance and gender in educational discourse: The role of Critical Discourse Analysis. *Discourse & Society,* 7(4), 453–479.

Bernstein, B. (1975). Class and pedagogies: Visible and invisible. *Class, codes and control: Vol. 3. Towards a theory of transmission* (pp. 116–156). London: Routledge & Kegan Paul.

Blommaert, J. (2001). Context is/as critique. *Critique of Anthropology,* 21(1), 13–32.

Bloome, D., & Power-Carter, S. (2001). Lists in reading education reform. *Theory Into Practice,* 40(3), 150–157.

Bourdieu, P. (1991). *Language and symbolic power.* Cambridge, England: Polity Press.
Bourdieu, P., & Wacquant, L. (1992). *An invitation to reflective sociology.* Chicago: University of Chicago Press.
Brandau, D., & Collins, J. (1994). Texts, social relations and work-based skepticism about schooling: An ethnographic analysis. *Anthropology & Education Quarterly, 25*(2), 118–136.
Bucholtz, M., Liang, A. C., Sutton, L. A. (Eds.). (1999). *Reinventing identities, The gendered self in discourse.* New York: Oxford University Press.
Burawoy, M. (1991). Restructing Social Theories. In M. Burawoy (Ed.), *Ethnography unbound: Power and resistance in the modern metropolis* (pp. 8–27). Berkeley: University of California Press.
Butler, J. (1990). Gender trouble: Feminism and the subversion of identity. New York: Routledge.
Chouliaraki, L. (1998). Regulation in "progressivist" pedagogic discourse: Individualized teacher–pupil talk. *Discourse and Society, 9*(1), 5–32.
Chouliaraki, L., & Fairclough, N. (1999). *Critical discourse analysis in late modernity.* Edinburgh, Scotland: Edinburgh University Press.
Clay, M. (1993). *Reading Recovery: A guidebook for teachers in training.* Portsmouth, NH: Heinemann.
Collins, J. (1989). Hegemonic practice: Literacy and standard language in public education. *Journal of Education, 17*(2), 9–34.
Collins, J. (1993). Determination and contradiction: An appreciation and critique of the work of Pierre Bourdieu on language and education. In C. Calhoun, E. LiPuma, & M. Postone (Eds.), *Bourdieu: Critical perspectives* (pp. 116–138). New York: Polity Press.
Collins, J. (1996). Socialization to text: Structure and contradiction in schooled literacy. In M. Silverstein & G. Urban (Eds.), *Natural histories of discourse* (pp. 203–228). Chicago: University of Chicago Press.
Collins, J. (2000). Bernstein, Bourdieu and the New Literacy Studies. *Linguistics and Education, 10*(4), 1–8.
Collins, J. (2001). Selling the market: Educational standards, discourse and social inequality. *Critique of Anthropology, 21*(1), 143–163.
Cook-Gumperz, J. (1986). *The social construction of literacy.* Cambridge, England: Cambridge University Press.
Cook-Gumperz, J. (1993). Dilemmas of identity: Oral and written literacies in the making of a basic writing student. *Anthropology and Education Quarterly, 24*(4), 336–356.
Cope, B., & Kalantzis, M. (Eds.). (1993). *The powers of literacy. A genre approach to teaching writing.* Pittsburgh, PA: University of Pittsburgh Press.
Corson, D. (2000). Emancipatory leadership. *International Journal of Leadership in Education, 3*(2), 93–120.
Cushman, E. (1998). *The struggle and the tools: Oral and literate strategies in an inner city community.* New York: SUNY Press, 1998.
Davies, B. (1993). *Shards of glass: Children reading and writing beyond gendered identities.* Cresskill, NJ: Hampton.
Davies, B., & Harre, R. (1990). Positioning: The discursive production of self. *Journal for the Theory of Social Behavior, 20*(1), 43–63.
Delgado-Gaitan, C. (1992). School matters in the Mexican-American home: Socializing children to education. *American Educational Research Journal, 29*(3), 495–513.
Delpit, L. (1988). The silenced dialogue: Power and pedagogy in educating other people's children. *Harvard Educational Review, 58*(3), 280–298.
Delpit, L. (1996). *Other people's children. Cultural con.ict in the classroom.* New York: The New Press.

Edwards, P. (1995). Empowering low-income mothers and fathers to share books with young children. *The Reading Teacher, 48*(7), 558–564.

Emerson, R. M., Fretz, R. I., & Shaw, L. L. (1995). *Writing ethnographic .Fieldnotes*. Chicago: University of Chicago Press.

Erickson, F. (1987). Transformation and school success: The politics and culture of educational achievement. *Anthropology and Education Quarterly, 18*, 335–356.

Evans, M. (1995). Ivory towers: Life in the mind. In L. Morley & V. Walsh (Eds.), *Feminist academics. Creative agents for change* (pp. 73–85). London: Taylor & Francis.

Fairclough, N. (1989). *Language and power*. London: Longman.

Fairclough, N. (1992a). *Discourse and social change*. Cambridge, England: Polity Press.

Fairclough, N. (1992b). Intertextuality in critical discourse analysis. *Linguistics and Education, 4*, 269–293.

Fairclough, N. (1995). *Critical discourse analysis: The critical study of language*. New York: Longman.

Fairclough, N. (2000). Multiliteracies and language: Orders of discourse and intertextuality. In B. Cope & M. Kalantzis (Eds.), *Multiliteracies: Literacy learning and the design of social futures* (pp. 162–181). London: Routledge.

Fairclough, N., & Wodak, R. (1997). Critical discourse analysis. In T. Van Dijk (Ed.), *Discourse as social interaction* Vol. 2, (pp. 258–284). Thousand Oaks, CA: Sage.

Fine, M. (1995). Silencing and literacy. In D. A. Wagner & V. Gadsden (Eds.), *Literacy among African-American youth: Issues in learning, teaching, and schooling* (pp. 201–222). Creskill, NJ: Hampton Press.

Fingeret, H., & Drennon, C. (1997). *Literacy for life: Adult learners, new practices*. New York: Teachers College Press.

Flowerdew, J. (1999). Description and interpretation in critical discourse analysis. *Journal of Pragmatics, 31*, 1089–1099.

Foucault, M. (1970). *The order of things: An archeology of knowledge*. London: Tavistock.

Foucault, M. (1977). *Discipline and punish: The birth of the prison*. New York: Pantheon.

Foucault, M. (1981) *Power/knowledge: Selected interviews and other writings, 1972–1977*. New York: Pantheon.

Foster, M. (1998). Educating for competence in community and culture: Exploring the views of exemplary African-American teachers. In M. Shujaa (Ed.), *Too much schooling too little education* (pp. 221–244). Trenton, NJ: Africa World Press, Inc.

Fowler, R., Hodge, B., Kress, G., & Trew, T. (1979). *Language and control*. New York: Routledge.

Freire, P., & Macedo, D. (1987). *Literacy: Reading the word and the world*. Westport, CT: Bergin & Garvey.

Gadsden, V. (1995). Introduction: Literacy and African American youth: Legacies and struggles. In V. Gadsden & D. Wagner (Eds.), *Literacy among African American youth: Issues in learning, teaching, and schooling*. Creskill, NJ: Hampton Press.

Gartner, A., & Kernzer-Lipsky, D. (1987). Beyond special education: Toward a quality system for all students. *Harvard Educational Review, 57*(44), 367–395.

Gee, J. (1991). What is literacy? In C. Mitchell & K. Weiler (Eds.), *Rewriting literacy: Culture and the discourse of the other* (pp. 3–12). New York: Bergin & Garvey.

Gee, J. (1992). *The social mind: Language, ideology and social practice*. New York: Bergin & Garvey.

Gee, J. (1993a). Critical literacy/socially perspective literacy. A study of language in action. *Australian Journal of Language and Literacy, 16*(4), 333–356.

Gee, J. (1993b). Quality, science and the lifeworld. *Critical Forum, 2*(3), 13–14.

Gee, J. P. (1994). First language acquisition as a guide for theories of learning and pedagogy. *Linguistics and Education, 6*, 331–354.

Gee, J. (1996). *Social linguistics and literacies: Ideology in discourses*. London: Falmer Press.

Gee, J. (1997). Foreword: A discourse approach to language and literacy. In C. Lankshear (Ed.), *Changing literacies* (pp. 1–3). Philadelphia: Open University Press.

Gee, J. (1999a). *An introduction to discourse analysis: Theory and method.* New York: Routledge.

Gee, J. (1999b). Reading and the new literacy studies. Reframing the National Academy of Sciences Report on Reading. *Journal of Literacy Research, 31*(3), 355–374.

Gee, J. (2000). The New Literacy Studies. From "socially situated" to the world of the social. In D. Barton, M. Hamilton, & R. Ivanic. (Eds.), *Situated literacies: Reading and writing in context* (pp. 180–196). London: Routledge.

Gee, J., & Green, J. (1998). Discourse analysis, learning, and social practice: A methodological study. *Review of Research in Education, 23,* 118–169.

Geertz, C. (1973). *The interpretation of cultures.* New York: Basic Books.

German, L. (1989). *Sex, class and socialism.* London: Bookmarks.

Gilbert, P. (1992). Narrative as gendered social practice: In search of different story lines for language research. *Linguistics and Education, 5,* 211–218.

Gilbert, P. (1997). Discourses on gender and literacy. In S. Musporatt, A. Luke, & P. Freebody (Eds.), *Constructing critical literacies* (pp. 69–75). Cresskill, NJ: Hampton.

Gipps, C. (1994). *Beyond testing: Toward a theory of educational assessment.* London: Falmer Press.

Giroux, H. (1997). *Pedagogy and the politics of hope: Theory, culture, and schooling.* Boulder, CO: Westview Press.

Gitlin, A. (Ed.). (1994). *Power and method. Political activism and educational research.* New York: Routledge.

Glaser, B., & Strauss, A. (1967). *The discovery of grounded theory: Strategies for qualitative research.* Chicago: Aldine.

Glesne, C., & Peshkin, A. (1992). *Becoming qualitative researchers: An introduction.* New York: Addison-Wesley.

Goffman, E. (1971). *Relations in public.* New York: Harper Colophon.

Goldstein, S., et al. (1980). An Observational Analysis of the IEP Conference. *Exceptional Children, 46*(4), 278–286.

Goody, J. (1987). *The interface between the written and the oral.* Cambridge, England: Cambridge University Press.

Gowen, S. (1991). Beliefs about literacy: Measuring women into silence/hearing women into speech. *Discourse & Society, 2*(4), 439–450.

Gowen, S. G. (1992). *The politics of workplace literacy. A case study.* New York: Teachers College Press.

Greenwood, B. (1998). *The last safe house: A story of the Underground Railroad.* New York: Kids Can Press.

Grice. (1999). Logic and Conversation. In A. Jaworski & N. Coupland (Eds.), *The Discourse Reader* (pp. 76–88). NY: Routledge.

Gumperz, J. (1982). *Discourse strategies.* Cambridge, England: Cambridge University Press.

Halliday, M. (1989). *Spoken and written language.* Oxford, England: Oxford University Press.

Halliday, M. (1994). *An introduction to functional grammar* (2nd ed.). London: Edward Arnold.

Halliday, M., & Hasan, R. (1989). *Language, context, and text: Aspects of language as a social-semiotic perspective.* Oxford, England: Oxford University Press.

Harris, B. (1992). *Cultural diversity, families, and the special education system.* New York: Teachers College Press.

Harris, V., Kamhi, A., Pollock, K. (Eds.). (2001). *Literacy in African American communities.* Mahwah, NJ: Lawrence Erlbaum Associates.

Harry, B., & Anderson, M. (1994). The disproportionate placement of African American males in special education programs: A critique of the process. *Journal of Negro Education, 63*(4), 602–619.

Heath, S. B. (1983). *Ways with words: Language, life and work in community and classrooms.* Cambridge, England: Cambridge University Press.

Hennimore, B. (2000). *Talk matters. Refocusing the language of public schooling.* New York: Teachers College Press.

Hicks, D. (2001). *Reading lives: Working class children and literacy learning.* New York: Teachers College Press.

Howarth, D. (2000). *Discourse.* Philadelphia: Open University Press.

Hughes, M. (1998). *Refusing ignorance: The struggle to educate Black children in Albany, New York 1816–1873.* New York: Mount Ida Press.

Hymes, D. (1974). Ways of speaking. In R. Bauman, & J. Sherzer (Eds.), *Explorations in the ethnography of speaking* (pp. 433–452). Cambridge, England: Cambridge University Press.

Janks, H. (1997). Critical Discourse Analysis as a Research Tool. *Discourse: Studies in the Politics of Education, 18*(3), 329–342.

Johnston, P. (1985). Understanding reading disability: A case study approach. *Harvard Educational Review, 55*(2), 153–177.

Johnston, P. (with Shannon, P., Murphy, S., & Hanson, J.). (1998a). The role of consequences. *Fragile evidence. A critique of reading assessment.* Portsmouth, NH: Heinemann.

Johnston, P. (1998b). *Knowing literacy: Constructive literacy assessment.* York, ME: Stenhouse.

Johnston, P. (1999). Unpacking literate achievement. In J. Gaffney & B. Askew (Eds.), *Stirring the Waters: The Influence of Marie Clay* (pp. 27–46). Portsmith: Heinemann.

Kamler, B. (1997). An interview with Terry Threadgold on critical discourse analysis. *Discourse: Studies in the Cultural Politics of Education, 18*(3), 437–451.

Kessler-Harris, A. (1990). *A woman's wage. Historical meanings & social consequences.* Lexington: University Press of Kentucky.

Ketter, J., & Lewis, C. (2001). Already reading texts and contexts: Multicultural literature in a predominantly White rural community. *Theory Into Practice, 40*(3), 175–183.

Key, D. (1998). *Literacy shutdown: Stories of six American women.* Newark, DE: International Reading Association.

King, C., & Barrett-Osborne, L. (1997). *Oh, freedom! Kids talk about the civil rights movement with the people who made it happen.* New York: Knopf.

Knobel, M. (1999). *Everyday literacies: Students, discourse, and social practice.* New York: Peter Lang.

Krais, B. (1993). Gender and symbolic violence: Female oppression in the light of Pierre Bourdieu's theory of social practice. In C. Calhoun, E. LiPuma, & M. Postone (Eds.), *Bourdieu: Critical perspectives* (pp. 156–177). New York: Polity Press.

Kress, G. (1985). *Linguistic processes in sociocultural practice.* Victoria, Australia: Deakin University Press.

Kress, G., & Hodge, B. (1979). *Language as ideology.* New York: Routledge.

Kumaravadivelu, B. (1999). Critical Classroom Discourse Analysis. *TESOL Quarterly, 33*(3), 453–484.

Labov, W. (1972). *Sociolinguistic patterns.* Philadelphia: University of Pennsylvania Press.

Labov, W., & Waletsky, J. (1966). Narrative analysis: Oral versions of personal experience. In J. Helm, (Ed.), *Essays on the verbal and visual arts* (pp. 12–44). Seattle: University of Washington Press.

Lagemann, E. C. (2000). *An elusive science: The troubling history of education research.* Chicago: Chicago University Press.

Lareau, A. (1989). Home advantage. Social class and parental intervention in elementary education. New York: Falmer Press.

Lather, P. (1986). Research as praxis. *Harvard Educational Review, 56*(3), 257–277.

Lather, P. (1991). *Getting smart: Feminist research and pedagogy with/in the postmodern.* New York: Routledge.

Lee, A. (1996). *Gender, literacy, curriculum: Re-writing school geography.* London: Taylor & Francis.

Leichter, H. (1984). Families as envionments for literacy. In H. Goelman, A. Oberg, & F. Smiths (Eds.), *Awakening to literacy* (pp. 38–50). Portsmouth, NH: Heinemann.

Lemke, J. (1995). *Textual politics: Discourse and social dynamics.* London: Taylor & Francis.

Lewis, C. (2001). *Literary practices as social acts: Power, status, and cultural norms in the classroom.* Mahwah, NJ: Lawrence Erlbaum Associates.

Lewis, C., Ketter, J., & Fabos, B. (2001). Reading Race in a Rural Context. *International Journal of Qualitative Studies in Education, 14*(3), 317–350.

Linnell, P. (1999). *Approaching dialogue. Talk, interaction, and contexts in dialogical perspectives.* Amsterdam: John Benjamins Publishing Company.

Luke, A. (1995). Texts and discourse in education: An introduction to critical discourse analysis. *Review of Research in Education, 21,* 3–48.

Luke, A., & Freebody, P. (1997). Critical literacy and the question of normativity. In S. Muspratt, A. Luke, & P. Freebody (Eds.), *Constructing critical literacies: Teaching and learning textual practice* (pp. 1–18). Creskill, NJ: Hampton.

Luke, C. (1997). Media literacy and cultural studies. In S. Muspratt, A. Luke, & P. Freebody (Eds.), *Constructing critical literacies: Teaching and learning textual practice* (pp. 19–50). Creskill, NJ: Hampton.

Luke, C., & Gore, J. (1992). Women in the academy: Strategy, struggle and survival. In C. Luke & J. Gore (Eds.), *Feminism and critical pedagogy* (pp. 192–210). New York: Routledge.

Luttrell, W. (1989). Working-class women's ways of knowing: Effects of gender, race and class. *Sociology of Education, 62,* 33–46.

Luttrell, W. (1996). Taking care of literacy: One feminist's critique. *Educational Policy, 19*(3), 342–365.

Luttrell, W. (1997). *School-smart and mother-wise. Working-class women's identity and schooling.* New York: Routledge.

Mathison, S. (1988). Why triangulate? *Educational Researcher, 17*(3), 13–17.

McCarthey, S. (2000). Home School Connections: A Review of Literature. *Journal of Educational Research, 93,* 145–153.

McDermott, R. (1987). Achieving school failure: An anthropological approach to illiteracy and social stratification In G. D. Spindler (Ed.), *Education and Cultural Process* (2nd ed., pp. 173–209). Prospect Heights: Waveland Press.

McDermott, R. (1996). The acquisition of a child by a learning disability. In S. Chaiklin & J. Lave (Eds.), *Understanding practice, Perspectives on activity and context* (pp. 269–305.) Cambridge: Cambridge University Press.

McNemar, B. S. (1998). The everyday literacy behavior of an adolescent mother for whom English is a second language. In T. Shanahan & F. V. Rodriguez-Brown (Eds.), *National Reading Conference Yearbook: Vol. 47* (pp. 274–284). Chicago: National Reading Conference.

Mehan, H. (1996). The construction of an LD student: A case study of the politics of representation. In M. Silverstein & G. Urban (Eds.), *Natural histories of discourse* (pp. 253–276). Chicago: University of Chicago Press.

Mehan, H., Hertweck, A., & Meihls, J. (1986). *Handicapping the handicapped: Decision making in students' careers.* Stanford, CA: Stanford University Press.

Mercado, C. I., & Moll, L. (1997). The study of funds of knowledge. Collaborative research in Latino homes. *Centro, 9*(9), 26–42.

Merriam, S. (1997). *Case study research in education: A qualitative approach.* San Francisco: Jossey-Bass.

Meyers, C. E., & Blacher, J. (1987). Parents' perceptions of schooling for severely handicapped children: Home and family variables. *Exceptional Children, 53*(5), 441–449.

Miles, M., & Huberman, A. (1984). *Qualitative data analysis: A sourcebook of new methods.* Beverly Hills, CA: Sage.

Moje, E. (1997). Exploring discourse, subjectivity, and knowledge in chemistry class. *Journal of Classroom Interaction, 32*(2), 35–44.

Moll, L. C., Amanti, C., Neff, D., & Gonzalez, N. (1992). Funds of knowledge for teaching: Using a qualitative approach to connect homes and classrooms. *Theory Into Practice, 31,* 132–141.

Morgan, M. (1999). No woman, no cry: Claiming African American women's place. In A. C. Liang, M. Bucholtz, & L. Sutton (Eds.), *Reinventing Identities: The gendered self in discourse* (pp. 27–45). New York: Oxford University Press.

Morrow, L. M. (Ed.). (1995). *Family literacy: Connections in schools and communities.* Newark, DE: International Reading Association.

Morrow, L. M., Tracey, D., & Maxwell, C. (Eds.). (1995). *A survey of family literacy in the United States.* Newark, DE: International Reading Association.

Moss, B. (2001). From the pews to the classrooms: Influences of the African American church on academic literacy. In J. L. Harris, A. Kamhi, & K. Pollock (Eds.), *Literacy in African American communities* (pp. 195–212). Mahwah, NJ: Lawrence Erlbaum Associates.

Moss, P. (1998). The role of consequences in validity theory. *Educational Measurement: Issues and Practices, 17*(2), 6–12.

Neuman, S., Celano, D., & Fischer, R. (1996). The children's literature hour: A socio-constructivist approach to family literacy. *Journal of Literacy Research, 28,* 499–523.

Ogbu, J. (1978). *Minority education and caste: The American system in cross-cultural perspective.* New York: Academic Press.

Olson, D. (1977). From utterance to text: The bias of language in speech and writing. *Harvard Educational Review, 47,* 257–281.

Orellana, M. (1999). Good guys and "bad" girls: Identity construction by Latina and Latino student writers. In M. Bucholtz, A. Liang, & L. Sutton (Eds.), *Reinventing identities: The gendered self in discourse.* (pp. 64–82). New York: Oxford University Press.

Paratore, J., Melzi, G., & Krol-Sinclair, B. (1999). *What should we expect of family literacy?* Newark, DE: International Reading Association.

Park, S. M. (1996). Research, teaching and service. Why shouldn't women's work count? *Journal of Higher Education, 67*(1), 46–75.

Patton, J. (1998). The disproportionate representation of African Americans in special education: Looking behind the curtain for understanding and solution. *The Journal of Special Education, 32*(1), 25–31.

Paulsen, G. (1993). *Night John.* New York: Delacorte.

Peshkin, A. (1988). In search of subjectivity: One's own. *Educational Researcher* (pp. 17–22).

Peterson, Penelope L. (1998). Why do educational research? Rethinking our roles and identities, our texts and contexts. *Educational Researcher, 27*(3), 4–10.

Peyton-Young, J. (1999). Critical literacy: Young adolescent boys talk about masculinity within a homeschooling context. In T. Shanahan & F. V. Rodriguez-Brown (Eds.), *National Reading Conference Yearbook: Vol. 48* (pp. 56–72). Chicago: National Reading Conference.

Peyton-Young, J. (2000). Boy Talk: Critical Literacy and Masculinities. *Reading Research Quarterly, 35*(3), 312–337.

Price, S. (1998). Critical discourse analysis: Discourse acquisition and discourse practices. *TESOL Quarterly, 33*(3), 581–595.

Price, S. (1999). Critical discourse analysis: Discourse acquisition and discourse practices. *TESOL Quarterly.*

Purcell-Gates, V. (1995). *Other people's words. The cycle of low literacy.* Cambridge, MA: Harvard University Press.

Richardson, L. (1995). Narrative and sociology. In J. Van Maanen (Ed.), *Representation in ethnography* (pp. 198–221). Thousand Oaks, CA: Sage.

Rockhill, K. (1987). Literacy as threat/desire: Longing to be SOMEBODY. In J. Gaskell & A. McLaren (Eds.), *Women and education: A Canadian perspective* (pp. 315–331). Calgary, Alberta, Canada: Detselig Enterprises.

Rockhill, K. (1995). Gender, language and the politics of literacy. In B. Street (Ed.), *Crosscultural approaches to literacy* (pp. 156–175). Cambridge, England: Cambridge University Press.

Rodriguez-Brown, E., & Mulhern, M. M. (1993). Fostering critical literacy through family literacy. A study of families in a Mexican-immigrant community. *Bilingual Research Journal, 17*(3 & 4), 1–16.

Rogers, R. (2000a). "It's not really writing. It's just answering the questions." *Language Arts, 77*(5), 428–437.

Rogers, R. (2001). Family literacy and the mediation of cultural models. *National Reading Conference Yearbook, 50,* 96–114.

Rogers, R. (2003). A Critical Discourse Analysis of the Special Education Referral Process: A Case Study. *Discourse.*

Rogers, R., (Ed.). *New directions in Critical Discourse Analysis,* Mahwah, NJ: Lawrence Erlbaum Associates.

Rogers, R. (2002a). Between contexts: A critical analysis of family literacy, discursive practices, and literate subjectivities. *Reading Research Quarterly, 37*(3), 248–277.

Rogers, R. (2002b). That's what you're here for, you're supposed to know": Teaching and learning critical literacy. *Journal of Adolescent and Adult Literacy, 45*(8), 772–787.

Rogers, R. (2002c). Through the eyes of the institution: A critical discourse analysis of decision making in two special education meetings. *Anthropology & Education Quarterly, 33*(2), 213–237.

Rogoff, B. (1995). *Apprenticeship in thinking: Cognitive development in social context.* New York: Oxford University Press.

Royster, J. J. (2000). *Traces of a stream: Literacy and social change among African American women.* Pittsburgh: University of Pittsburgh Press.

Sawin, P. (1999). Gender, context and the narrative construction of identity: Rethinking models of "women's narrative." In M. Bucholtz, A. Liang, & L. Sutton (Eds.), *Reinventing identities: The gendered self in discourse* (pp. 241–258). New York: Oxford University Press.

Scribner, S., & Cole, M. (1981). *The psychology of literacy.* Cambridge, MA: Harvard University Press.

Shanahan, T., Mulhern, M., & Rodriguez-Brown, F. (1995). Project FLAME: Lessons learned from a family literacy program for linguistic minority families. *Reading Teacher, 48*(7), 586–593.

Shepard, L. (1997). The centrality of test use and consequences for test validity. *Educational Measurement: Issues and Practice, 16*(3), 5–8, 13.

Silverstein, M., & Urban, G. (Eds.). (1996). *Natural histories of discourse.* Chicago: University of Chicago Press.

Solsken, J. (1992). *Literacy, gender and work: In families and in school.* New York: Ablex.
Sparks, B. (2001). The gendered construction of the adult education and family literacy act. *New Directions for Adult and Continuing Education, 91,* 47–54.
Spradley, J. (1980). *Participant observation.* New York: Holt, Rinehart & Winston.
Stangvik, G. (1998). Conflicting perspectives on learning disabilities. In C. Clark, A. Dyson, & A. Millward (Eds.), *Theorising special education* (pp. 137–155). London: Routledge.
Stanley, L. (1995). My mother's voice? On being "A Native on Academia." In L. Morley & V. Walsh (Eds.), *Feminist academics: Creative agents for change* (pp. 183–193). London: Taylor & Francis.
Sternberg, R., & Grigorenko, E. (1999). *Our labeled children.* Reading, MA: Perseus Books.
Stevens, L. (2001). South Park and society: Instructional and curricular implications of popular culture in the classroom. *Journal of Adolescent and Adult Literacy, 44*(6), 548–555.
Sticht, T. G., & McDonald, B. A. (1989). *Making the nation smarter: The intergenerational transfer of cognitive ability* (Technical Report). San Diego, CA: Applied Behavioral & Cognitive Sciences.
Street, B. (1984). *Literacy in theory and practice.* Cambridge, England: Cambridge University Press.
Street, B. (Ed.). (1995). *Cross-cultural approaches to literacy.* Cambridge, England: Cambridge University Press.
Stuckey, E. (1991). *The violence of literacy.* Portsmouth, NH: Boynton Cook.
Taylor, D. (1983). *Family literacy: Young children learning to read and write.* Portsmouth, NH: Heinemann.
Taylor, D. (1997). *Toxic literacies: Exposing the injustice of bureaucratic texts.* Portsmouth, NH: Heinemann.
Taylor, D., Coughlin, D., & Marasco, J. (Eds.). (1997). *Teaching and advocacy.* New York: Stenhouse.
Taylor, D., & Dorsey-Gaines, C. (1988). *Growing up literate: Learning from inner-city families.* Portsmouth, NH: Heinemann.
Teale, W. (1986). Home background and young children's literacy development. In W. Teale & E. Sulzby (Eds.), *Emergent literacy: Writing and reading* (pp. 173–206). Norwood, NJ: Ablex.
Teale, W., & Sulzby, E. (Eds.). (1986). *Emergent literacy: Writing and reading.* Norwood, NJ: Ablex.
Test of Adult Basic Education. (1987) Monterey, CA: CTB/McGraw-Hill.
Tierney, W., & Lincoln, Y. (Eds.). (1997). *Representation and the text: Reframing the narrative voice.* Albany, NY: SUNY Press.
Titscher, S., Meyer, M., Wodak, R., & Vetter, E. (2000). *Methods of text and discourse analysis.* London: SAGE.
Toolan, M. (1997). What is Critical Discourse Analysis and why are people saying such terrible things about it? *Language and Literature, 6*(2), 83–103.
Urwin, C. (1998). Power relations and the emergence of language. In J. Henriques, W. Holloway, C. Urwin, C. Venn, & V. Walkerdine (Eds.). *Changing the subject: Psychology, social regulation and subjectivity* (pp. 264–322). London: Methuen.
U.S. Department of Commerce, Bureau of the Census. (1990). *Block statistics census tracts, Albany, NY.* Washington, DC: U.S. Government Printing Office.
van Dijk, T. (1993). Principles of critical discourse analysis. *Discourse and Society, 4*(2), 249–283.
van Dijk, T. (1998). Discourse and ideology [Editorial]. *Discourse and Society, 9*(3), 307–308.

Walkerdine, V. (1990). *Schoolgirl fictions*. New York: Verso.
Weinstein-Shr, G. (1993). Literacy and social process: A community in transition. In B. Street (Ed.), *Cross-cultural approaches to literacy* (pp. 272–291). Cambridge, England: Cambridge University Press.
Wenger, E. (1998). *Communities of practice: Learning, meaning and identity*. Cambridge, England; Cambridge University Press.
Widdowson, H. G. (1998). The theory and practice of critical discourse analysis. *Applied Linguistics, 19*(1), 136–151.
Willis, P. (1977). *Learning to labor: How working class kids get working class jobs*. Farnborough, England: Saxon House.
Wodak, R. (Ed.). (1997). *Gender and discourse*. London: Sage.
Wodak, R. (1999). Critical discourse analysis at the end of the 20th century. *Research in Language and Social Interaction, 32*(1 & 2), 185–193.
Wolcott, H. (1990). *Writing up qualitative research*. Thousand Oaks, CA: Sage.
Wolcott, H. (1995). Making a study "more" ethnographic. In J. Van Maanen (Ed.), *Representation in ethnography* (pp. 79–111). Thousand Oaks, CA: Sage.
Wortham, S. (2001). *Narratives in action: A strategy for research and analysis*. New York: Teachers College Press.
Young, J. P. (2000). Boy talk: Critical literacy and masculinity. *Reading Research Quarterly, 35*, 312–337.
Ysseldyke, J. E., Algozzine, B., Richey, L., & Graden, J. (1986). Declaring students eligible for learning disabiilty services: Why bother with the data? *Learning Disability Quarterly, 5*, 37–42.

Author Index

Subject Index

LaVergne, TN USA
30 August 2010
195134LV00004B/280/P

9 780805 847840